JUST MARRIED & COOKING

Brooke Parkhurst & James Briscione

200 Recipes for Living, Eating, and Entertaining Together

SCRIBNER

New York London Toronto Sydney

SCRIBNER
A Division of Simon & Schuster, Inc.
1230 Avenue of the Americas
New York, NY 10020

First Scribner hardcover edition May 2011

SCRIBNER and design are registered trademarks of The Gale Group, Inc.,
used under license by Simon & Schuster, Inc., the publisher of this work.

For information about special discounts for bulk purchases,
please contact Simon & Schuster Special Sales at 1-866-506-1949
or business@simonandschuster.com.

The Simon & Schuster Speakers Bureau can bring authors to your live event. For more information or to book an event,
contact the Simon & Schuster Speakers Bureau at 1-866-248-3049 or visit our website at www.simonspeakers.com.

DESIGNED BY ERICH HOBBING

Manufactured in the United States of America

1   3   5   7   9   10   8   6   4   2

Library of Congress Control Number: 2010033053

ISBN 978-1-4391-6998-8
ISBN 978-1-4516-2557-8 (ebook)

Brooke's Dedication

For Jamie, Parker Lee, and my mother—

you always taste, you never complain, and you always inspire.

Jamie's Dedication

For my top two sous chefs, Brooke and Parker,

who I learn from and love more every day.

And to my family for all the years of love and support.

ACKNOWLEDGMENTS

We consider ourselves very fortunate to be with such a supportive publishing house. Who else gets to commemorate their first year of marriage with a collection of recipes? Nan Graham, you're the strong leader who always has a twinkle in her eye. Whitney Frick, you're the hippest, most thoughtful sounding board that we could have asked for. Thank you for your insight, your thorough edits, and your undeniable love of good food. And we are very thankful for our acquiring editor, Beth Wareham, who wasn't afraid to take a leap of faith. We hope we've made you proud.

Brooke would like to thank her mother for her love and patience and, more specifically, for a childhood filled with layer cakes and lattice-topped pies. She'd also like to thank Bill Contardi for six good years.

Jamie would like to thank Frank Taylor and Frank Stitt, who were willing to take a chance on a young kid, teach him how to cook, and introduce him to the world of food. He also thanks his family for their unwavering love and support, and for their relentless willingness to show up and eat.

CONTENTS

PART 1

Life As We Know It

New Traditions

JUST MARRIED & COOKING

INTRODUCTION

JUST MARRIED AND COOKING is the foodie soundtrack of our lives.

It's as if we made a mixed tape—filling it with ingredients, flavors, textures, and memories—and dedicated it to each other and to new beginnings. If a moment in our life together merits a song, then it also deserves a really wonderful recipe. Because cheesy popovers, sizzling skirt steak, and strawberry layer cake say as much about us as does our favorite Jack Johnson tune.

We knew we had to get down the flavors of our elopement and marriage in South Carolina, along the banks of the May River. We wanted to record salty afternoons at the Gulf when our skin tasted like a margarita glass (and our bodies were warm as hotcakes from the noontime sun). We needed to remind ourselves of the sweetness, the light, the reckless happiness of welcoming a baby girl into this world. Could anything replicate those newborn days? Jamie came close with his Nilla-laden, creamy New Baby Banana Pudding—one of the stars of our "Everyday Desserts."

But, of course, we didn't just write this book for each other. We wrote it for you—the newlyweds, the kitchen-shy, the would-be and budding cooks who need a little push. After you rinse and put away all the gorgeous new gear that friends and family have given you from your kitchen registry, you're suddenly going to realize that you'll be sharing meals with someone for the next sixty years (at least!).

Budgeting, grocery shopping, cooking dinner for each other seven nights a week until old age . . . what to do?!

We experienced the same mini-crisis, so we designed a cookbook that jazzes things up, making your kitchen and its bar stools the hottest place in town (or at least in your cul-de-sac). This is more than just a collection of recipes, it's an instruction manual and tip sheet on how to make easy, elegant food at home. These chapters are our glam-on-a-budget plan for eating and entertaining well 365 days a year.

This book is organized into two sections. "Life As We Know It" is the workhorse, focusing on everyday dinners like Jamie's rustic Eggplant and Tomato Gratin, an earthy platter of Pork Chops with Bourbon and Prunes, and big bowls of Whole-Wheat Pappardelle with Butternut Squash and Blue Cheese. We want you to mix and match our greatest hits, pulling a vegetable recipe from "Fixin's, or Second Thoughts," a protein from "The Lighter Side," and a bake-on-the-run bite of something sweet from "Everyday Desserts."

But every once in a while, we know that you need to slip into a pair of heels and a little knit dress and sip a champagne cocktail. So we created complete menus in the "New Traditions" section of the book to help you turn out showstopping plates and drinks for special occasions. Sicilian Lobster Salad, Crispy Skate with Spinach, Brown Butter, and Lemon, and our potent Blood Orange Old-Fashioned transform an evening with friends and family into an event. Our food is simple, but it might just inspire a new celebration.

At this point, you might be wondering, Who are these people? And why should I make their food?

Jamie is an alumnus of Daniel Boulud's 4-star kitchen and he's worked with some of the best chefs in New York City and the Southeast. He considers Frank Stitt, the James Beard Foundation Award–winning chef of Highlands Bar & Grill and Bottega, in Birmingham, Alabama, to be his culinary mentor. While Jamie was the chef de cuisine at Highlands, Stitt instilled in him a deep appreciation for the growing seasons as well as for the local, farm-fresh produce. Jamie's take-aways as a young chef: nothing that's been unloaded from a plane can taste as good as what you've dug up in your backyard; what grows together, goes together; a little French finesse makes everything taste better. He's one Southern boy who's just as comfortable stirring a pot of grits as he is searing a lobe of foie gras. And maybe it's this combination of cosmopolitan and country that gives him a leg up on the culinary competition: when Jamie appeared on Food Network's competition series *Chopped,* he walked away the grand champion.

Brooke, for her part, grew up on the Gulf Coast surrounded by amazing Southern lady cooks. Her mother and her aunts cooked what they knew and cooked it well, always with style and love for big, bold flavors. Almost every dish that came from their kitchens featured the fruits of local waters—sweet Gulf shrimp, briny Apalachicola oysters, line-caught flounder, deep-sea grouper—or, simply, fruit that grew on the family's farm fence, like tiny, tart summer blackberries and sweet cherry tomatoes. Good, honest cooking was the focus of everyday life. So when Brooke moved to New York City after college, with the intent of pursuing journalism, it's no surprise that she fell in love with the city's culinary scene . . . and a handsome Alabama chef. Eventually, Brooke found a way to combine her two loves, writing and cooking, by publishing her novel with recipes, *Belle in the Big Apple,* and by writing a daily online food column, Full Plate, for the *New York Daily News.*

But it's been Jamie's latest gig, as a chef-instructor at the Institute of Culinary Education in Manhattan's Flatiron District, that's afforded us a glimpse into the culinary lives and kitchens of our peers, engaged and newlywed couples. While Jamie works with the professional students during the week, Fridays and Saturdays are reserved for the Date Night Couples Cooking series that we teach together. The weekend gig is our research lab, our playground, our time to figure out just what makes your kitchens tick. We've learned the dishes you can't live without (bacon-studded mac-n-cheese, juicy roasts, interesting salads), the techniques you're dying to learn (roasting, sauce-making, fish cookery), and how you really cook during your hectic workweek. Our students keep us, and the food in this book, real.

Think of *Just Married and Cooking* as our life together in recipes. This is the book we wrote during the craziest time in our lives, when a church ceremony made us husband and wife, two lines on a pregnancy test made us a family of three, and a shared set of pots and pans made everything official. We hope you find as much joy in these dishes as we did creating them. Put down those takeout menus and get cooking!

KITCHEN REGISTRY

What Your Family and Friends Should Fork Over
for Your Starter Kitchen

One of the best things about getting married is "the gun"—that all-powerful, bar-code-scanning do-dad that zaps, then stores your wedding, birthday, or anniversary wish list. Every recipe in this book can be prepared using the list of tools below. Zap these kitchen items and you should be set for a lifetime of culinary bliss.

KITCHEN DRAWER—Absolute essentials that don't require a plug, a set of double A's, or an instruction manual:

- measuring cups
- measuring spoons
- citrus press (Brooke calls it a "lemon squeezer")
- Microplane zester
- can opener
- vegetable peeler

KITCHEN CABINET—Bulkier pieces that are stashed out of the way but never out of reach:

- colander/pasta strainer (large and small)
- stainless-steel mixing bowls (a set of nesting bowls will come in at least three sizes)
- salad spinner
- cutting boards (one large for chopping, one small for cutting little things like fruit and cheese)
- box grater

NEXT TO THE STOVE—Keep these essentials handy and organized in a tool caddy next to your stovetop:

- good wooden spoon
- tongs
- whisk

- metal spoon
- slotted spoon
- skimmer
- mesh strainer with handle
- ladle
- fish spatula
- regular metal spatula
- rubber spatula
- salt pig
- pepper mill

COUNTERTOP/STASHED AWAY IN THE PANTRY—Electric appliances that will cost a little money but are worth it:

- KitchenAid standing mixer*
- food processor
- handheld mixer
- immersion blender
- spice grinder
- food mill or potato ricer

THINGS THAT CUT

- serrated/bread knife
- chef's knife
- paring knife
- kitchen scissors
- mandoline

BAKING

- 2 baking sheets (with lip)
- 2 cookie sheets (no lip)
- 12-cup muffin pan
- 13- x 9-inch baking dish

* Put this on your wish list. But if you don't have the space to keep it on your countertop, it's not worth the expense or the trouble of lugging it in and out of the pantry (unless you plan on opening a bake shop out your back door).

- 8- x 8-inch baking dish
- 1- to 2-quart oval gratin dish
- 2 loaf pans (bread or meatloaf)
- wire cooling rack
- three 9-inch cake pans
- cake or tart pan with removable bottom
- popover pan

POTS AND PANS

- 2 small saucepots, 1 or 1½ and 2 quarts
- 1 large saucepot, 6 to 8 quarts ("pasta pot")
- 1 round Dutch oven, enamel covered, 6 quarts or more
- 8-inch nonstick sauté pan (omelet pan)
- 10- or 12-inch nonstick sauté pan
- 10- or 12-inch regular sauté pan
- large sauté pan
- cast-iron skillet
- cast-iron grill pan (if you don't have an outdoor grill)

THE BAR—Steer your "in between jobs" friends to this section of your registry. Inexpensive, perfectly suitable bar equipment and glasses can be found at nearly every housewares or kitchen store. Crate and Barrel and CB2 have the most stylish, well-priced selections.

- cocktail shaker/strainer set
- wooden muddler
- wineglasses, start with one nice set before you worry about having a different glass for each wine
- champagne flutes
- rocks glasses
- collins glasses

CHEF'S PANTRY

Seasoning—Turning out tasty, well-seasoned food takes a little more than that starter spice rack you got for your first apartment. This is a fantastic list of fundamentals that'll get you through every recipe in this book. Buy whole spices when possible and grind them (with an inexpensive coffee bean grinder) as needed. If that's not an option, buy them in ground form and be sure to store in a cool, dark area (directly above the stove is not the best place to store spices). Vinegars and oils are also best kept in a cool, dark place.

- kosher salt
- whole black peppercorns, for your pepper mill
- cumin
- coriander
- paprika
- smoked paprika
- cayenne
- dried basil
- dried marjoram
- dried oregano
- fennel seed
- mustard seed
- ground cinnamon
- ground ginger
- nutmeg, buy whole and grate on a Microplane as needed
- onion powder
- garlic powder

Non-Spice Essentials
- vanilla extract
- almond extract
- honey
- sriracha hot sauce
- vinegar-based hot sauce—Tabasco or Cholula
- soy sauce
- fish sauce

- Worcestershire sauce
- sesame oil
- vegetable oil
- olive oil (see page 16)
- vinegars: balsamic, red wine, white wine, cider

Herbs—Whether you're an urban dweller with a window box, you've cultivated an acre of countryside, or you find yourself somewhere in between, planting your own herbs is the perfect way to brighten up your surroundings and your cooking. It's a great money saver too. A few young plants from your local farmers' market or garden center will produce fresh herbs all season long and cost the same as one dinky bunch of herbs from the grocery store.

Essentials: If you only have room to grow a few herbs, try these. They grow very well in most environments and are the most commonly used in our kitchen.
- basil
- parsley
- cilantro
- mint
- thyme
- rosemary

If you have the space, add these to your garden:
- dill
- tarragon
- marjoram
- oregano
- chives
- sage

CHEF'S GLOSSARY

You see a word in a recipe and you don't know what it means, so you scrap the whole thing. (Even though you really wanted Striped Bass with Roasted Fennel and Grapefruit Supremes for dinner. "Supremes? Like The Supremes as led by Diana Ross?!" you're wondering.) We don't want you to be intimidated and we want to educate you! Throughout this book, you'll find words that are included in the Chef's Glossary. If one throws you for a loop, flip back here and you'll be on your way to a delicious meal.

Al dente—A term typically reserved for pasta but used to describe properly blanched vegetables too. In Italian, *al dente* literally means "to the tooth." It refers to a state of doneness that is tender but retains a slight bite.

Blanch—An invaluable process of precooking vegetables. Chefs use this technique to prepare items, especially green vegetables, ahead of time so they only need to be reheated and seasoned before serving. Blanching helps green vegetables keep their vibrant color. To blanch, bring a pot of well-salted water to a boil, add the vegetables, and cook until tender. Remove from the boil and plunge into ice water to stop the cooking process.

Boil v. Simmer—These two words describe a similar action, at different levels. Boiling water is turbid, with bubbles constantly breaking the surface, or rolling. Simmering is gentle. Bubbles form on the bottom of the pot and slowly, but consistently, break the surface. When simmering, bubbles are typically first seen around the edge of the pot.

Chiffonade—When herbs or leafy green vegetables are cut into thin strips. The easiest way to achieve this is to bundle the herbs (or lay one on top of the other), roll them, and then begin cutting from the stem end to the tip of the leaf.

Deglaze—To add liquid (typically wine or stock) to a pan to release the fond from the bottom. Deglazing is the first step in making a great sauce after searing meat in a pan.

Dice—To cut any item into small cubes. A proper dice is most easily achieved by first cutting items into thin strips (or a julienne), then slicing the strips into cubes. Don't get discouraged; good dicing requires lots and lots of practice.

Dredge—To lightly coat in flour or another fine, dry coating. To dredge, fill a plate or shallow dish with flour. Season the item to be coated, then drag both sides through the flour. Pat off all the excess flour. Dredging should only be done immediately before cooking.

Fold—A gentle mixing motion done with a spatula or broad spoon. Proper folding is done in a bowl, cutting through a mixture with the edge of a spatula, then turning the ingredients at the bottom of the bowl over to the top. This motion is repeated until the contents are evenly mixed. This method is typically employed when incorporating ingredients with large amounts of air whipped into them (egg whites, whipped cream).

Fond—Those tasty brown bits that appear on the bottom of your sauté pan or pot. Technically, they're the caramelized juices of meats or vegetables, but all you need to know is they're big-time flavor (if you don't burn them).

H.o.d.—An hors d'oeuvre or pre-dinner nibble. Forget the pronunciation. And who could even remember how to spell it? This is how we always abbreviate this French tongue twister.

Julienne—To cut into thin strips. To make a julienne, first cut thin slices, then cut those slices into strips that are as wide as they are thick. Julienne pieces are typically 2 to 3 inches in length. Julienne examples: strips of peppers (think fajitas) or french fries.

Microplane—The brand name of a wandlike handheld grater that creates very finely grated product. Excellent for grating hard cheeses like Parmesan and Pecorino, creating a paste of raw garlic or ginger, and zesting limes and lemons.

Reduce—To simmer a liquid mixture to decrease its volume. Reducing thickens and concentrates flavor. The process only removes water, so overreducing can be corrected by adding water or stock back to the mixture.

Render—The process by which fatty ingredients are cooked to melt the fat contained in them, leaving the leaner pieces brown and crisp. Rendering should be done over low heat and requires frequent stirring.

Resting—An essential part of properly cooking meats. It involves removing the meat from the heat source and placing it on a cooling rack to help keep juices inside. Resting also allows the juices to redistribute inside the meat so they won't be lost when you do dig in. As a general rule, resting time should be half the cooking time.

Sauté—To quickly cook something in a flat-bottomed pan in a small amount of fat over high heat.

Sear—To quickly brown an item on the exterior without cooking it through. Searing requires very high heat and nearly smoking hot oil. This method is also the best way to set off your smoke detector or stink up the apartment for two days.

Supremes (sou-PREMS)—Jewel-like segments of citrus fruit with all of the rind, pith, and membrane removed (see page 14).

Sweat—To sauté without browning. This is a technique for cooking vegetables, usually members of the onion family. Adding a pinch of salt or 2 to 3 tablespoons water helps the process of sweating. For sweating, cook in preheated fat (butter or oil) over low to medium heat; add liquid to the pan or reduce the heat if items begin to color.

"White part only"—Scallions and leeks have two parts: the onion part and the herb part. If a recipe asks for "white part only," it's really talking about the onion part, and not just the part that is white in color. In fact, the usable part could be up to one-third white and two-thirds green. The good, cookable part ends where the scallion or leek splits into dark green leaves or shoots. The green tops have little flavor, so use them to garnish as you would an herb.

Cutting Supremes of Citrus Fruit

This is the most important technique you might not know. We love including all citrus fruits in savory dishes for their ability to brighten and lighten a dish. By cutting supremes, you eliminate the bitter pith (the white part) and the tough membrane, leaving just jewel-like pieces of tender fruit—pure flavor.

Trim all the pith and zest from the citrus fruit. Begin by cutting a small slice from the top and bottom, so the inner fruit is just exposed. Position the fruit so it sits squarely on your cutting board. With a sharp knife, follow the contour of the fruit from the top to the bottom, removing all the white pith along the way. Turn the fruit and continue cutting until you have gone all the way around. With all of the white stuff now gone, cut in between the membranes to release the clean fruit in perfect, crescent-shaped wedges. Work over a bowl the entire time to catch the juices and reserve for a dressing.

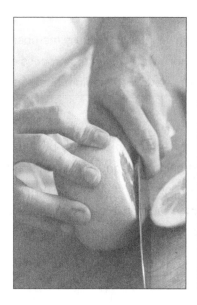 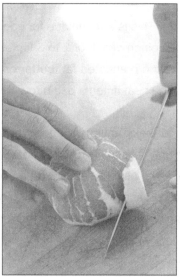 

CAVEATS

- If a recipe calls for salt, we mean kosher salt unless otherwise noted. Chefs and experienced home cooks lean toward kosher salt instead of sea salt because it's tactile—the texture is coarse and uniform and easier to pinch. Also sea salt is too expensive to cook with on a daily basis.
- Pepper should always be freshly ground. Don't buy those little boxes of pepper in the spice section of your grocery store. You can never know how long ago the peppercorns were ground, processed, and packaged, which means they may have lost most of their flavor and bite along the way.
- The term "to taste" means what tastes good to you. But you won't know unless you, well, taste. Then season and taste again and continue gradually adding seasoning until it couldn't taste better. Don't stop when it's pretty good. We worked too hard on these recipes for them to only be pretty good. Keep seasoning and tasting until it's great.
- A little common sense goes a long way. But don't be afraid to cook and make mistakes. We have learned more from the many, many, many bad things we cooked over the years than we have from the dishes that came out flawless.
- You know your stove better than we do, so adjust the heat as necessary, whether the recipe tells you to or not.
- We take no responsibility for the results of any dishes made with cheap cookware. Good pots and pans and sharp knives won't make you a great cook, but they sure help.
- You need two bottles of extra virgin olive oil in your kitchen. One should be less expensive and for cooking and incorporating into the recipes. The second olive oil should be pricier and have a more nuanced flavor. (This is the one that you'll dramatically pour over a finished dish in a way that will convince everyone you really know what you're doing.) FYI—olive oil is not like wine; it does not get better with age. Unfiltered oils keep for three months, while premium, filtered olive oils have a much longer shelf life of twelve to eighteen months. Still a little confused? Check out our olive oil guide on page 16.

Olive Oil

After saying your vows, you're exclusive with your honey. But when it comes to olive oil, we absolutely encourage you to play the field.

Bucking our Southern roots and our families' love of butter, we cook just about everything with olive oil. The key has been to find our perfect "everyday" oil (it goes with everything—like Brooke's Old Navy tanks) and then to find one that's for special occasions (like Jamie's brown wingtips that he only hauls out for church and 4-star restaurants). When you see *cook, sauté*, or any other verb that denotes a *prolonged period of heat*, use your less-expensive oil. The oil's nuanced flavors will be cooked out—so why waste your money? When you see the words *fresh* or *finish* in a recipe—like with fresh greens, vegetables, and simple pastas—consider splurging with your nicer oil.

Over the past five years together, we've been adventurous—dare we say, promiscuous?—with our olive oil tasting. In our kitchen, we've hopped from country to country and tasted oils from everywhere. Jamie, more of a Francophile, prefers the lighter, more fragrant oils of southern France and northern Italy. Brooke likes more robust oils from southern Italy and Sicily, with the occasional Tuscan thrown into the mix. If she's feeling crazy, she'll hop over to Greece for one of their super-smooth, low-acidity extra virgin olive oils and make plans to pour it on a dinner of super-simple grilled fish.

Instead of buying the regular 16- or 20-ounce glass bottles, we economize and buy a big, 3-quart jug from our trusty discount Italian food store, Buon Italia, located in New York City's Chelsea Market. But we wouldn't have made that investment without a thorough tasting. Imagine being stuck with 3 liters of olive oil that's only good for greasing up squeaky door hinges (though we have plenty of those in our old apartment)!

OLIVE OIL LABELS—CUTTING THROUGH THE CLUTTER

This is all the confusing stuff you might find on the label of your olive oil and what it means. Warning: don't buy a bottle before reading this!

ACIDITY—Always expressed as a percentage, it is the best indicator of oil quality, though it gives no indication of flavor. The better the olive (and the resulting oil), the lower the acidity.

- **0–0.8% acidity—Extra Virgin Olive Oil**—highest quality, no taste defects
- **up to 2% acidity—Virgin Olive Oil**—lower quality than extra virgin
- **up to 3.3% acidity—Ordinary Virgin Oil**—lower quality than virgin, though some may still be acceptable
- **above 3.3% acidity—Refined Oil**—these oils are processed (or refined) before being considered fit for human consumption

FIRST PRESS OR COLD PRESS—The best oil is extracted from olives on their first pressing and without heat. A first cold-pressing of great olives makes a great oil, but a first cold-pressing of bad olives . . . you got it, bad oil. "First Press" and "Cold Press" are great things to see on a label, but they don't guarantee that the contents of the bottle will be great.

OLIVE OIL OR 100% PURE OLIVE OIL—Remember when Mom used to tell you if you can't say anything nice, don't say anything at all? Well, this is about the last thing that could be said about this oil before having to say nothing at all. Typically oil with this label is a mixture of refined and virgin oils.

LIGHT OR EXTRA-LIGHT OLIVE OIL—This oil has the same amount of calories as all other oils. It's the flavor that it is "light" on.

OLIVE-POMACE OIL—This oil is extracted from the remnants from a first pressing through solvents or other physical means. Avoid at all costs.

PART 1

Life As We Know It

Everyday eating can be a joy or a chore—you're the one in charge. In the past, we've found that people tend to fall into two major categories. Either you're a utilitarian kind of eater, grocery shopping once a week and seasoning up just enough protein to get you through the day. Or you're like us—unstoppable foodies who anchor your days with food fantasies and meal preparation.

Writing this cookbook, we realized there should be a middle ground. You should be able to look forward to a simple, delicious dinner without it taking up your entire day. Because isn't it more important to know how to make drool-worthy Monday lunches and Thursday-eve dinners (the stuff that gets you through the workweek) than being able to cook up a Christmas Day *abbondanza* once a year? That standing rib roast isn't going to give you 364 days of leftovers.

The "Life As We Know It" section of this book was written with interesting, everyday eating in mind. The recipes manage to be easy and elegant. You won't need more ingredients than can fit inside your messenger bag, and the meals can be put together in an hour or less. Jamie listened to the seasons with his ingredient pairings, and Brooke tried to keep things healthful. And although these recipes are simple, we also want to inspire you, so we made sure to slip in a few more sumptuous, gourmet items like coriander and lime vinaigrette–dressed carrots and sautéed lettuce. We've also included tips and information about things like seasoned salts, homemade sausage, curing fish, and making the best dang bowl of risotto to ever be prepared outside of Venice. We want this book to help you see the same old food in a whole new way.

Although we've organized the recipes in "Life As We Know It" into different chapters, the most important thing is that you enjoy a selection of these dishes together. So figure out what you've both been craving and then mix and match recipes. If you want one of our Afterwork Apps for dinner and blueberry pancakes for dessert, go for it! The key is to experiment, try things out, and discover what you love to cook and eat together. Pour yourselves two glasses of wine and enjoy your time in the kitchen instead of staring at a screen while sitting on the couch. Pinch hit—he chops, you sear, and you both do the dishes. You'll see that everything tastes better when you make it together.

MORNINGS

Just the Two of Us and for a Crowd

When we first met, Brooke was always up early, putting together a simple, healthful breakfast. Jamie would lie in bed until the absolute last moment, and with just enough time to down a cup of coffee, he'd rush out the door. When he figured out that mornings with Just the Two of Us could mean bowls of homemade granola, lemony blueberry muffins, or a skillet of bubbling goat cheese frittata, his bachelor taste for energy bars and bad deli muffins became a thing of the past.

While we love our morning meal together, we also enjoy sleeping late. In an effort to have more time beneath the covers, we never let that first meal get too complicated. If anything takes more than half an hour, we'll do a little measuring and mixing the night before and then sleep easy, knowing that something delicious will greet us in the morning.

Sometimes, when the mood strikes just right, or Brooke drops enough heavy-handed hints, Jamie'll get his act together for a real treat: breakfast in bed. It can't be beat. It's totally romantic, but, we admit, totally hard to pull off with ease. It should be about assembling, not cooking. Because no matter how stealthy you are, your honey's probably going to wake up as you fumble around for your robe and shuffle off to the kitchen. That means you have about twenty minutes to pull off something delicious before toting it back under the covers. After all, breakfast in bed isn't half as fun if you're not, well, in bed.

Forget the eggs and bacon—nothing's sexy about sticky, yellow yolks or the smell of smoked pork clinging to your fine cotton sheets. (Well, Jamie might disagree about the bacon part.) Instead, think of stirring together muffin batter the night before, then dropping in the berries and baking the day of. Diced fruit, warm bowls of café au lait, and hot muffins with good butter are a delicious start to a lazy day.

Other mornings, we just want to be with friends. The night before, we stock the fridge with prosecco and exotic fruit juices and whip up a batch of focaccia dough (for our breakfast pizza) and a couple of baked treats. We hit the sheets knowing that in the morning our kitchen will be the hottest brunch spot in town. The beauty of breakfast foods, at least those you'll find in this book, is that they're almost as easy to make for ten as they are for two. Make sure to take a look at our sidebars for tips about which elements can be made ahead and which should be made once your friends are well into their mimosas.

Brooke's mom always told her breakfast was the most important meal of the day. We say it should be the most enjoyable one as well.

Better Morning Muffins

A good muffin is a sort of breakfast bribe, making it a little easier to heave off the covers and confront a new day. Because we both feel we deserve a prize for getting out of bed in the morning (to the sound of buses trundling up 6th Avenue), we knew we had to experiment and come up with an outrageously good recipe for an outrageously good muffin. After fiddling around with a lot of batter and licking dozens of beaters, we decided that the perfect breakfast muffin contained yogurt (for moistness), lemon zest (for bright flavor), and cornmeal (for texture). Pile a pyramid of these beneath your cake dome and start your day with a smile.

makes 1 dozen muffins

8 tablespoons (1 stick) unsalted butter, at room
temperature, plus more for the pan

1¼ cups all-purpose flour, plus more for dusting
the pan

¼ cup cornmeal

1 teaspoon baking soda

1½ teaspoons baking powder

½ teaspoon kosher salt

6 ounces fresh or frozen blueberries, raspberries,
or strawberries, rinsed and dried

grated zest of 1 lemon

1 cup granulated sugar, plus more for sprinkling

2 large eggs

2 teaspoons vanilla extract

2 tablespoons milk

Preheat the oven to 375 degrees.

Butter a 12-cup muffin pan, dust it with flour, and tap out the excess. Set aside.

In a large bowl, whisk together the flour, cornmeal, baking soda, baking powder, and salt. Mix the dry ingredients well, then add the berries and stir to coat.

Using an electric mixer, beat the butter, lemon zest, and sugar until light and fluffy, about 3 minutes. Beat in the eggs one at a time and then the vanilla, beating well after each addition. Reduce the mixer speed to low and add the milk. Add the flour mixture and mix with a wooden spoon or spatula until just combined. Be careful to not overmix. With a large spoon, fill the muffin cups three-quarters full with batter. Sprinkle each filled cup with a generous pinch of sugar.

Bake the muffins until a toothpick inserted into the center of one muffin comes out clean, 25 to 30 minutes. Place the pan on a wire rack and allow the muffins to cool for 15 minutes. Once you can handle them, remove the muffins to a wire rack and allow them to cool. Serve warm.

TECHNIQUE TIP: VARY BERRY

You can swap berries in this recipe according to the seasons. The key is that the berries should be bite-size or smaller, which means most strawberries need to be cut into quarters for this recipe. If using frozen berries, there is no need to thaw—or rinse—before adding.

Good French Butter

Would you pour vegetable oil on your organically grown lettuce or on farm-fresh vegetables? We didn't think so. So never use margarine in—or on—your homemade baked goods. Unsalted butter is best for baking and cooking. To serve with your muffins, splurge on a good French butter such as Celles sur Belle or Isigny Ste. Mère.

French or European-style butter (though some are made in the good ol' U-S-of-A, such as Vermont Butter & Cheese Company) has a richer, fuller flavor than the everyday butters that line the shelves of the average supermarket. The cows that produce these top-shelf butters graze on thick, lush grasses often found in cool coastal areas or valleys. A rich, healthy diet means richer, more flavorful milk, and butter that has a bright golden color and smooth, satisfying taste.

What's a Quick Bread?

Quick breads—unlike yeast breads—are leavened, or made to rise, with eggs or chemical leaveners like baking powder, sodium bicarbonate, or cream of tartar. They are quick to make and the results are, for the most part, uniform. Popovers, muffins, scones, banana bread, biscuits, and pancakes all fall into this category.

Popovers

Popovers seem extravagant because of their whimsical shape. The puffy tops, bursting above the rims of the muffin cups, make them look like fat, fairy-tale mushrooms. They're also a lot of fun because of their wonderful contrasting textures—crispy on top, chewy and eggy at their center. Even though they're considered a "quick bread," they make your plate feel fancy. After Brooke's twenty-ninth birthday dinner at BLT Steak—where everyone fell in love with the bread basket of enormous Gruyère-Parmesan popovers—we always try to incorporate them into our nice dinners. Recently, breakfast has become our newest excuse to eat popovers. For relaxed family mornings like Mother's Day, we take the sweet route and bake them with cinnamon and sugar.

makes 6 popovers

4 tablespoons (½ stick) unsalted butter, melted,
      plus more for buttering the pan
1 cup milk
1 teaspoon kosher salt
1¼ cups all-purpose flour
1 cup grated Gruyère or Monterey Jack cheese
2 large eggs
¼ cup grated Parmesan cheese, for topping

If you didn't snag a popover pan from your wedding registry, you can make popovers in a muffin pan. They won't be as tall and impressive looking, but they'll taste great just the same. Fill each muffin cup with batter just above halfway.

Preheat the oven to 400 degrees.

Lightly butter a 6-cup popover pan or coat with nonstick spray.

Place the butter, milk, salt, flour, Gruyère, and eggs in a food processor or blender and process until smooth, about 30 seconds. Pour the batter into the cups of the popover pan; each should be one-third to one-half full. Scatter the Parmesan cheese into each of the cups. Bake on the middle rack of the oven for 40 minutes. Remove the pan to a cooling rack before removing the popovers from the cups. Serve warm.

Cinnamon-Sugar Popovers

Omit the Gruyère and Parmesan and turn your popovers into a sweet treat by topping the plain popovers with cinnamon and sugar.

makes 6 popovers

2 tablespoons ground cinnamon
¼ cup granulated sugar
2 tablespoons unsalted butter, melted

Prepare the popovers as directed above, omitting the cheeses from the recipe. Combine the cinnamon and sugar in a small bowl or on a plate and mix well. When the popovers are finished baking and cool enough to handle, brush the top of each with melted butter. Dip or roll the tops of the popovers in the cinnamon sugar and serve warm.

Brooke's Breakfast Granola

Brooke's granola looks as good as it tastes. It's the perfect combination of honey-toasted oats, dried fruit, and nuts. Around the corner from our apartment, at our local bakery, they charge a fortune for a bag of this. Stir up a batch of Brooke's and don't look back! And even if yours is a meat-and-potato kind of guy (like Jamie), pair the granola with a bowl of tart, plain yogurt and wait for him to ask for seconds. To impress out-of-town guests, pull out the stemless wineglasses that were on your kitchen registry and create a colorful parfait of fruit (winter: bananas, strawberries; summer: peaches, blueberries), yogurt (plain, vanilla), and granola.

makes 10 cups granola

3½ cups old-fashioned rolled oats

¾ cup slivered almonds or chopped pecans

⅔ cup shredded dried coconut

½ cup sunflower seeds or pumpkin seeds (if using
    salted seeds, omit the salt from the recipe)

½ teaspoon kosher salt

1 tablespoon ground cinnamon

4 tablespoons (½ stick) unsalted butter

3 tablespoons honey

3 tablespoons brown sugar

¼ cup golden raisins

½ cup dried cranberries

⅔ cup dried apricots, cut into quarters

½ cup dried banana chips, roughly chopped

Preheat the oven to 325 degrees.

In a large bowl, combine the oats, almonds, coconut, sunflower seeds, salt, and cinnamon. In a small saucepan, melt the butter with the honey and brown sugar over low heat, stirring until the sugar is dissolved. Pour the butter mixture into the oat mixture and stir until well combined.

Spread the granola evenly on a large rimmed baking sheet or 2 half sheet pans. Bake in the middle of the oven until golden brown, about 15 minutes. Remove the pan about halfway through the cooking and stir well. Return to the oven. After 15 to 20 minutes, the oats should be golden and fragrant. Remove the pan from the oven and let cool completely on a rack. Stir in the dried fruits. Granola can be kept in an airtight container at cool room temperature for up to 2 weeks.

Blueberry Pancakes with Maple Sauce

Only Clinton Street Baking Company, on Manhattan's Lower East Side, makes blueberry pancakes that are as lip-smacking good as Jamie's. The restaurant's are so delicious that half the city lines up for an order. Brooke thought that a Saturday morning, three-plus-hour Clinton Street ritual was quaint; Jamie found it maddening. We both got our way when Jamie wrote this recipe. His final touch of make-at-home genius was figuring out a way to combine the pancakes' favorite condiments, butter and maple syrup, into one rich, smooth sauce.

serves 4

2 cups all-purpose flour

2 teaspoons baking powder

1 teaspoon kosher salt

2 tablespoons granulated sugar

2 cups milk or buttermilk

1 large egg

4 tablespoons (½ stick) unsalted butter, melted

vegetable oil or nonstick spray

1 pint blueberries

Maple Sauce (recipe follows)

In a large bowl, whisk together the flour, baking powder, salt, and sugar. In a separate bowl, whisk the milk, eggs, and melted butter together until thoroughly mixed. Pour this mixture into the dry ingredients and stir with a wooden spoon or spatula until just combined. Set the batter aside to rest for at least 30 minutes or refrigerate, up to overnight.

Place a cast-iron skillet or nonstick pan over medium-low heat and add just enough oil to cover the bottom. Pour some of the batter into the heated skillet, using a ¼-cup measure as a scoop. When the batter is poured into the pan and has stopped spreading, press 4 or 5 berries into each cake. Cook until bubbles form in the center and the edges are firm. Turn and cook about 2 minutes more.

Serve with Maple Sauce.

TECHNIQUE TIP

Make sure to avoid an ugly, gray batter full of burst berries by not mixing the blueberries into the bowl of batter. Placing blueberries in each pancake once they're formed in the skillet also ensures no one ends up with a berryless pancake.

Maple Sauce

½ cup maple syrup
4 tablespoons (½ stick) unsalted butter

Heat the maple syrup in a small saucepot over low heat until bubbling and slightly darkened in color. Cut the butter into small pieces and stir in gradually.

YUMMY MISTAKES

Turning out perfect pancakes is all about the heat, and getting it right requires a little fine-tuning. Tradition says the first pancake is always for the cook—that's because the first one usually burns or comes out very pale. As you cook the first few pancakes, adjust the heat so that the first side is golden brown just as the bubbles start to form in the center of the cake, then flip and cook until golden on the second side. The adjustments take a little practice, but don't worry—you'll get it down and you'll have some delicious mistakes to comfort you until then.

THE NEXT LEVEL

Breakfast for Dessert—We love to indulge our inner child when it comes to dessert time: S'mores (page 214), milkshakes (page 110), and blueberry pancakes! To give them an elegant touch, buy nice bamboo skewers. Make a half batch of pancakes and maple sauce and get some extra berries. Cut the cooked pancakes into 1-inch squares and place on small skewers or toothpicks, alternating pieces of pancake with the fresh berries. Three pieces of pancake and two berries drizzled with sauce make the perfect bite.

Banana-Pecan Bread

When Brooke accidentally buys a bunch of bananas better suited for the appetite of an adult chimpanzee than a tiny baby, she makes this bread with the leftover ripened fruit. But, really, the comingling of the bourbon and banana flavors is so right on, it's worth it to purposefully overshoot the numbers on your grocery list and patiently wait for the bananas to ripen. And you didn't misread the recipe—we really want you to mash up four to five ripe ones. Hey, it's called "banana bread" for a reason!

makes 1 loaf, serving 8 or more

BATTER

8 tablespoons (1 stick) unsalted butter, at room temperature, plus more for the pan
1 cup all-purpose flour, plus more for dusting the pan
¾ cup dark brown sugar
¼ cup granulated sugar
2 large eggs
2 cups mashed ripe bananas (4 to 5 bananas)
¼ cup bourbon (optional)
1 cup whole-wheat flour
1 teaspoon baking soda
¼ teaspoon kosher salt
½ teaspoon ground cinnamon

TOPPING

¼ cup roughly chopped pecans
2 teaspoons granulated sugar
2 teaspoons brown sugar
¼ teaspoon ground cinnamon
¼ teaspoon ground nutmeg
⅓ cup semi-sweet chocolate chips (optional)

Preheat the oven to 350 degrees.

Butter and lightly flour a 9- x 5-inch loaf pan. Combine the butter and sugars in a large bowl and beat with an electric mixer until light and fluffy. Add the eggs one at a time, beating well after each addition. Mix in the mashed bananas and bourbon with a spatula or wooden spoon.

Combine the flours, baking soda, salt, and cinnamon in a separate bowl and mix well. Add half of the dry ingredients to the banana batter and stir until just combined. Add the remaining dry ingredients and mix again. Pour the batter into the prepared pan.

Stir together the topping ingredients and sprinkle over the batter.

Bake until a toothpick inserted into the bread comes out clean, about 1 hour 10 minutes. Place the pan on a rack and let cool for 20 minutes. Run a knife around the edges to loosen the bread from the sides of the pan. Invert onto a plate and transfer to a wire rack to cool.

Serve with morning coffee.

HURRY UP!

You can speed along the ripening process by placing your bananas with an apple in a brown paper bag on the kitchen counter. The gases emitted by the apple help fruits like bananas and pears ripen more quickly.

Café au Lait

Drink your coffee like you're on Boulevard St. Germain

On weekends, Jamie trades in his coffee mug for a café au lait bowl. (We love Anthropologie's inexpensive, brightly colored ceramic bowls.) And instead of pouring cold cream into his coffee, he warms a bit of milk. All of this, he says, makes him feel like he's having breakfast on Boulevard St. Germain instead of on a couch in the Village. If a piece of inexpensive china and a dash of warm milk can transport you across the Atlantic, why not? For your little taste of France, spoon the desired amount of sugar into the bottom of a café-au-lait-size bowl. (We find that sugar dissolves better when hot liquid is poured over it as opposed to sugar being added to hot liquid.) Fill the bowl three-quarters full with strong coffee. Top it off with warm whole milk that you've either heated on the stovetop or in your microwave. Serve with a plate of buttery croissants and pretend you're on the sidewalk terrace of Café de Flore.

Buttermilk Biscuits and Sawmill Gravy

In high school, Jamie and his best friend, Patrick, landed their first kitchen jobs at a brunch joint on Pensacola Beach. Not surprisingly, every Sunday, the two teen-agers got stuck with 6 A.M. biscuit duty. It wasn't long before Jamie was turning out light-as-air biscuits. His hard-won secret? Gently folding and then rerolling the biscuit dough to create light layers. Here, he decides to gild the lily and make a batch of sawmill gravy to pour over the biscuits. Instead of buying a roll of Jimmy Dean preseasoned breakfast sausage, he seasons plain pork with his own blend of spices.

makes about 12 biscuits

1 cup (2 sticks) unsalted butter, chilled
2½ cups all-purpose flour, plus a bit more for rolling
1 tablespoon baking powder
1 teaspoon kosher salt
¾ cup buttermilk, or ¾ cup whole milk mixed with
    1 teaspoon distilled white vinegar
melted butter for brushing the baked biscuits
Sawmill Gravy (recipe follows)

FOLDING THE DOUGH

Love the buttery layers of those biscuits that come in a can? Folding and layering the dough, as in the recipe above, gives you those same perfect layers. Dough Boy, be damned! But if you're not up for the whole layering process, just gently roll the dough out ¾ inch thick, punch out the biscuits, and continue with the recipe as directed above.

Preheat the oven to 425 degrees.

Cut the butter into a small dice and freeze until ready to use. Add the flour, baking powder, and salt to the bowl of a food processor and pulse to combine. Add the butter from the freezer and continue pulsing until the butter is in pieces no larger than a green pea. To make the dough without a food processor, rub the butter into the flour mixture by hand in a large bowl.

Transfer the flour mixture to a bowl and add all of the buttermilk at once. Stir with a wooden spoon until just combined. The mixture will look a little dry and uneven. Turn the dough onto a well-floured work surface and knead for 3 to 4 minutes to make a smooth, even dough; add flour as needed if the dough is too sticky.

With well-floured hands and working on a well-floured surface, press the dough into a flat sheet, about 1 inch thick. Fold lengthwise into thirds (as you would fold a letter). Repeat this process 2 more times.

After folding the dough the third time, roll the dough into a ¾-inch-thick sheet, using a rolling pin. Cut rounds out of the dough and place them on a lightly oiled baking sheet or on parchment paper so that they just touch those next to them. After cutting the biscuits, gather the scraps and reroll until all the dough is used. Cut biscuits can be refrigerated overnight.

Bake until golden and risen, about 15 minutes. Remove from the oven and immediately brush with melted butter.

To serve biscuits and gravy, remove 2 biscuits from the pan and split them in half. Lay them open-faced on a plate and spoon a generous amount of the sausage gravy over the biscuits.

Ideally, use a 2½-inch round cutter for the biscuits. If you do not have one, punch out the biscuits with one of your sturdier wineglasses—the opening of most wineglasses is just the right size for biscuits.

Sawmill Gravy

serves 6 to 8

2 tablespoons canola oil
1 pound pork Breakfast Sausage (page 138)
6 cups milk
¼ cup all-purpose flour
kosher salt and freshly ground pepper to taste

Place a wide, heavy-bottomed pot over medium-high heat and add the oil. When the oil is hot, add the seasoned pork and cook until the fat is rendered and the meat is well browned.

While the pork is cooking, warm the milk in a separate pot over low heat. Stir the flour into the browned pork mixture, reduce the heat to medium, and cook, stirring, until the flour is golden in color, about 5 minutes. Slowly stir in the milk. The mixture will thicken immediately. Continue stirring over medium heat until all the milk is incorporated, the mixture has thinned, and no lumps of flour remain.

Stop stirring and allow the mixture to come to a boil over medium heat. Simmer for 15 minutes more, stirring often to ensure that nothing sticks to the bottom of the pot. Season with salt and pepper; the gravy should be fully flavored with a little kick. Cover and keep warm over the lowest possible heat until the biscuits are ready.

Our Southern Secret

Even though you might be a Yankee, we'll share with you our Southern biscuit-making secret: White Lily all-purpose flour. Ssshhhh. . . . It's so revered by Southerners that it's called "Sunday flour" because it was only used for special dishes. Brooke's mother wouldn't consider baking with anything else. But why is White Lily so special? The flour is made from soft, red winter wheat, which is the low-protein, low-gluten variety. While other all-purpose flours are made from a blend of wheat, White Lily is finer, lighter, whiter. Many master bakers say that it even feels silky in their hands. If you live down South, you can find White Lily in the baking aisle of any grocery store. For you dedicated biscuit makers in the other thirty states, check out the White Lily website to place your order at www.whitelily.com.

Asparagus and Goat Cheese Frittata

Frittatas are like omelets without the fuss. They're perfect for when you have company. Instead of making eight individual omelets, you can make one frittata and then slice it as you would a pizza. Just pick out a few great ingredients, scramble the eggs halfway, pop it under the broiler for a minute, and breakfast is done. The great trick in this recipe is blanching the asparagus in the sauté pan so that it's perfectly tender. The last thing anyone needs in the morning is one more pot to wash.

serves 2

1 tablespoon unsalted butter

1 shallot, minced, or 2 tablespoons minced yellow
    onion

1 clove garlic, sliced

½ cup ¼-inch pieces asparagus

¼ teaspoon kosher salt, plus a pinch

2 tablespoons water

4 large eggs

¼ cup crumbled goat cheese

GO ELEGANT, AND GREEN

The frittata is delicious when topped (like a pizza) with lettuces—think frisée, arugula, watercress, baby spinach—dressed with lemon juice and olive oil.

Preheat the broiler.

Cook the butter, shallot, and garlic in an 8-inch nonstick sauté pan (omelet pan) over medium heat. When the shallot begins to sizzle, add the asparagus and a pinch of salt. Sauté the mixture for 1 minute, then add the water. Bring to a boil, then simmer until all the water has evaporated from the pan and the shallot begins to sizzle again (this will ensure the asparagus is cooked through).

In a separate bowl, beat the eggs with ¼ teaspoon salt. Add the eggs to the pan and stir with a rubber spatula, scraping down the edges and across the bottom to mix the eggs thoroughly with the asparagus. Cook, without stirring, over medium heat until the edges firm and begin to set. Add the goat cheese to the still-runny eggs and transfer the pan to a rack positioned directly underneath the broiler. If you do not have a pan with an ovenproof handle, leave the door of the oven open and let the handle partially hang out. Broil until the eggs in the center are firm and the edges are slightly brown, about 2 minutes.

Run a spatula all the way around the edges of the pan and underneath the frittata. Slide the frittata out onto a plate and cut it like a pizza.

Simple Breakfast Focaccia with Spinach, Butternut Squash, and Fontina

Pizza for breakfast is nothing new. Jamie ate his share over many spring breaks, and Brooke ate pizza for breakfast (and lunch and dinner) while living in Rome. But a breakfast pizza is something altogether different. You take the best of breakfast (eggs and bacon) and the best of pizza (the crust) and throw them together. At Morandi, a great Italian spot near our apartment in the West Village, the chef turns out focaccia occhio di bue. *The "bull's eye" is a fried egg. Pancetta, or Italian bacon, studs the dough and a dusting of Pecorino finishes things off. We love that combination and we also love ours, which is meant for a crowd. Our dough is rolled out and stretched to fit a full-size cookie sheet (using the entire dough recipe) and then topped with sautéed spinach and butternut squash, and six eggs. Each person gets a square of pizza and an egg, or a "bull's eye." This is filling, and because the recipe is so easy to double or triple, it's a perfect dish to serve when you've got company.*

serves 6

2 tablespoons unsalted butter

1 shallot, minced (1½ to 2 tablespoons)

1 clove garlic, crushed

2 cups diced peeled butternut squash

1 teaspoon kosher salt, plus more to taste

freshly ground pepper

6 ounces fresh spinach

1 recipe Focaccia Dough (recipe follows)

extra virgin olive oil

1 cup grated fontina, provolone, or mozzarella cheese

6 large eggs

Preheat the oven to 450 degrees.

Melt the butter in a large, heavy-bottomed pan over medium-low heat. Add the shallot and garlic and sweat until very aromatic but not browned. Add the squash and season with 1 teaspoon salt and a few grinds of fresh pepper. Cook, stirring often, over medium heat until the squash is partially tender, about 5 minutes. Increase the heat to high, add the spinach, and cook until completely wilted. Spread the mixture on a large plate lined with paper towels and refrigerate until you're ready to use.

Spread the dough in the pan as directed in the recipe or hand shape rounds for individual pizzas. Rub the surface of the dough with olive oil. With clean hands, dimple the dough all over with your fingertips. (Running your hands quickly under cold water will keep them from sticking to the dough.) Scatter the cooked squash and spinach mixture over the surface of the dough. Spread half of the cheese over the squash mixture.

Visually divide the pan into 6 equal sections. Crack an egg in the center of each section and season well with salt and pepper. Top with the remaining cheese. Gently slide the pizza into the hot oven. Cook for 7 minutes; then turn the oven to broil and cook for an additional 4 minutes. Remove from the oven and cool slightly before slicing to serve.

Focaccia Dough

Jamie's had a lot of experience pullin' dough. He began making pizza and focaccia at Frank Stitt's Bottega Café when he was in his early twenties and hasn't stopped since. The difference is that now he makes them with Brooke in a small apartment oven, not in a big, high-temp forno a legna (wood-burning oven). This focaccia is perfect for the newbie home cook because you won't need to have logged dozens of hours working with dough. Really, very little skill is required. You just stretch and then fit the dough into half sheet pans or a full-size baking sheet, dimple it with your fingers, coat it with olive oil, and pop it into a hot oven. And there's no slow-simmering tomato sauce for any of our seasonal combinations. We prefer to quickly sauté fresh veggies (like butternut squash, zucchini, artichokes, or asparagus) and pair them with full-flavored cheeses.

makes two 8- to 10-inch round pizzas,
two 13- x 9-inch focaccias,
or one 18- x 13-inch pizza

MAKE AHEAD

Make the dough the night before and keep well covered in the refrigerator. Precook the vegetables and prepare the cheeses. With a little planning, you'll go from a fridge full of ingredients to hot-out-of-the-oven pizza in about 15 minutes.

1½ cups lukewarm water
1 teaspoon honey
1 packet (2¼ teaspoons) active dry yeast
1 teaspoon kosher salt
3½ cups all-purpose flour, plus more as needed
¼ cup extra virgin olive oil, plus more for greasing

Whisk together the water, honey, and yeast in a small bowl; set aside for 5 minutes. In a separate bowl, combine the salt, flour, and olive oil and blend well. Stir the yeast mixture into the flour mixture with a wooden spoon. The mixture should pull into a smooth ball. Transfer the dough to a clean bowl that has been lightly greased with olive oil. Cover with plastic wrap or a clean kitchen towel and set aside for 45 minutes. For best results, refrigerate overnight.

Remove the dough from the bowl to a floured work surface. Punch the dough down by pressing the air out of it with floured hands until completely flattened. Gently knead the dough until smooth and roll into one large ball.

For focaccia, lightly oil a 13- x 9-inch baking pan and place the dough in the center of the pan. With floured fingertips, pull the dough to the corners of the pan. Continue stretching and pulling until the dough fills the bottom of the pan in an even layer. The dough is now ready to top.

To make a round pizza, divide the dough in half and roll each half into a ball under the palm of your hand. Roll into flat discs with a rolling pin. Lift the flattened disc of dough from the work surface one hand at a time. Hold the disk by its edge with two hands so that the rest of the dough hangs above the surface. Gently stretch the edges of the dough between your hands. Rotate the dough in a hand-over-hand motion—like turning a steering wheel—until the dough measures 8 to 10 inches across. Repeat with the other disc. The pizzas are now ready to top.

CALL IN THE SUBS

Make this dough with any mixture of flour from 100 percent all-purpose to 100 percent whole wheat—whatever you like—as long as the total is 3½ cups. We often prefer to substitute 1 cup whole-wheat flour for 1 cup of the all-purpose. But be warned: a 100 percent whole-wheat crust will be awfully chewy.

Seasonal Toppings

Seasonal substitutions that are great for brunch, bar food, or a fun dinner:

- Summer—Sliced zucchini or other squash, tomatoes, and mozzarella cheese
- Fall/Winter—Caramelized onions, sautéed mushrooms, ricotta cheese, and/or Italian sausage
- Spring—Cooked artichokes, asparagus, and fontina cheese

Crustless Quiche Lorraine

If you're going to make quiche with a crust, that buttery, golden, flaky sucker had better be perfect. None of this translates into easy-breezy, low-stress morning eats. So why not scrap the crust? These crustless beauties have the same creamy, eggy deliciousness without getting your pajamas covered in flour.

makes 12 individual quiches

2 tablespoons unsalted butter, plus more for the
    muffin pan
dry breadcrumbs as needed (about 6 tablespoons)
4 cups leeks, diced
4 cloves garlic, minced
2 cups diced smoked ham or bacon
1½ cups half-and-half
2 large eggs
2 large egg yolks
1 teaspoon kosher salt
¼ teaspoon freshly ground pepper
1 cup grated cheese, such as Parmesan, Gruyère,
    fontina, and so on

Preheat the oven to 325 degrees.

Prepare a 12-cup muffin pan by rubbing the inside of each cup with a nub of cold butter to coat it completely. Add ½ tablespoon breadcrumbs to each cup and roll and shake the pan around so that every bit of butter is covered with breadcrumbs. Tap out the excess and set aside while you prepare the custard.

To prepare the leeks, trim the dark green leaves from the main stalk of the plant. The remainder should be white and shades of green, but solid through, like an onion. Cut the stalk in half through the root end. Insert the tip of your knife into the stalk just behind the root and cut back lengthwise to the end of the plant, creating long, thin strips, about ¼ inch wide, that are all held together by the root, like that fringe trim on your dad's old suede jacket.

Fill a large pot with cool or room-temperature water. Slice the strips of leek across the width, beginning at the green end and working toward the root. Discard the root end. Toss the cut pieces of leek into the bowl of water, agitate with your hand, and leave to settle for 5 minutes. The leeks will float on the surface of the water while the dirt and grit drop to the bottom of the bowl. Scoop the leeks from the surface of the water with a slotted spoon or your hands.

Melt the butter in a large sauté pan over medium heat. Add the leeks; don't worry about transferring some water with them, for the little bit of extra water will help them cook without browning. Sauté the leeks until tender, about 5 minutes. Add the garlic and ham and cook for 3 minutes more, making sure not to burn the garlic. Remove the pan from the heat and stir in the half-and-half. Add the eggs, egg yolks, salt, and pepper to the pan and whisk to combine. Using a slotted spoon, scoop the leeks and ham from the custard mixture and distribute evenly among the prepared muffin cups. Then pour in the custard to reach ¼ to ⅛ inch from the top of each cup. Sprinkle the top of each cup with a bit of cheese.

Bake until just a bit wobbly but set, about 15 minutes. Give the pan a jiggle to test. Cool for 10 minutes before unmolding.

Sweet and Spicy Bacon

A touch of brown sugar and cayenne gives plain bacon extra crunch and bite. There's also that fun interplay of salty and sweet.

serves 4

12 slices thick-cut smoked bacon
cayenne
brown sugar

Preheat the oven to 375 degrees.

Arrange the bacon slices in a single layer on a wire rack set on top of a baking sheet (you may need 2 baking sheets and racks to keep the slices in a single layer). Lightly sprinkle with cayenne, then brown sugar.

Bake until the bacon has rendered its fat and the sugar begins to bubble and caramelize, about 7 minutes.

BRINGING HOME THE BACON

When Jamie appeared on the first season of Food Network's *Chopped,* he made it to the final dessert round only to be confronted with a stack of sliced bacon. He reached back into the recesses of his exhausted brain for this Sweet and Spicy Bacon recipe and partnered it with a chocolate-espresso sauce, orange sabayon, and fresh fruit salad. His spin on "breakfast for dessert" was enough to sway the judges in his favor and send him home the champion.

Bacon, Bacon, Bacon!

Pancetta—Pancetta is pork belly that hails from Italy and is cured with salt and a mixture of spices that includes black pepper. But pancetta, unlike bacon, is not smoked. We think it's great for pastas and other dishes where porky richness is a must but smoke might overwhelm more delicate flavors in the dish.

Canadian Bacon—Bacon that comes from north of the border is the loin of a pig that is cured with salt and smoked in a style similar to American bacon. Canadian bacon can be used interchangeably with smoked ham. This is actually a much leaner option than regular bacon. It adds a meaty, smoky flavor to a dish without the fat.

American Bacon—The stuff we grew up eating at the breakfast table is salt-cured pork belly that is smoked after it's cured. Hundreds of variations exist, depending on the methods and ingredients used for curing and the type of wood used for smoking. American bacon comes in regular cut (which is quite thin), thick cut (still relatively thin slices), and slab from the butcher counter.

Sherry Shrimp and Grits

Our Southern remedy for a long night of drinks on the town. Instead of a burger and fries the morning after, sauté some sweet Gulf shrimp and make a pot of lightly salted grits. The sherry is a quick flavor enhancer, adding a lot of depth to an otherwise simple recipe. Even though this dish originated on the South Carolina coast (as an early morning breakfast for shrimpers), it's just as tasty eaten at noon in the comfort of your own apartment.

serves 4

1 cup dry stone-ground grits, prepared (page 40)
2 pounds (26/30 count or smaller) fresh shrimp,
    peeled and deveined
kosher salt and freshly ground pepper to taste
cayenne or Creole Seasoning (page 63)
4 tablespoons (½ stick) unsalted butter
1 medium green bell pepper, diced
1 shallot, minced
2 cloves garlic, minced
1 cup dry sherry
½ cup cream
2 tablespoons chopped fresh parsley
1 cup cherry tomatoes, quartered
8 slices bacon, cooked crisp and crumbled

Prepare the grits.

In a small bowl, toss the shrimp with 1 teaspoon kosher salt, ¼ teaspoon black pepper, and a pinch of cayenne or 2 teaspoons Creole Seasoning. Set aside if using immediately, or cover and refrigerate up to 12 hours if preparing later.

Melt the butter in a large sauté pan over high heat. Add the bell pepper, shallot, and garlic. Season lightly with salt and pepper; cook until the garlic and shallot are tender and lightly browned. Deglaze the pan with the sherry and reduce by three-quarters. Stir in the cream and bring the mixture to a boil. Add the seasoned shrimp and cook over medium-high heat until the shrimp are bright pink and the liquid is reduced by approximately one-quarter.

Remove from the heat and stir in the parsley, tomatoes, and bacon. Serve with the grits.

MAKE AHEAD

Prepare a pot of grits and keep them over very low heat, covered with a lid, or in a large casserole, covered with aluminum foil, in a 200-degree oven for up to 2 hours. For the shrimp, prepare the recipe up to the point the shrimp are to be added to the cream. Turn off the heat after the cream comes to a boil and hold the pan on top of the stove. About 5 minutes before you're ready to serve, bring the mixture to a boil, add the shrimp, and continue as directed.

Frank Stitt's Southern Restaurant Empire

Frank Stitt opened Highlands Bar & Grill in Birmingham, Alabama, in 1982, about twenty years before grits became a fashionable (or acceptable, for that matter) side dish in fine-dining restaurants. From the beginning, Frank championed Alabama's great local ingredients and the strong food traditions of the South—instilling those values first in his cooks, then the community, and eventually shaping the new face of cooking in the American South. Jamie was fortunate enough to spend six years working under the great chef and spent his first year at Highlands making two gallons of grits every day for the restaurant's signature appetizer Baked Grits with Ham, Wild Mushrooms, and Parmesan. Through the years, Stitt's cooking at Highlands has garnered innumerable awards and recognition, including being named one of the "Top 5 Outstanding Restaurants" in the country in 2009 and 2010 by the James Beard Foundation.

Highlands Bar & Grill—The flagship restaurant and the one that's garnered the most awards and praise over the years. Highlands is a fixture on Birmingham's south side, and the main reason that neighborhood remains the town's number-one nighttime destination. Dinner at Highlands is a top priority for any trip to central Alabama.

Bottega—Stitt's Italian joint, set in a nearly century-old building designed by the same architects that drew up the plans for the New York Public Library, is a favorite spot for Birmingham foodies in the know. And for those truly in the know, there's no better seat in the house than at the newly redesigned bar with Ward, the town's favorite bartender/storyteller/confidant, and a shiny Berkel slicer that pumps out paper-thin slices of the world's finest cured meats.

Bottega Café—The wood-burning pizza oven is the heart of Bottega's casual sister restaurant. The menu features hand-stretched pizzas, baked pastas, roasted meats, and fish from the oven, plus innovative salads and sandwiches. But there is nothing casual about this place; it is THE spot to see and be seen. Especially on Mondays, or—as Brooke knows it—Crab Cake Night.

Chez Fon Fon—There's no finer spot on a cool Alabama night than under the trellis, next to the *boule* court, on Chez Fon Fon's back porch. A glass of champagne and one of the best steak tartares we've ever tasted make the experience complete.

Quartet of Creamy Grits

Thanks to chefs like Frank Stitt, who first taught Jamie how to make this dish, grits are not just for breakfast anymore. On menus from Apalachicola to Seattle, this Southern-style polenta is happily accompanying every-thing from grilled pork to roasted fish for dinner. But still, for us, there's nothing more comforting than a warm bowl of grits with a little extra cheese on top for those chilly New York mornings.

serves 6 to 8

9 cups water

2 teaspoons kosher salt, plus more to taste

2 cups stone-ground grits

6 tablespoons (¾ stick) unsalted butter, cut into bits

1 cup grated Parmesan cheese

freshly ground pepper to taste

Tabasco sauce to taste

Combine the water and salt in a medium pot and bring to a rapid boil. Add the grits in a slow stream, whisking constantly. Turn off the heat and allow the grits to settle. Some husk will rise to the top. Skim the small white flecks from the surface of the water

What's a Grit?

If you want to drive someone from the South mad, tell them that grits are the same thing as polenta. Grits are coarsely ground dried corn; polenta is dried corn with a medium grind. The difference may seem small, but after cooking, they're a world apart (literally, like, Italy to Alabama). Good grits should have the words "stone-ground" and/or "organic" on the label. Quick or instant grits are merely a shell of their former selves, not worth the time or money (even though they're cheap). The best grits likely won't be found at your local grocery store (unless you live in a great Southern town). They will, how-ever, turn up at the farmers' market. When all else fails, do what you do for all of your problems these days—turn to the Internet. Small mills that produce the finest grits in the world offer their wares via mail order; check them out at:

McEwen & Sons—Our favorite by far! Grown and milled just outside of Birmingham, Alabama.
www.mcewenandsons.com

Anson Mills—Delicious grits steeped in South Carolina tradition. www.ansonmills.com

Louisiana Pride Grist Mill—This is another great source for grits just north of Baton Rouge.
www.louisianapridegristmill.com

using a fine-mesh skimmer or a spoon and discard. Whisk the grits again, breaking up any clumps that may have formed on the bottom. Turn the heat back to high and stir constantly until the mixture returns to a boil. Reduce the heat to a simmer and cook for approximately 45 minutes. Stir occasionally to make sure nothing sticks to the bottom of the pot. When finished, the grits should be well thickened and tender (though they will retain a good bit of texture). If the grits are extremely thick and still tough, add more water, ½ cup at a time, as they cook.

Add the butter and cheese and stir until melted. Adjust the seasoning with salt, pepper, and hot sauce.

For creamy grits, serve immediately. To make grits cakes, cook a bit longer until very thick, spread evenly onto a greased baking sheet, and refrigerate until cooled completely. Cut into the desired shapes and gently remove with a spatula. Grits cakes can then be reheated in a cast-iron skillet, on a VERY hot grill, baked, or fried.

Once the grits are cooked, you can add any number of garnishes to the pot, in addition to the Parmesan and Tabasco.

FOUR FAVORITES

Fresh Jalapeño and Cheddar Cheese—Substitute Cheddar cheese for the Parmesan and add minced fresh jalapeños for a spicy, Southwestern-flavored treat.

Prosciutto and Sautéed Mushrooms—Pile thinly sliced prosciutto and sautéed mushrooms on top of cooked grits with extra Parmesan to give Southern goodness an Italian flair.

Chopped Fresh Tomatoes, Sweet Peppers, and Cheddar Cheese (aka Nassau Grits)—Substitute Cheddar cheese for the Parmesan and simmer in the cooked grits diced tomatoes and sweet peppers for 5 to 10 minutes until tender. Though the name comes from the Bahamas, we know them from the famed Pensacola, Florida, breakfast spot The Coffee Cup.

Sautéed Sweet Corn—Cut fresh corn from the cob, sauté in butter until tender, and season with salt and pepper. Stir the cooked corn into the cooked grits to take their corn flavor to the next level.

SUNRISE COCKTAILS

One of our favorite parts of brunch is that it provides an acceptable reason to have a drink before noon. The trick is to stir up something that makes you feel bubbly—not buzzed—after a few sips. Brunch is about mimosas, not Manhattans! The best way to go about serving drinks to a crowd is to let them serve themselves. Set up a buffet with all of the necessary elements and set out a recipe card by each station. Everyone will love playing bartender, and you'll have a chance to get the food on the table.

Champagne Buffet

Champagne and brunch go hand-in-hand. Why tear them apart? There's something about popping a cork before noon that makes the headache you created last night, and the worries of Monday morning, float away with the bubbles.

Start out with a bottle of champagne or good-quality prosecco. Nino Franco and Zardetto are the best brands of Italian bubbly for celebrations with friends because they're as economical as they are delicious. To get more bang for your buck—and give your guests a buffet of options—set a few of the following juices out on a nice tray along with your chosen bubbly on ice and let them mix their own drinks:

- orange juice
- blood orange juice
- apricot nectar
- peach/white peach juice
- passion fruit puree

Boiron is a French company that produces the highest-quality pure frozen fruit purees in the world. Look for them in the freezer section of high-end grocery stores or on the web at www.boiron freres.com/uk_index.html. Also, nectars and purees tend to be more concentrated, so you need to use less of these than you would juice.

French 75

serves 4

2 ounces fresh lemon juice
2 ounces gin
1 ounce (2 tablespoons) Simple Syrup (recipe
    follows)
champagne
1 strip lemon twist for each glass

Shake the lemon juice, gin, and simple syrup together
with ice and strain evenly into 4 glasses. Fill each
glass with champagne and top with the lemon twist.

Simple Syrup

1 cup granulated sugar
2 cups water

Combine the sugar and water in a small pot. Bring the
mixture to a boil and stir until the sugar is dissolved.
Cool and store in the refrigerator for up to 4 weeks.

Champagne Cocktail

*If you think Samuel Langhorne Clemens's (aka Mark
Twain) greatest contribution to American culture was
The Adventures of Tom Sawyer, think again. Legend has
it that Clemens stirred up the world's first champagne
cocktail, a simple mixture of brut champagne, a bit of
brandy, a touch of sugar, and a drop of spice or bitters.*

serves 1

5 drops Angostura bitters
1 sugar cube
champagne or prosecco
1 strip lemon twist

Add the 5 drops bitters directly to the sugar cube
inside an empty champagne flute. Fill the glass with
champagne or prosecco and garnish with the lemon
twist.

Kir Royale

serves 1

1 ounce (2 tablespoons) crème de cassis

champagne or prosecco

Pour the cassis into a champagne flute and fill with bubbly.

Ramos Gin Fizz

The gin fizz is the only beautifully bubbly drink on our list without champagne. Here Jamie gives you the quick-and-easy version of the New Orleans brunch classic made by the finest old-school bartenders.

serves 2

6 ounces gin
juice of 1 lemon
juice of 1 lime
1 tablespoon powdered sugar or superfine
    granulated sugar
1 large egg white (optional)
2 tablespoons cream
ice cubes
soda water

Combine the gin, lemon and lime juices, sugar, egg white, and cream in a shaker with 2 ice cubes and shake until frothy—a good minute of vigorous shaking. Strain into highball glasses filled with ice and top off with a splash of soda water.

AFTERWORK APPS

Sometimes Brooke does a Ryan Seacrest–style countdown to 5 P.M. "Four, three, two, one, WHITE WINE!" Is that so wrong? There's just something so exhilarating about leaving the workday behind and doing what we really want: nibbling on delicious apps and sipping drinks while catching up with our friends.

The trick here is to serve social food that invites you to step away from the dinner table and relax. We love our dips and passable h.o.d.s because it's just as easy to enjoy them on the couch—just you and your honey catching the day's episode of Jon Stewart—as it is to share them with a crowd. We swear Brooke has made three best girlfriends on the merit of the ratatouille recipe alone. Jamie, for his part, likes to bribe our building's superintendent with the tangy, unctuous goodness of our feta dip and a bag of pita chips. (Hey, our rent didn't go up this year and our dishwasher always works!)

More than anything, we think it's really comforting to have one or two of these sitting in the fridge, waiting for us when we come home after a long ride on the F train. If friends can't make it, we can still call an "emergency happy hour" any day of the week and unwind with delicious, simple bites. The best part of all is the easy cleanup; our food doesn't require forks and knives—thumbs and index fingers only!

Mix and match from the list below, and you and your happy hour friends will be ready to munch faster than you can open that bottle of vino. There's just enough food to keep everyone happy—and to keep them coming back for more.

Easy Add-Ons for Your Afterwork Apps

- assortment of nuts (hickory-smoked almonds, peanuts, cashews, Marcona almonds)
- olives
- hard cheeses (like hunks of Parmesan and Manchego)
- avocado-oil- or olive-oil-fried potato chips

Blue Cheese, Apple, and Walnut Spread

There's something so delicious and gutsy about blue cheese and walnuts together in a salad that we thought the combo would make a fabulous spread. It's savory, sweet, crunchy, and absolutely irresistible with a lightly toasted baguette. You'll never again be as rewarded for five minutes of chopping and a quick stir as you will with this app!

serves 4 to 6

2 apples (Honeycrisp, Gala, or Golden Delicious)
grated zest of ½ lemon
juice of 1 lemon
pinch of kosher salt
freshly ground pepper
2 tablespoons extra virgin olive oil

8 ounces blue cheese (Danish, Maytag, Bleu
        d'Auvergne, Roquefort, or Stilton), crumbled
1 cup walnut pieces, toasted and roughly chopped
2 tablespoons chopped fresh chives or parsley

Cut the apples into slices approximately ¼ inch thick, discarding the cores. Cut the slices into strips ¼ inch wide, then cut again crosswise to form small cubes. (Remember, these will be served on crackers or a baguette, so they should be very small cubes.) Place the apples in a medium bowl and toss with the lemon zest and juice, salt, and a few grinds of pepper. Add the olive oil, blue cheese, walnuts, and chives and mix well. Store, tightly covered, in the refrigerator for up to 10 days. Serve with toasted bread, whole-wheat crackers, or celery sticks.

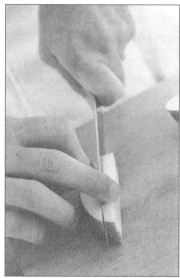
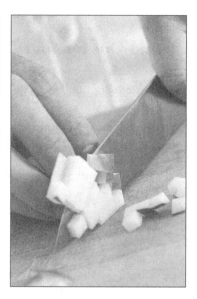

Feta and Sun-Dried Tomato Tapenade

If you're like us and believe that foods can enhance your mood—even transport you—then throw away the Prozac and pack your passport. Our tapenade pairs the salty tang of feta and olives with handfuls of brightly flavored parsley. The result is this amazing mixture that will whisk you away to the sun-baked beaches and breezy port towns of Greece.

serves 6 to 8

¼ cup sliced scallions

½ cup pitted Kalamata olives, chopped

½ cup sun-dried tomatoes (oil packed), chopped

2 cups (firmly packed) flat-leaf parsley leaves

2 cups cow's milk feta cheese, crumbled

1 tablespoon red wine vinegar

2 tablespoons extra virgin olive oil

Combine the scallions, olives, sun-dried tomatoes, and parsley in a food processor. Pulse in short bursts of 3 to 4 seconds until all the ingredients are well chopped but not pureed. Stop and scrape down the sides as needed. Add the feta and pulse again briefly to combine. Transfer the mixture to a bowl and stir in the vinegar and olive oil. Serve with fresh pita, pita chips, or toasted pieces of bread (baguette or focaccia). Keeps refrigerated for 2 weeks.

Getting a Little Nutty

Our spring trip to Napa Valley and San Francisco yielded two cases of delicious wine and one fantastic, surprise find—an organic almond farm just southeast of San Fran. We both fell in love with Alfieri Farms' hickory-smoked almonds—we feel they must be the "good-for-you" alternative to barbecue potato chips. They're the perfect thing to snack on throughout the day and even better when enjoyed during "app hour," poured into little dishes of our wedding china and served with a strong cocktail. Once we finish our last bag, we're going to reorder through their website. G. L. Alfieri Organic Almond Farms, 19465 S. Carrolton Avenue, Ripon, California 95366; www.alfierifarms.com.

Roasted Eggplant, Tahini, and Basil Dip

The Middle Eastern staple baba ghanoush took a road trip to southern Italy and this is the fabulous, very flavorful result. Roasted eggplant is very simply mixed with tahini (a paste of ground sesame seeds), garlic, sun-dried tomatoes, and basil. Our friends love the dip with our happy hour staple, pita chips, as much as they do with a plate of crudités—small sticks of zucchini, fennel, carrots, and celery.

serves 6 to 8

2 medium Italian eggplants (about 2 pounds)

1 head garlic

¼ cup extra virgin olive oil, plus more as needed

2 teaspoons salt, plus more as needed

½ teaspoon freshly ground pepper, plus more as needed

3 tablespoons tahini

½ cup sun-dried tomatoes, finely chopped

½ cup fresh basil leaves, finely chopped

Preheat the oven to 325 degrees.

Remove the skin from the eggplants with a vegetable peeler and cut the eggplants into 1-inch cubes. Place in a large baking dish. Break the head of garlic into cloves, smash each clove with the side of a heavy knife, and remove the skin. Add the crushed cloves to the eggplant. Pour the olive oil evenly over the eggplant and season with the 2 teaspoons salt and the ½ teaspoon pepper. Mix well to distribute evenly.

Cover the baking dish with aluminum foil and place in the preheated oven to cook. After 1 hour of baking, uncover the dish and stir the contents well. Return to the oven and bake for 15 minutes. If after this time there is still a good bit of moisture in the dish, stir again, and bake, uncovered, until nearly dry. Cool completely before continuing. (This step can be done 1 to 3 days in advance if the roasted eggplant is cooled and kept covered in the refrigerator.)

Transfer the cooked eggplant and garlic to a food processor. Puree until smooth. Add the tahini, tomatoes, and basil and puree again to incorporate. Taste and adjust the seasoning with salt and pepper as needed and add more olive oil if the mixture becomes too thick. Serve with fresh pita, pita chips, or toasted pieces of bread (baguette or focaccia). Keeps refrigerated for 2 weeks.

Ratatouille Crostini

Ratatouille is a Provençal staple and every French(wo)man has her or his favorite list of veggies that they throw in the pot. This dish, originally a stew, features warm-weather produce such as tomatoes, zucchini, eggplant, bell peppers, onions, garlic, and basil. Whether you layer the veggies "gratin-style" before baking them or dice them and throw them all in a pot to simmer, the result is a ripe taste of summer. Instead of serving our 'touille as a side dish to accompany grilled fish or meat, we make it an h.o.d. The brightly colored bits of veggies spooned onto toasted rounds of baguette spread with creamy goat cheese make it a gorgeous bite. This is Brooke's absolute favorite summer appetizer.

serves 8 to 12

2 tablespoons extra virgin olive oil, plus more
    for the baguettes
½ cup diced yellow onion
pinch of kosher salt, plus more to taste
1 tablespoon minced garlic
1 cup finely diced eggplant
½ cup finely diced zucchini
½ cup finely diced yellow squash
1 red bell pepper, seeded and diced
freshly ground pepper to taste
1 cup finely diced tomato
4 branches fresh thyme
1 tablespoon chopped fresh basil
1 baguette
8 ounces fresh goat cheese

Heat the olive oil in a large, heavy-bottomed pot over medium-high heat. Add the onion with a pinch of salt and cook, stirring often, until softened, about 5 minutes.

Stir in the garlic and cook until aromatic, about 30 seconds. Add the eggplant, zucchini, squash, and bell pepper. Season well with salt and pepper. Cook, stirring occasionally and being careful not to let anything stick to or brown on the bottom of the pot, until the vegetables are halfway tender, about 7 minutes. Add the tomato and thyme, mix well, and bring to a simmer. Cook until thickened. Remove from the heat and stir in the basil. Adjust the seasoning and set aside to cool.

Drizzle a sliced baguette with olive oil and toast in a preheated 350-degree oven. Spread the toasted slices with goat cheese and top each with a spoonful of the room-temperature ratatouille.

THE NEXT LEVEL

Take a little time and cut the vegetables properly. Remember that spoonfuls of your ratatouille are going to rest atop small slices of toasted bread. Roughly chopped, chunky vegetables don't make for delicate bites.

Brooke on *the* Bottle—Sauvignon Blanc: What Women Want

The trick to serving wine to a gaggle of girls is to choose one crowd-pleaser. That way, as the hostess, you can wordlessly refill glasses instead of cutting in on the conversation to ask, "Chardonnay or Pinot Grigio?"

But how to choose just one wine? What *do* women want?

I've joined the ranks of Nancy Meyers and Freud as I try to crack the code, and after exhausting, tipsy research—countless lunches, showers, girl dinners, and gab fests—I think I've come up with the answer! Women want Sauvignon Blanc.

First, to understand a girl's favorite grape, you have to know how wines are classified. In America, Chile, and New Zealand—where you'll find many wonderful, well-priced Sauvignon Blancs—wines are named by the predominant grape used. So when your wine-store savior asks you, "Are you looking for a Chardonnay, Pinot Grigio, or a Sauvignon Blanc?" he's really wondering which variety of grape you prefer.

In western Europe, however, wines are labeled according to the region in which they're grown. Sancerre, for example, comes from the lovely hilltop town of Sancerre in France's Loire Valley. It also happens to be made from 100 percent Sauvignon Blanc. It's just tradition in France to name the wine after the geographic region instead of the grape.

If one girlfriend declares Sauvignon Blanc is the best, while the other insists Sancerre is the bomb, you can play peacekeeper and tell them they're both right.

But enjoying wine isn't about labels—it's about taste. A good Sauvignon Blanc is light and lively and pairs perfectly with so many "girl" foods (salads, seafood, veggies, and lighter cheeses). The majority of Sauvignon Blancs are crisp and dry and work just as well as an apéritif before the food is served as they do during the meal. There's an herbal scent, pleasant tartness, and lemony zip to the grape that keeps it refreshing—whether you're on your first glass or your third.

An assignment for you: sample a variety of Sauvignon Blancs from different countries and with different price ranges. Choose a favorite based on your taste and your pocketbook. Then order a case or two for your next get-together. Hostessing will be that much easier once you've selected a crowd-pleasing wine that all your girlfriends will want again and again.

BEST SAUVIGNON BLANC REGIONS

New Zealand—Best bang for your buck, tart, crisp, pepperoncini-like spiciness (pepperoncini are the pickled hot peppers you find on your Greek salad)

Chile—Good value and very similar flavor profile to New Zealand's Sauvignon Blancs, though not as consistently pleasing

France, Loire Valley—Expensive (but worth every penny), minerally, light floral quality, depth, some fruit, very well balanced

California—Less expensive than French versions but prices vary widely, melon-like flavor, touch of butter, grassiness

Sweet Pea–BLT Wraps

The seven-layer salad is a Southern Junior League staple that both Brooke and Jamie grew up on. Bacon, lettuce, tomato, mayo, shredded Cheddar, green bell peppers, and sweet peas are layered in a trifle bowl (or any high-sided, clear glass bowl) and then served up to a lot of oohs and aahs. We like to think of these wraps as a portable, updated version of that Southern sellout salad. The Cheddar is replaced by blue cheese and we've omitted the iceberg in favor of fragrant basil and pretty red-leaf lettuce.

serves 6 to 8

4 ounces sliced bacon
one 16-ounce package frozen sweet peas
1 cup cherry tomatoes
1 tablespoon torn fresh basil
2 tablespoons mayonnaise
¼ cup crumbled blue cheese
salt and freshly ground pepper to taste
1 head red- or green-leaf lettuce

TO FRY OR NOT TO FRY

When crisping bacon to turn into crumbles as in this recipe, you may pan-fry or bake the strips of bacon. By baking on a rack, the fat drips away as it cooks, leaving the strips crisp without the risk of burning and marginally leaner than pan-frying. Pan-frying is comforting and delicious, though we think it the better option when you want bacon more on the chewy side than the crispy. Both methods of cooking are certain to fill your house with the glorious smell of smoked pork, but only pan-frying will leave it smelling like that until tomorrow.

Preheat the oven to 350 degrees.

Arrange the bacon in a single layer on a baking sheet and bake until crisp, about 10 minutes. Remove the browned bacon from the oven and drain on paper towels.

Bring a large pot of salted water to a boil and add the peas. Cook until tender, approximately 3 minutes. Refresh under cool water and set aside in a colander to drain. Cut the tomatoes into quarters and combine with the peas in a bowl. Crumble in the bacon; add the basil, mayonnaise, and blue cheese and mix well. Season to taste with salt and pepper, then transfer to a clean bowl.

Separate the leaves of lettuce, tearing them from the core. Do your best to keep them whole. After giving them a good wash and drying well, arrange them on a platter. Place the bowl of the pea mixture in the center of the platter and serve by letting everyone spoon some of the pea mixture into a lettuce leaf to make their own wraps.

Seasonal Fruit Wrapped in Prosciutto with Thyme-Honey Cream

Jamie has a serious food crush on salty and sweet, calling it the culinary world's greatest combination. Honey-roasted peanuts, toffee bars, and chocolate-covered pretzels are some of his favorites. When he takes a spin on the healthier side, he slices up a big ol' platter of melons, peaches, or figs, wraps them in prosciutto, and finishes everything off with this easy-to-make sweet cream. Follow our recipe and capitalize on the perfect salty-and-sweet marriage year-round.

serves 6

CREAM

1 cup cream

1 sprig fresh thyme

1 lemon, zest grated and juiced

1 teaspoon wildflower honey

4 ounces prosciutto di Parma, very thinly sliced

1 cantaloupe or honeydew melon (March through August) *or*

2 peaches or nectarines (June through September) *or*

12 fresh figs (August through December)

THE NEXT LEVEL

For an extra treat, cook the prosciutto-wrapped fruit on a very hot, lightly oiled grill, or line them up on a baking sheet, drizzle with olive oil, and broil until the prosciutto is just crisped and the fruit warmed through. The peaches and figs are especially good when cooked.

For the cream, combine the cream, thyme, and zest in a small saucepot. Bring the mixture to a simmer over medium heat and cook at a simmer for 5 minutes. Turn off the heat, whisk in the honey, and pour the mixture through a fine-mesh strainer into a plastic, ceramic, or glass container. Stir in the lemon juice and place in the refrigerator. The cream can be made up to 2 days in advance.

No matter which fruit you're using, you'll need to cut the prosciutto into 1-inch-wide strips (just big enough that a bit of the fruit will stick out from either end once it's wrapped).

For the melon, remove the rind and seeds and cut the fruit into bite-size pieces. Wrap in prosciutto and stick a toothpick through where the ends of the prosciutto meet. Arrange on a platter.

For the peaches or nectarines, cut the fruit in half and discard the pits. Slice each half into 4 to 6 wedges (2 pieces of fruit will yield 16 to 24 pieces). Wrap 1 slice of prosciutto around the center of each piece of fruit. Be sure to wrap completely and the ham will stick to itself.

For the figs, cut in half through the stem and wrap in prosciutto. If you've got good ham, it will stick to itself and you won't need a pick to secure it. Arrange on a platter lined with fig leaves if you can get your hands on them.

Come party time, remove the cream from the fridge and let it warm up a little. Drizzle it over the fruit and spoon some into a little bowl to serve alongside in case anyone wants a little extra.

STICK A PICK IN IT

No matter which fruit you're using, securing the prosciutto with a toothpick will ensure your pretty packages stay together and make them easier to pick up, dip, and eat; but only the melon requires it. Because the melon has a much higher water content, sometimes those extra juices can cause the prosciutto to unstick itself.

HOW TO SELECT A CANTALOUPE

- When shopping for your cantaloupe, make sure there is no stem attached, because a ripe melon will pluck right off the vine.
- Don't worry about looks—care about what's on the inside. The tastiest melon probably isn't going to be the prettiest one.
- Go for the khaki-colored melon—not a green one.
- Sniff the stem end—it should smell a little sweet and melony.

Pro-SHOO-toe

Think of prosciutto as the Madonna of the ham world. It made its big, stateside splash back in the '80s and no one could get enough. In short order, critics predicted its rise and fall—surely we'd all move on to a bigger, better, younger Italian export. But the dry-cured hindquarters of the pig, deriving their name from the Italian verb *prosciugare*, meaning "to dry," held their own. Americans quickly developed such a taste for the nutty, lightly smoky, vibrantly complex slices of pig that they began to endeavor to make their own. Iowa native Herb Eckhouse and his wife, Kathy, own and operate La Quercia, a much-lauded and loved company dedicated to producing European-quality cured meats here in the States. Their salty-sweet prosciutto is available at Whole Foods, by mail order, and in fine-dining establishments like New York City's Babbo and Gramercy Tavern. To eat it is to believe it. And we love it!

Broccoli Rabe and Ricotta Bruschetta

Our broccoli rabe preparation is fantastic in so many different ways—hot out of the sauté pan as a side dish, cool and straight from the fridge as part of a lunchtime salad, and, finally, at room temperature, nestled atop a toasted baguette smeared with ricotta cheese. We're more than a little proud of ourselves for sneaking a folic-acid- and phytochemical-packed vegetable into our happy hour lineup. Served with a cocktail, dark greens are much less painful. For good measure, give your plate of ricotta and rabe a final drizzle of fruity, super-high-quality extra virgin olive oil.

serves 4 to 6

1 bunch broccoli rabe

¼ cup extra virgin olive oil, plus more as needed

3 cloves garlic, crushed

½ teaspoon red pepper flakes

½ cup olives (Kalamata or Picholine), pitted and
    roughly chopped

grated zest of ½ lemon

kosher salt and freshly ground pepper to taste

1 baguette

8 ounces fresh ricotta cheese

best-quality extra virgin olive oil for drizzling

Preheat the oven to 325 degrees.

Trim the tough stem ends from the broccoli rabe (approximately 1½ inches). Bring a large pot of well-salted water to a rapid boil. Add the broccoli rabe and cook for 3 minutes. Drain and refresh under cold water to cool completely. Dry thoroughly by squeezing in a clean kitchen towel.

Place the olive oil, garlic, and red pepper flakes in a large sauté pan over high heat. Cook until the garlic begins to lightly brown around the edges. Add all of the broccoli rabe to the pan and cook until heated through and the leaves are tender. The stems will remain a bit tough. Stir in the olives and lemon zest and mix well. Adjust the seasoning with salt and pepper. Transfer to a plate or platter to cool.

Slice the baguette diagonally so that each slice is 5 to 7 inches long and ½ inch thick. Brush the bread with olive oil and toast on a baking sheet in the preheated oven until crisp but not completely dry, about 8 minutes. Remove the bread from the oven and cool. The toasted bread can be stored in an airtight container or ziplock bag in a cool, dry place for 1 week.

To serve, spread 2 tablespoons ricotta onto each toasted slice of bread. Top with the cooked broccoli rabe and drizzle each bruschetta with a small amount of extra virgin olive oil.

EVERYDAY DINNERS

This is where things get tough in a marriage. . . . How do you keep it interesting night after night?

No one tells you that the food is the first thing to go.

Wait, did you think we were talking about something else?

In our house, we argue about the type of meal. Brooke prefers a big lunch and a small dinner. So come supper-time, all she wants is a baguette, a few slivers of cheese, a light salad, and then to call it a night. Jamie, on the other hand, fantasizes about ending his day with bacon-wrapped pork roast and a pile of mashed potatoes. After a string of unsatisfying meals (for one or the other), we've broached creative compromise territory. Here's what we decided:

- A protein is a must and vegetables are nice.
- Two vegetables, if cooked simultaneously, are even nicer.
- Starches (pasta, rice, orzo, couscous) that incorporate protein and veggies are the quickest dinners of all and make for even better lunches the next day.
- Thin cuts of beef or pork don't overwhelm one on the calorie front and cook up faster than a pot of Uncle Ben's.

Really, we think this is the most important part of this cookbook, because everyday dinners are the ones we remember the most—the warm butternut squash soup after a day in the cold and snow, pork tenderloin for friends on a Tuesday night, and spring vegetable cannelloni for the first warm evening. Because this is what marriage is all about: sharing a life, meals, and moments together day in and day out, even when it's not a special occasion.

TACO NIGHT

Mexican food makes people smile. (Mention soft tacos and then talk about wienerschnitzel—see which one gets a bigger grin.) So in the summer, when we go down to the Gulf of Mexico and rent a beach house with our families, we always squeeze in a taco night. The warm weather already has everyone in the mood for fun, easygoing eats, and the promise of a "build-your-own buffet" with platters of sautéed onions and peppers, spiced grilled chicken, marinated beef, and bacony black beans brings everyone to the stove. Easy-as-pie garnishes become kids' work; the tiniest ones grate the cheese, the midsizers chop the tomatoes, and the burgeoning chefs-to-be whip up a big bowl of guacamole. But, really, what sets our taco night apart are the seasoned salts (page 61) that make every protein flavorful.

serves 4 to 6

Fajita-Style Onions and Peppers

2 tablespoons vegetable oil
¼ teaspoon ground cumin
½ teaspoon ground coriander
½ teaspoon smoked paprika
2 cups thinly sliced yellow onion (1 medium)
1½ teaspoons kosher salt
3 cloves garlic, grated
¼ teaspoon dried oregano
freshly ground pepper to taste
3 bell peppers, cut into julienne

Add the vegetable oil, cumin, coriander, and paprika to a wide-bottomed pot over medium-high heat. When the oil is very hot and the spices are fragrant, add the onion and stir rapidly until the sizzling stops. Stir in the salt, garlic, oregano, and ground pepper. Cook for 5 minutes more. Add the peppers and continue cooking until the vegetables are tender.

Chicken

1 teaspoon kosher salt, plus more as needed
½ teaspoon freshly ground pepper, plus more
    as needed
2 cloves garlic, grated
¼ teaspoon dried oregano
1 lime, juiced
1 tablespoon extra virgin olive oil
4 boneless, skinless chicken breasts

Whisk together the salt, pepper, garlic, oregano, lime juice, and olive oil. Add the chicken breasts, turn to coat well, and leave to marinate for 30 to 60 minutes at room temperature or refrigerate overnight.

Remove the chicken from the marinade, brush off the excess, and season lightly with salt and pepper. Cook the chicken on a hot well-oiled grill or roast on a foil-lined baking pan in a preheated 425-degree oven until cooked through, 8 to 12 minutes. Rest the cooked chicken on a rack for 2 to 3 minutes before slicing.

Beef or Pork

grated zest of 1 lime
½ lime, juiced (about 1 tablespoon)
1 clove garlic, grated
3 tablespoons fish sauce or soy sauce
1 tablespoon sesame oil
¼ teaspoon red pepper flakes
¼ teaspoon ground ginger or grated fresh ginger
    (optional)
1 pound flank or skirt steak, or 1 pork tenderloin
    (1 to 1½ pounds)
kosher salt and freshly ground pepper

Combine all the ingredients except the meat in a bowl and whisk to combine. Trim any excess fat from the meat and add the meat to the marinade. Marinate for 1 to 2 hours at room temperature or refrigerate overnight.

Remove the meat from the marinade, brush off the excess, and season lightly with salt and pepper. Cook on a hot well-oiled grill or roast on a foil-lined baking pan in a preheated 425-degree oven. For beef, cook 4 to 6 minutes each side. For pork, cook 8 to 10 minutes each side. Rest the meat on a rack for 4 to 6 minutes before slicing.

Fish

1 to 1½ pounds boneless, skinless firm white fish
    fillets (mahi mahi, halibut, or striped bass)
1 large egg
2 tablespoons milk
1½ cups cornmeal
½ cup all-purpose flour
1 tablespoon Creole Seasoning (page 63)
canola or vegetable oil for frying
kosher salt to taste

Cut the fish into strips about the size of your pointer finger (a touch thicker if you have skinny fingers). Beat the egg and milk together in a small bowl. In a separate bowl, combine the cornmeal, flour, and seasoning.

Dip the pieces of fish into the egg mixture, then coat in the cornmeal mixture. Rest the pieces in a single layer on a clean plate or tray until all the fish is battered. Place a medium sauté pan or cast-iron skillet over medium heat and fill with oil to a depth of ½ inch. Test the oil by dipping the end of one of the pieces of fish into it. If it bubbles rapidly, you are ready to fry. Set a plate lined with paper towels next to the stove. Add the battered fish to the pan to cook, being careful not to overcrowd the pan. Turn each piece once with a pair of tongs and cook until they are golden brown on both sides. Transfer the cooked pieces to the towel-lined plate to drain. Sprinkle lightly with salt and serve immediately.

KISS—KEEP IT SIMPLE, STUPID

It's one of the great rules in the kitchen—and in life for that matter—and something that Jamie heard as a young cook more times than he cares to remember. While our fried fish tacos are plenty simple and even more delicious, grilled fish tacos are even easier. Once the fish is cut and seasoned, they'll be on the table in just about 5 minutes.

Cut the fish into strips, season with Ultimate Grill Salt (page 61)—approximately 2 teaspoons per pound of fish—and cook on a very hot grill for 2 minutes per side, or until cooked through. When the fish comes off the grill, give the whole plate a good squeeze of lime before serving.

Seasoned Black Beans

4 ounces bacon, chopped

½ cup diced yellow onion

1 teaspoon ground cumin

1 jalapeño, diced

2 cloves garlic, minced

1 beefsteak tomato, diced

one 15-ounce can black beans, drained

2 tablespoons chopped fresh cilantro

Place a large sauté pan over high heat, add the bacon, and cook until lightly browned. Stir in the onion and continue cooking until it is very tender. Add the cumin and jalapeño and cook for 2 minutes. Stir in the garlic and cook until aromatic but not browned. Add the tomato and heat through, about 2 minutes. Add the black beans, bring the mixture to a simmer, and cook for approximately 10 minutes to allow the flavors to come together. Remove from the heat and stir in the cilantro.

Serve sautéed vegetables, cooked meat, and warmed tortillas on a platter accompanied by the black beans and dishes of sour cream and grated Cheddar cheese. Warm tortillas by tightly wrapping a stack of them in aluminum foil and heating them in a 350-degree oven for 5 to 7 minutes. After that, the oven can be turned off and the tortillas kept warm for up to 30 minutes.

Mexican Make-Ahead

Fajita-Style Onions and Peppers and Seasoned Black Beans can be made a day in advance, kept in the fridge, and rewarmed just before serving. Or just chop the veggies up to 24 hours in advance and keep refrigerated in ziplock bags to cook just before serving. Marinating the chicken, beef, or pork is best done in ziplock bags up to 36 hours in advance. Store the marinated meats in the fridge and remove 1 hour before cooking, so the meat can warm slightly.

Greta's Spicy Avocado Crema

Our good friends Greta and Mark were married last year in the Hamptons on the most stunning late-summer day. Spanish blue skies and the shimmering Atlantic Ocean welcomed Mark, a fisherman-turned-finance guru, and his bride into married life. In the months since their big day, we've enjoyed some amazing meals at their apartment in Battery Park City, especially pan-fried fish tacos with all the fixings. We always thought it was the groom's longshoreman past that gave the couple a leg up on the preparation of the spicy fish nestled into warm flour tortillas. Only after about our fifth dinner did we realize that it was Greta's "secret sauce"—a sort of avocado-cilantro cream sauce—that put their dinners in another stratosphere. Kind of like our Spanish Romesco sauce (page 86), this Tex-Mex winner is meant to be made in large batches and then enjoyed with everything from fish to chicken to green salads to plain ol' tortilla chips.

serves 12 or makes 2 cups

2 cups fresh cilantro leaves

1 jalapeño, seeded

1 ripe avocado, halved, pitted, and cut into large
    chunks

½ teaspoon grated lime zest

1 lime, juiced

½ teaspoon ground cumin

1 teaspoon kosher salt, plus more as needed

½ teaspoon freshly ground pepper, plus more as
    needed

one 16-ounce container sour cream

1 tablespoon extra virgin olive oil

1 tablespoon hot sauce

In a food processor, pulse together the cilantro, jalapeño, avocado, lime zest and juice, cumin, salt, and pepper. Once the cilantro and spice mixture is blended together smoothly, spoon in the sour cream and olive oil. Add the hot sauce and continue to blend until a smooth, creamy consistency is reached. Taste and adjust the seasoning. Transfer to a bowl and refrigerate for at least 15 minutes before serving.

FLOUR OR CORN?

To wrap up all the delicious bits, you need a pliable, "accepting" tortilla. And that's why, when we're cruising the grocery store, we choose flour tortillas over corn. While we love the flavor of the corn, they can get a little fussy if they're not just the right temperature. And you need a tortilla that can roll—and roll with the punches of a long dinner.

JAMIE'S KICK-BUTT SEASONED SALTS

If you're from the South, chances are you know someone who swears by the culinary magic of Dale's Seasoning sauce. The common refrain heard around the grill is "Man, I don't know what's in that stuff, but it sure makes a mean steak." If you're not from the South, think of Dale's as the Southern version of soy sauce. It's a dark, thin liquid with a distinguished bouquet of herbs and spices, but, more than anything, it has a meat taste and a heart-stopping amount of sodium. For some reason, it's this key ingredient—salt—that most often escapes people. Everyone gets so caught up trying to identify the oil, herb, or spice in which they drown their favorite cut of meat that they forget the most essential components of any cook's arsenal. When they ask me for my "secret ingredient," I invariably answer, "Salt and pepper."

First of all, let it be known that I am not a proponent of marinating good cuts of meat. I believe in spending a little extra to get a great piece of meat and seasoning it with salt and pepper. However, there are times that I want to add certain flavors to a piece of meat to enrich a dish or to help tenderize and add flavor to a lesser cut. In these situations, I still don't turn my back on salt and pepper. Salt naturally enhances the flavor of almost any food. It really is a sort of culinary magic.

The idea behind seasoned salts is to combine strong flavors with a specific amount of salt, which allows the strong flavors to be transferred into the meat very quickly—much more quickly than the time it takes to marinate. The only advantage marinating may hold over seasoned salt is its ability to tenderize the meat, given time and the proper level of acidic ingredients. And don't forget—sometimes salt comes in a liquid form, like fish sauce, soy sauce, or, of course, Dale's. Below are my favorite formulations for seasoned salts. Marinades, for their part, are scattered throughout the book.

Use these seasoned salts as you would any other seasoning. Sprinkle on meats or vegetables before or during cooking. While seasonings should always be added to taste—starting with a moderate amount and adding until the desired taste is achieved—for proteins, which you can't sample as they cook, a good rule is ½ to 1 teaspoon for an average-size chicken breast. Always season both sides of the meat, so you'll be sprinkling ¼ to ½ teaspoon seasoned salt on each side.

Ultimate Grill Salt

This is our signature salt—and Jamie's culinary secret weapon. Brooke likens it to "fairy dust" because she thinks it magically makes everything taste better. For fish taco night, this is the best, quickest way to season your mahi mahi, grouper, or triggerfish. It also gives chicken and beef a delicious Tex-Mex accent.

makes ½ cup

¼ cup kosher salt
1 teaspoon finely grated lime zest
1 clove garlic, finely grated on a Microplane,
    or 1 teaspoon garlic powder
1 tablespoon freshly ground pepper
1 teaspoon smoked paprika
1 teaspoon ground cumin
1 teaspoon ground coriander
2 teaspoons lime juice
1 tablespoon onion powder

Combine all ingredients in a bowl and blend well. Store in the refrigerator in an airtight container, up to 10 days.

Fajita Salt

Cumin, coriander, and paprika conspire in this mix to give your "grillables" a ton of zing. The only thing that makes this salt any better is a bottle of tequila and a good sunset.

makes ¼ cup

¼ teaspoon ground cumin

½ teaspoon ground coriander

½ teaspoon smoked paprika

1½ teaspoons kosher salt

3 cloves garlic, grated

¼ teaspoon dried oregano

freshly ground pepper to taste

Combine all the ingredients in a small bowl and store in the refrigerator, covered, for up to 10 days.

Italian Salt

"Chicken . . . again?" We've all heard it; we've all thought it. But use a healthy dash of our Italian mix— with just enough oregano and marjoram to keep it interesting—and you'll get excited again about those hunks of white meat.

makes ¼ cup

1 tablespoon kosher salt

½ teaspoon freshly ground pepper

1 teaspoon garlic powder

1 teaspoon dried oregano, or 2 teaspoons chopped fresh

1 teaspoon dried marjoram, or 2 teaspoons chopped fresh

1 teaspoon dried basil

Thoroughly mix all the ingredients and store in an airtight container. Brush the meat or vegetables with olive oil, then sprinkle with this seasoning before cooking. Store in an airtight container, up to 3 months.

Creole Seasoning

A few chefs with oversized personalities (and bellies) would be more than happy to sell a small shaker of this stuff, with their face on it, for five bucks. Since we can't get away with that kind of capitalism quite yet, we'll hand over this awesome, all-purpose seasoned salt recipe that's perfect for chicken, fish, and shrimp. You can also top oysters with a mixture of the salt and butter before popping them in the oven. This is the good stuff that's the key ingredient for our Bar-B-Qued Shrimp (page 104).

makes ⅓ cup

2 tablespoons kosher salt

1 tablespoon sweet paprika

1 teaspoon smoked paprika

1½ tablespoons garlic powder

1 tablespoon onion powder

2 teaspoons freshly ground pepper

1 teaspoon cayenne

2 teaspoons dried oregano

2 teaspoons dried thyme

Thoroughly mix all the ingredients and store in an airtight container, up to 3 months.

Thai Marinade

When you want to replicate the unmistakable flavors of your favorite Thai/Vietnamese place, pull out a jar of this and go to town. It pairs the best with sliced steaks like skirt, flank, and hanger. Sprinkle, grill, and fan your steak on a bed of red lettuces, thinly sliced cucumber and onion, and shredded carrot. Retire those take-out menus forever!

makes ½ cup

grated zest of 1 lime

juice of ½ lime (about 1 tablespoon)

1 clove garlic, grated

3 tablespoons fish sauce or soy sauce

1 tablespoon sesame oil

¼ teaspoon red pepper flakes

¼ teaspoon ground ginger, or 1 tablespoon grated
    fresh ginger

Whisk all the ingredients together in a bowl. Add meat and turn to coat well. Leave to marinate for 1 hour at room temperature or overnight in the refrigerator.

Roast Pork Tenderloin and Autumn Vegetable Puree with Brown Butter and Balsamic

Pork tenderloin is found between the shoulder and the leg of the pig—essentially, it's the meat that runs opposite the loin. Because these muscles aren't primarily used for movement, the meat is super tender and lean and our fail-safe choice for quick and delicious weeknight meals. (Save that pork shoulder for lazy Saturdays of braising and hanging around the house.) Jamie perfumes the loin with a traditional bouquet of rosemary and thyme and then the side dish—Autumn Vegetable Puree—really gets down to business. Brown butter makes the puree luscious and smooth, and a few drops of balsamic vinegar give it a little kick of genius. The flavors are deep and rich, exactly what you want to come home to. Brooke thanks her lucky stars whenever she opens the door to find Jamie and this warm, savory meal.

serves 4 to 6

TRIMMING UP YOUR PORK

Pork tenderloin is one of the quickest and easiest of all cuts to prepare for cooking. To trim it, take a small, sharp knife and cut away any of the small bits of fat that cling to the meat. Next cut away the silver skin, the shiny connective tissue that adheres to the surface of the top side on the thickest end of the loin. Slip the tip of the knife underneath the silver skin, hold it tightly, and continue to slide the knife underneath as you push the blade away from you to cut the tough pieces away.

Roast Pork Tenderloin

1 tablespoon extra virgin olive oil
1 tablespoon unsalted butter
2 cloves garlic, crushed
2 branches fresh thyme
1 branch fresh rosemary
2 pork tenderloins (about 3 pounds), trimmed
kosher salt and freshly ground pepper

Preheat the oven to 425 degrees.

Combine the olive oil, butter, garlic, and herbs in a small saucepot. Heat over medium heat until the mixture begins to bubble. Set aside to cool slightly.

Pat the tenderloins dry and season well with salt and pepper on all sides. Place the tenderloins in a medium roasting pan or an ovenproof sauté pan that is just big enough to hold them. Pour the olive oil mixture over the meat and turn until well coated. Roast in the hot oven for 6 minutes; turn and cook for 6 minutes more. Remove the meat to a rack to rest and pour the roasting juices over the meat. Rest for 5 minutes before slicing.

COOK LIKE A PRO

All meats cook best when removed from the refrigerator 30 to 60 minutes before cooking.

Autumn Vegetable Puree

2 pounds mixed autumn vegetables (butternut
squash, sweet potato, potato, parsnip, carrot)
12 tablespoons (1½ sticks) unsalted butter
1 small yellow onion, diced
1 teaspoon fresh thyme leaves, or ½ teaspoon dried
3 cloves garlic, minced
kosher salt and freshly ground pepper to taste
2 cups chicken stock or water
2 teaspoons balsamic vinegar

Peel and trim the vegetables as necessary and cut into similar-size chunks, roughly 1½ inches.

Melt 2 tablespoons of the butter in a large, heavy-bottomed pot over medium heat. Add the onion and sweat until tender. Stir in the thyme and garlic and cook for 30 seconds more.

Add the vegetables and mix well to coat with the butter and onion. Season with salt and pepper. Continue stirring until a sizzle returns to the pan. Add the stock and bring the mixture to a simmer over medium heat. Cook, partially covered, until all the vegetables are tender, 15 to 20 minutes. You should be able to easily crush one of the vegetables against the side of the pot with the back of a spoon.

While the vegetables are simmering, place 6 tablespoons butter in a small pan over medium heat. Allow the butter to melt completely. It will then begin to boil. When the boiling stops, all the water has been cooked out and the butter should be lightly golden and clear. This stage is known as clarified. Leave the butter over the heat until it begins to darken, eventually turning a deep brown color and smelling well toasted, nearly burned. This is the brown butter stage; strain immediately through a fine-mesh strainer and reserve. Be careful—it is extremely hot!

Remove the vegetables from the liquid with a slotted spoon and place in a food processor or food mill. Process the vegetables until smooth, adding some of the cooking liquid as needed if the mixture is too thick.

Working quickly while the puree is still hot, stir in the strained brown butter, the balsamic, and the remaining 4 tablespoons whole butter. Taste and adjust the seasoning with salt and pepper.

COOK LIKE A PRO

Brown butter, or *beurre noisette,* has a roasted, nutty taste that adds depth to the flavor of many foods. It's easier to make in large batches, so make a half pound or more at a time. It will keep in the fridge or freezer indefinitely.

Filet of Beef with Grilled Asparagus and Roasted Potatoes

There are a lot of date-night traditions, but none are as timeless—or make a couple feel as fancy—as a nice steak dinner. In the 1950s, Brooke's grandparents Pete (named so because she was so petite) and Pappy would fly to New York for a Broadway show and proper steak and sides at Keens Steakhouse. While they definitely squeezed in some culture during their visits, Brooke's pretty sure that a juicy rib-eye and a good gin martini were the ultimate purpose of the 1,500-mile trek. We do all that—but make it just under thirty dollars. Stay in, save a little money, and sear up your own steak date-night.

serves 2

Filet of Beef

2 beef tenderloin filets (also known as filet mignon),
    6 to 8 ounces each
kosher salt

canola oil (about 1 tablespoon)
freshly ground pepper

Unwrap the meat and season lightly with salt on both sides, approximately ⅛ teaspoon per side. Leave the meat at room temperature, uncovered, for 30 to 45 minutes before cooking.

Place a heavy sauté pan or cast-iron skillet over high heat; add enough canola oil to cover the bottom of the pan. Pat any moisture off the surface of the meat and season again with salt (about the same amount you used the first time) and pepper. When the oil begins to shimmer or lightly smoke, add the beef, making sure the pieces are not touching. Cook on one side until a deep brown crust develops. Turn the meat and brown equally on the second side. Reduce the heat in the pan if the meat becomes dark before the proper cooking time is reached (see the guideline below). Remove to a rack to rest before serving.

Cooking Times for Steaks (approximately 1 inch thick)

Rare: 3 to 4 minutes per side
Medium-rare: 4 minutes per side
Medium: 5 to 6 minutes per side
Medium-well: 6 to 7 minutes per side, medium to medium-high heat
Well-done: 8 to 10 minutes per side, medium to medium-high heat

Times do not include "resting time," the time that the meat should sit on a rack after it has been cooked. Shoot for 3 to 7 minutes of "rest" for your meat, time that is crucial for proper cooking and the proper reabsorption of juices.

WHY CANOLA OIL? THE TIPPING POINT OF SMOKING POINTS

No, "smoke point" is not the rocky outcropping you used to sneak out to for a cigarette as a teenager; smoke point refers to how hot a fat can get before it goes bad. Olive oil, for all its wonderful and delicate flavor, can be destroyed by heat quickly. In fact, the temperature required for proper browning of meat is way outside of olive oil's comfort zone, imparting a bitter or off flavor to the meat before it has finished cooking. Canola or vegetable oil (like corn, cottonseed, grapeseed, and so on) has a neutral flavor and is more stable at high temperatures, making it a better choice for high-heat cooking. Olive oil remains a favorite for gentle cooking and imparting its flavor as a finishing oil or in making dressings.

What to Look for at the Meat Counter

The meat counter can be an intimidating place if you're unsure what you're looking for. This recipe calls for a cut that goes by many names—beef tenderloin, filet of beef, or filet mignon. You can be certain that all cuts are coming from the same place, the tenderloin of mature beef cattle. When picking out the right piece, whether it's filet, rib-eye, or strip, look for these things:

Color—The meat should have a bright red color. Pass if the muscles look anemic (light red or pink) or too dark (red turning to brown)—a sure sign of meat that has been sitting in the case a little too long.

Marbling—You've probably heard a lot about marbling. It's those little white flecks you see in the meat—the little bits of fat interspersed between the muscles that help give a steak flavor and keep it from drying out when cooking.

Feel—If you can get your hands on the meat before you buy it, it should be firm to the touch. Avoid meat that seems mushy, unless it's dry aged, which is another story.

Tip—For the most flavorful steaks (or pork or chicken), unwrap the meat as soon as you get home and pat off any excess moisture with a paper towel. Lightly season the meat with kosher salt, wrap in paper or leave loosely covered with plastic, and store in the fridge until ready to cook, up to 4 days. Season the meat again just before cooking.

Grilled Asparagus

There are plenty of reasons to love good, grilled aspara-gus—and let's be honest, who doesn't? But beyond the simple-delicious-easy factor, we love grilled asparagus because it's special. Not special, as in only for "nice" company, like our wedding registry water goblets that Jamie's not even allowed to touch. Ever. Special as in we only eat this vegetable when it is fresh, local, and perfect. Of course, you can get asparagus any time of the year, but if you've ever whipped up a side of the tender green spears in the icy months, you know they lose more than a little of their delicate flavor during that three-and-a-half-thousand-mile journey from Peru. So in late spring and throughout the summer, when it's easy to grab a bunch of local asparagus, we pack in all the spears we can. At other times of the year, we go with sautéed or "super-green" spinach (page 293) or broccoli rabe (page 54) to make our at-home steakhouse complete.

> 1 bunch jumbo asparagus, trimmed and peeled
> 2 tablespoons extra virgin olive oil
> kosher salt and freshly ground pepper
> grated zest and juice of ½ lemon

Preheat the grill or broiler.

Bring a large pot of salted water to a rapid boil. Drop the asparagus into the water and cook for 2 minutes. Drain and refresh immediately in ice water.

Pat the asparagus dry and toss with 1 tablespoon of the olive oil. Season well with salt and pepper. Cook on a hot grill or under the broiler until tender and lightly charred. Remove to a plate and dress with the remaining 1 tablespoon olive oil and the lemon zest and juice.

Roasted New Potatoes

New potatoes are those perfect, tiny red-skinned tubers. Look for ones that are no bigger than a golf ball.

> ½ to 1 pound new potatoes
> 4 to 6 branches fresh thyme
> 2 cloves garlic, crushed
> ¼ cup olive oil
> 2 teaspoons kosher salt
> freshly ground pepper

Preheat the oven to 425 degrees.

Cut the potatoes in half and place in a large bowl with the thyme, garlic, olive oil, salt, and a few grinds of pepper. Toss well to combine. Turn the contents of the bowl into a baking pan lined with aluminum foil. Arrange the potatoes in a single layer with the cut sides down. Roast in the oven until easily pierced with a knife, 20 to 25 minutes. Cool briefly in the baking pan and serve hot.

THE NEXT LEVEL

For extra flavor, toss the warm cooked potatoes with fresh chopped herbs (thyme, rosemary, or parsley), lemon zest, or finely grated Parmesan cheese.

Brooke on the Bottle—Chile and Argentina: Thrifty, Crowd-Pleasing Reds (a Little Oak, a Little Spice, a Little Tannin)

When you're on a newlywed budget, you have to branch out from Bordeaux. With your new social whirl, you need to have bottles of wine on hand for showers, dinners, impromptu parties, cozy nights on the couch, barbecues, and quick gifts. You want vino you can enjoy NOW, and you want to be able to buy it without breaking the bank. (And, in fact, if you buy a case of it, most wine purveyors will give you a 15 percent discount.)

Think about yourself and your new spouse: you're charming and hardworking. At a party, people surround you. And that's exactly what you want from your wine!

Chile and Argentina are a long way from the French countryside, but they offer the most consistent "best-buys" in the wine world. Their cost/quality ratio can't be beat. With a killer combination of style and substance, or, in "wine-speak," depth of flavor, complexity, and palate-pleasing fruitiness, the Chilean and Argentine wines really work for their titles of Mr. and Mrs. Popularity.

Argentina: For a sure bet, think red and think Malbec. Argentina's most famous grape, Malbec, is primarily grown in Mendoza. These guys produce 75 percent of all wines exported from Argentina and they know what they're doing! When you snag a Malbec from the shelf, you're picking up a bottle with rich blueberry and blackberry flavors that possesses a light smokiness and soft tannins. This is a wine for all seasons and every occasion.

Chile: Cabernet Sauvignon, Merlot, and Carmenere are the holy trinity for Chile's winemakers. While each grape is delicious on its own, their flavors hit a Marvin Gaye groove when combined to make a "blend" or a "meritage" wine. For a young, well-priced wine, a Chilean blend is as smooth as it gets.

Roasted Lamb Loin with Tomato-Cucumber Salad

The beautiful (fleeting!) part of being a newlywed is that you care about everything—how you look in the morning, how a recipe appears on the plate, and if your meal impresses your mate. A few months into our marriage, however, we had both exhausted our list of quick, healthful meals. Jamie immediately thought that super-tender lamb loin (instead of the tougher, gamier leg of lamb) would be a nice change of pace. Brooke, convinced that her bloodline must be half Greek because of her love of feta cheese, imagined that chic Athenians would couple the meat with a classic cucumber and tomato salad—and maybe a spoonful of feta thrown in for good measure. In the end, we came up with a rustic, wonderful meal.

serves 4

Roasted Lamb Loin

2 lamb loins, about 8 ounces each

1½ teaspoons kosher salt mixed with ½ teaspoon chili powder, or 2 teaspoons Ultimate Grill Salt, Fajita Salt, or Creole Seasoning (pages 61 to 63)

canola oil (about 1 tablespoon)

Pat the lamb loins dry and season both sides with all of the salt mixture. Place a heavy sauté pan or cast-iron skillet over high heat; add enough canola oil to cover the bottom of the pan. When the oil begins to ripple or lightly smoke, carefully lay the lamb in the pan. Reduce the heat slightly and cook for 3 to 4 minutes on the first side until the meat is well browned. Turn and cook the same on the second. Rest for 4 minutes on a rack before slicing.

CALL IN THE SUBS

Where's the Beef?—Lamb loins are tasty, tender, and cook up in a flash, but if you can't find them at your local market, try this recipe with steak—skirt or flank is excellent.

Tomato-Cucumber Salad

We love to make this salad in summer when cucumbers and vine-ripened tomatoes are at their best. Kirby cucumbers—the little guys that don't have many seeds—are ideal for this, though English or hothouse cucumbers make a nice substitute year-round. To seed the cucumbers, split them in half lengthwise and scrape the seeds out with a teaspoon.

2 to 3 cups seeded and sliced cucumbers (4 kirby or 1 hothouse), ¼ to ½ inch thick

1 teaspoon kosher salt, plus more as needed

1 teaspoon granulated sugar

1 cup thinly sliced yellow onion

2 tablespoons white wine vinegar

freshly ground pepper

2 beefsteak tomatoes

2 teaspoons chopped fresh dill, or ½ teaspoon dried dill mixed with 1 tablespoon fresh parsley leaves, chopped together

2 tablespoons extra virgin olive oil

8 ounces feta cheese, crumbled (optional)

Toss the cucumber slices in a colander with 1 teaspoon salt and the sugar. Place a clean bowl with a can of vegetables in it as a weight on top of the cucumbers to squeeze out the excess liquid. Leave the colander in the sink to drain, about 15 minutes.

While the cucumbers are draining, toss the onion with the vinegar, a pinch of salt, and a few grinds of black pepper. Cut the tomatoes into cubes.

Quickly rinse the cucumbers under cold water and press dry. Remove the onion from the vinegar and toss with the cucumbers, tomatoes, herbs, and olive oil. If you want to add the feta, stir it in now. Season to taste with salt and pepper. Serve at room temperature.

"No Rotten or Underripe Tomatoes, Please!"

For a few wonderful months of the year, freshly picked, locally grown tomatoes are available around the country. Getting your hands on these great summer tomatoes is pretty darn easy, assuming the weather holds up (ask any farmer and he'll tell you that continual rain wreaks havoc on a crop). But when the cool winds of fall begin to blow, decisions must be made. Are you willing to go on a nine-month tomato fast? If you simply can't make it through the cool months without your fresh tomato fix, follow our tips for selecting the best from the bunch.

Delicate little flowers—Remember, tomatoes are like guys' egos—they bruise easily. So while squeezing is a great way to determine a tomato's ripeness, be gentle. You want a tomato that yields to light pressure but isn't too soft, and if it seems that it may bounce if dropped on the floor, pass.

Don't think big—Often smaller varieties of tomatoes do better in the off-season. Look to Roma, Campari, or "on-the-vine" tomatoes to give you more flavor year-round.

Take it from the top—Any good, standard breed of tomato should have brightly colored red flesh. But check the top, right around the stem, to see if the tomato was plucked from its vine a little early. A ring of color from pale yellow to green indicates that the tomato is still slightly underripe.

Need a good tomato, eh?—Though most people feel "hothouse" and "greenhouse" are dirty words, many farmers are now growing organic, sustainable produce out of greenhouses with little to no environmental impact. So rest easy if the sticker on that juicy, plump tomato reads "Canada"—that's where a majority of wintertime tomatoes come from and that's still a heck of a lot better than the trip from South America.

Spring Vegetable Cannelloni

When Jamie lived in Birmingham, he taught cooking classes every Monday night (his one night off from the restaurant) to an adorable group of ladies. On one of Brooke's many trips down from New York, she joined the class full of grandmothers, bridge champions, and Chardonnay connoisseurs and sat in the back row, hoping no one would pay her any attention. Of course, that's exactly when Jamie introduced Brooke as his new girlfriend and asked her to join him behind the stove. Would she help him make the cannelloni for the class? Fresh pasta? Mornay sauce for a crowd? Brooke freaked out. Then Jamie showed her just how easy this recipe was. Now you and your honey can try this one together too.

serves 4 to 6

Think of cannelloni as individual lasagnas. Instead of layers of pasta and filling, all the good stuff is rolled up in a single sheet of cooked pasta, then baked with a creamy, cheesy sauce on top. We give this dish a lively and light spring touch with lots of good green veggies and herbs, but don't skimp on the cheese either. Cannelloni are the stuff that leftover dreams are made of, so take the time to make a batch and enjoy it for days.

Mornay Sauce

Mornay is simply a béchamel (roux-thickened milk sauce) with the addition of cheese.

3 tablespoons unsalted butter
¼ cup all-purpose flour
3 cups whole milk
1 cup grated Asiago cheese (you may substitute Parmesan or Gruyère)
kosher salt and freshly ground pepper
Tabasco sauce (optional)

In a heavy-bottomed saucepan, melt the butter over medium heat. When the foam subsides, add the flour. Turn the heat to medium-low and stir often with a whisk, making sure to get the flour that will try to stick to the edges of the pan. Cook for approximately 3 minutes. It will be ready when the mixture sounds like Rice Krispies, smells like popcorn, and looks like wet sand. Once it reaches this stage, whisk in the milk little by little.

As you whisk in the first drops of milk, the flour will immediately solidify. By continuing to whisk the milk gradually (about ¼ cup at a time) into the flour mixture (aka roux), you will ensure a smooth sauce with no lumps. Keep whisking until all of the milk is incorporated. Cook over medium-low heat, stirring often (remember to scrape the edges with a spoon). If anything sticks to the bottom, it will burn and ruin the whole sauce. Cook the sauce at a simmer until thickened, approximately 5 minutes. Remove the pan from the heat and stir in the cheese. Season to taste with salt and pepper, and a few dashes of hot sauce if using. Set aside to top the pasta dish. The sauce can be refrigerated for up to a week.

Cannelloni

1 pound fresh pasta sheets (if possible), or 1 box
    lasagna sheets (flat edges)
1 cup ricotta cheese
½ cup grated Parmesan cheese
1½ cups Mornay Sauce (recipe precedes)
1 cup frozen green peas, blanched
1 cup blanched chopped asparagus
2 tablespoons chopped fresh mint, or basil and
    parsley
½ to 1 cup finely diced boiled ham or smoked ham,
    or finely chopped prosciutto (optional)

Bring a pot of well-salted water to a boil. Fill a large bowl with cold water (no ice) and set it next to the stove. Drop the pasta sheets into the boiling salted water one at a time to make sure they don't stick together (cook in batches of 6 to 8 sheets). Cook until tender, 3 to 4 minutes for fresh sheets, 8 to 10 for dried. Transfer the cooked pasta to the bowl of cold water to stop the cooking and to keep the sheets from sticking.

In a separate bowl, combine the ricotta, Parmesan, and ½ cup of the Mornay sauce. Blend well, then stir in the peas, asparagus, herbs, and ham if using.

Preheat the oven to 450 degrees.

Working with one sheet at a time, remove the pasta to a clean cutting board and pat dry with a clean kitchen towel. Cut each pasta sheet crosswise in half to make 2 nearly square-shaped pieces. Spoon 2 to 3 tablespoons filling onto each half-sheet and roll into the shape of a thick cigar. Place seam side down in an ovenproof dish. Repeat for as many servings as needed. Pack the rolls into the baking dish side by side and spoon the remaining 1 cup sauce over the top.

Bake on the top rack of the preheated oven until brown and bubbling on top, about 15 minutes.

MAKE AHEAD

A fully assembled pan of cannelloni can be held tightly covered in the refrigerator for 2 to 3 days or in the freezer for up to 3 months before baking.

Marinated Skirt Steak with Scallion Potato Cakes

This is Brooke's please-your-hubby meal because men are really never as happy as when they're eating steak and potatoes. Lucky for the ladies, skirt steak is a nice, inexpensive cut similar to flank steak, but tastier. Marinate the meat in our salsa verde, don't cook it beyond medium-rare, and you'll have a wonderfully tender hunk of steak that makes you look like a high roller (even though your grocery bill will be but a blip on the credit card statement). Golden, crispy-edged scallion pancakes round out the dish—and any leftover pancakes make a fabulous next-day brunch. We stole the idea from Brooke's mom, Suzanne, to crown the cakes with a sunny-side-up egg. We haven't looked back since.

serves 4

Marinated Skirt Steak

1 bunch parsley, leaves picked from the stems
    (about 2 cups)
1 tablespoon capers
2 teaspoons fresh thyme leaves
1 tablespoon dried marjoram
1 clove garlic, grated
¼ cup extra virgin olive oil
2 teaspoons red wine vinegar
kosher salt and freshly ground pepper
1½ pounds skirt steak, trimmed

Combine the parsley, capers, thyme, marjoram, garlic, oil, and vinegar in a food processor and pulse to chop well, but do not puree it. Season to taste with salt and pepper. Take ½ cup of the salsa verde (or more as needed) and rub it onto both sides of the steak. Leave to marinate for 30 to 60 minutes at room temperature or refrigerate overnight.

Preheat a grill, grill pan, or broiler to high.

Brush the marinade off the steak and season with salt and pepper. Cook on a preheated grill or on a baking pan underneath the broiler for 4 minutes per side. Remove to a rack to rest before slicing. Slice the meat against the grain, arrange on plates, and spoon over the remaining salsa verde. Serve with scallion potato cakes.

GO AGAINST THE GRAIN

Slicing meats against the grain or perpendicular to the direction of their muscle fibers makes the meat seem more tender because the fine connective tissue that bundles the muscle fibers is cut into smaller pieces.

Scallion Potato Cakes

makes 6 to 8 medium cakes

2 Idaho or russet potatoes
1 teaspoon kosher salt, plus more to taste
2 tablespoons all-purpose flour
1 bunch scallions (6 to 8), thinly sliced
freshly ground pepper
canola oil

Peel the potatoes and grate them on the coarse side of a box grater. Toss with the salt and place in the center of a clean kitchen towel or length of cheesecloth and squeeze as tightly as possible to extract the excess moisture. Mix the squeezed potatoes with the flour and scallions. Season lightly with salt and pepper.

Heat a thin layer of canola oil in a cast-iron or nonstick skillet over medium heat. Divide the potato mixture into 6 to 8 portions and form into small cakes by patting small balls of the mixture between your hands. The cakes should be the size of your palm. Slip the cakes into the oil and brown slowly on one side before flipping to do the same on the other. Do not allow the heat to get too high or the potatoes will burn before they cook through. When the cakes are cooked through, remove to a plate lined with paper towels and sprinkle with salt.

TECHNIQUE TIP

If the potatoes brown on the outside before they are cooked through, transfer them to a 350-degree oven and bake a few minutes to finish cooking without burning the exterior.

Chicken Simmered with Tomatoes, Peppers, and Pancetta

Brooke loves to see the word "simmer" in a recipe. It means she can pour herself a glass of wine and relax a little while the recipe cooks along, bubbly and independent (like a good Southern woman). This earthy chicken Basquaise—basically a Spanish take on the Italian classic chicken cacciatore—is right up her alley with just about fifteen minutes of attended cooking time and thirty minutes in the oven. After a good, long simmer—and two glasses of vino for the cook—canned tomatoes, sweet peppers, and ham stew together to make a moist, juicy chicken dinner.

serves 2 to 4

¼ cup chopped pancetta or bacon

2 tablespoons extra virgin olive oil

4 chicken leg quarters, or 8 chicken thighs

kosher salt and freshly ground pepper

1 yellow onion, thinly sliced

1 tablespoon piment d'Espelette or red pepper flakes

4 cloves garlic, crushed

one 14.5-ounce can chopped tomatoes

2 red bell peppers, peeled and cut into julienne

2 cups chicken stock

2 tablespoons excellent olive oil, for finishing

1 baguette

Preheat the oven to 325 degrees.

Place the pancetta and 1 tablespoon of the olive oil in a cold ovenproof pan and gently heat over medium heat, stirring occasionally, until crisped and brown.

Remove the pancetta to a paper-towel-lined plate to drain. Season the chicken with salt and pepper and sear on both sides in the rendered pancetta fat. When well browned on both sides, remove to the plate with the pancetta.

Wipe the excess fat from the pan and add the remaining 1 tablespoon olive oil. Heat over medium heat, add the onion, and sauté until tender and translucent. Stir in the red pepper and garlic and cook until aromatic. Add the tomatoes and bell peppers. Return the chicken and pancetta to the pan and bring the mixture to a boil. Cook until the tomatoes are nearly dry, 4 to 6 minutes. Stir in the chicken stock. Cover with a tight-fitting lid or aluminum foil, transfer the mixture to the oven, and bake for 30 minutes.

Remove the pan from the oven, uncover, and let rest a minimum of 5 minutes before serving. Drizzle with good olive oil and serve from the pan with crusty bread.

TECHNIQUE TIP

Whole, uncooked peppers can be peeled with a standard vegetable peeler, just like apples, peeling in strips from the stem to the base. The peeler won't remove all of the skin, especially in the creases of the vegetables, but taking off the majority of the skin makes the peppers much easier to eat when cooked.

Spicy Anchovy and Caper Tomato Sauce with Eggplant

Think of this as a chunky puttanesca sauce—the quick-cooking Italian standby that features capers, anchovies, and red pepper flakes—with eggplant thrown in for a little heft. Our sauce is spicy, tangy, salty, and can be made in a snap. (Hey, if certain Italian ladies purportedly whip this up in between clients, you can stir it up between work and your prime-time show.) Ours will definitely become your new go-to pasta recipe.

makes 1 quart sauce, serving 4 to 6

4 cloves garlic, grated

4 to 6 anchovy fillets, packed in olive oil

3 tablespoons capers

¼ cup extra virgin olive oil

1 large Italian eggplant, cubed (about 4 cups)

one 28-ounce can peeled plum tomatoes, roughly
      chopped, with their juice

1 cup water

½ teaspoon red pepper flakes

¼ teaspoon dried marjoram or oregano

kosher salt and freshly ground pepper

1 pound rigatoni pasta, cooked

fresh basil leaves as needed

grated Pecorino or Parmesan cheese as needed

Place the garlic, anchovies, and capers in the center of a cutting board and mince them together to form a paste—it won't be terribly smooth. Set aside.

Heat the olive oil in a large, heavy-bottomed saucepot. When the oil is very hot, add the eggplant and cook over high heat, approximately 3 minutes. The eggplant will absorb all of the olive oil, but frequent stirring will prevent sticking. Though you'll be tempted, DO NOT add extra oil. Stir in the garlic paste and cook until very aromatic. Add the canned tomatoes and water to the pot. Continue stirring until the mixture comes to a boil, then reduce the heat to a simmer. Stir in the pepper flakes and marjoram. Season to taste with salt and pepper. Simmer for 30 minutes and adjust the seasoning.

Add the cooked pasta to the sauce and stir in the torn basil leaves. Divide among bowls and top with grated cheese.

THREE THINGS TO DO WITH FLANK STEAK: ROPA VIEJA, SPICY BEEF SALAD, AND SLOW-ROASTED FLANK STEAK SANDWICHES

Beef feels a little fancy—even when the price tag corresponds to Grade A chuck instead of dry-aged filet. While we might splurge on the lean, expensive stuff (aka filet mignon) for at-home date nights, Jamie's heart really belongs to the more challenging, inexpensive "off" cuts that require a little love and a few tricks before they reveal their true flavor and tenderness. All you need to turn an otherwise ho-hum cut like flank steak into a dreamy, exotic meal is to become acquainted with your spice cabinet. In the following three recipes, we take flank steak (the well-exercised muscle of the cow that would be something like the oblique muscles in your body) to Cuba, then Thailand, and back around stateside with a few different cooking techniques and plenty of interesting spices. Before you know it, boldly flavored beef is on the dinner table and a week's worth of lunches are tempting you from the fridge.

Five Flavor Boosters: Ingredients

Easy-to-find ingredients that pump up the flavor of any dish.

1. Sriracha hot sauce
2. Good Dijon mustard
3. Parmigiano Reggiano, or her less-expensive cousin grana Padano
4. Vinegars (good-quality white wine, red wine, and balsamic)
5. Zests (orange, blood orange, lemon, Meyer lemon, lime, grapefruit)

Ropa Vieja

Flank steak is commonly known as "fajita beef" or "stir-fry beef" because it's the inexpensive cut of choice for less-than-Michelin-quality Mexican and Chinese joints. The meat that might naturally be a little tough can become extraordinarily tender and flavorful if cooked with a little love and care—just ask your Dominican or Cuban abuela. Ropa vieja is Latin America's iconic stewed beef dish that simmers otherwise tough beef into submission. After the cubed flank steak cooks in a spicy tomato sauce for almost two hours, it's moved beyond its "old clothes" moniker to become the stuff of juicy, tender meat dreams. We love our ropa vieja on a little bed of rice or nestled into soft corn tortillas. Either way, a topping of fresh avocado slices is a must.

serves 4, but we always make it for 2
and enjoy the leftovers

1 to 2 pounds flank steak, cut into 2-inch cubes
    (1 pound for a fancier stew, 2 pounds for a
    dish you can sink your teeth into)
2 teaspoons kosher salt
1 teaspoon dried oregano
1 teaspoon chili powder
1 medium yellow onion, diced (about 1½ cups)
5 cloves garlic, sliced
1 to 2 jalapeño peppers, seeded and diced (2, if you
    like it spicy)
2 tablespoons extra virgin olive oil
one 14.5-ounce can chopped tomatoes
1 cup water

In a medium bowl, toss the cubed flank steak with the salt, oregano, and chili powder to coat well. Set aside while you prepare the onion, garlic, and jalapeños.

Place a large sauté pan over high heat. Add the olive oil and wait for it to heat through. Carefully slide the seasoned beef cubes into the pan, shake them to form a single layer on the bottom (if it does not fit in a single layer, remove some of the meat from the pan and cook in a second batch), and let them sear for 2 to 3 minutes on the first side. Turn the meat and brown well on the second side. When the meat is deeply colored on each side, add the onion and garlic and reduce the heat to medium. Sauté the beef with the onion and garlic until tender, about 5 minutes. Stir in the jalapeños and cook for 2 minutes more.

In a medium saucepot, bring the tomatoes and water to a gentle simmer over medium heat. Transfer the beef and vegetable mixture to the tomatoes and continue to simmer, uncovered, for 1½ hours. Be sure to keep the pot at a gentle simmer for the entire cooking time or the meat will become tough.

Alternatively, you can break out that Crock-Pot you never use and cook the entire mixture on low for 3 hours or on high for 1½ hours. Cool completely before storing in the refrigerator. The meat will improve over the course of a day or two as it sits in the sauce. Reheat in a sauté pan over high heat.

Spicy Beef Salad

We ordered spicy beef salad so many times from our downstairs Thai take-out joint in the Village that we finally decided to write a recipe of our own. The citrus and vinegar in the marinade does an awesome job of tenderizing the meat and making it taste like the most exotic thing that's ever graced your kitchen table. Dinner will be ready in a snap if you use the Microplane from your kitchen registry to create a quick paste from the garlic and ginger. And don't worry about chopping your carrots—use that other registry gadget, the box grater—to shred them.

serves 4

2 pounds flank or skirt steak

1 recipe Thai Marinade (page 63)

1 cup seeded and sliced cucumber

1 cup shredded carrot

juice of 1 lime

1 teaspoon grated fresh ginger

1 teaspoon grated fresh garlic

1 tablespoon chopped fresh cilantro

3 scallions, thinly sliced

kosher salt and freshly ground pepper

1 pint cherry tomatoes, cut in half

1 tablespoon sesame oil

1 head red- or green-leaf lettuce, washed and chopped

Trim any excess fat from the steak and combine the meat with the marinade. Leave to marinate for at least 1 hour.

While the steak is marinating, combine the cucumber, carrot, lime juice, ginger, garlic, cilantro, and scallions in a large bowl. Mix well and leave to marinate until ready to serve.

Preheat a grill.

Remove the steak from the marinade, brush off the excess, and season well with salt and pepper. Cook on the hot grill until well charred and medium-rare, 4 to 6 minutes per side. Remove the steak and cool for 5 minutes before slicing.

While the steak cools, add the cherry tomatoes and sesame oil to the marinated vegetables and toss to combine. Season to taste with salt and pepper. Make a pile of the clean, chopped lettuce in the center of each plate or on one platter. Top the lettuce with the marinated vegetables and then the sliced steak. Pour any of the steak juices over the plates and serve immediately.

TECHNIQUE TIP

Without a grill, the steak can be seared in a sauté pan or cast-iron skillet on top of the stove or roasted underneath the oven's broiler for 4 to 6 minutes on each side.

Slow-Roasted Flank Steak Sandwiches with Watercress and Horseradish Cream

Think of it as barbecuing in your oven. When we roast our flank steak, we go slow and low and make sure to season the uncooked meat with a generous hand. After it's roasted and then cooled, we apply a little weight and pressure (via the backside of a big cast-iron skillet) to compact the meat and make it a juicy foil for that classic New York City sandwich meat—brisket. (We're tempted to say that ours rivals Katz's deli on the Lower East Side . . . but we won't go that far.) We finish off our juicy steak sandwich with the lightness—and bite—of our own homemade horseradish cream sauce.

serves 4

1½ pounds flank steak

1 tablespoon Ultimate Grill Salt or Creole Seasoning (pages 61 and 63), or 2 teaspoons salt mixed with 1 teaspoon chili powder

2 tablespoons olive oil, plus more as needed

2 large onions, thinly sliced

6 cloves garlic, thinly sliced

3 or 4 branches fresh thyme

2 or 3 branches fresh rosemary

HORSERADISH CREAM

2 tablespoons horseradish, freshly grated or prepared from a jar (squeeze out the juice before measuring)

¼ cup sour cream

Worcestershire sauce

freshly ground pepper

4 brioche rolls or fresh hamburger buns

melted butter for toasting the rolls

2 cups fresh watercress, thick stems removed, or arugula

Preheat the oven to 325 degrees.

If the piece of steak is longer than 10 inches, cut it into 2 pieces. Season the meat with grill salt, Creole Seasoning, or the salt–chili powder mixture. In a large baking dish, combine the olive oil, onions, and garlic; toss well to coat. Place the seasoned meat on top of the onions and place the fresh herbs on top of the meat. Cover the pan with aluminum foil and place in the preheated oven. Cook until the meat is falling-apart tender, about 2 hours. Test for tenderness by pinching a piece of the meat near the side. If it easily breaks away in your fingers, the meat is done. Remove the pan from the oven and transfer the meat to a cooling rack. Discard the whole herbs and transfer the onions and garlic to a plastic container and reserve for sandwiches. Clean the baking dish. When the meat is cool to the touch, wrap it tightly in plastic wrap. Return the wrapped meat to the clean baking dish and place another dish or other flat, heavy object on top of the steak. Refrigerate overnight to compress the meat and make better slices for sandwiches.

To make the sauce for the sandwiches, stir together the horseradish, sour cream, and a few dashes Worcestershire sauce; season with a few grinds of pepper.

Brush the rolls with melted butter and toast under the oven's broiler set to high or in a toaster oven. Cut the beef into thin slices.

To assemble the sandwiches, spread a spoonful of the horseradish cream on the base of each bun. Top with the reserved onions and then the sliced beef. Lightly dress the watercress with olive oil and layer on top of the beef. Spread the remaining horseradish cream on the inside of the bun tops. Serve immediately or wrap in aluminum foil and pack for a gourmet picnic!

Horseradish cream is an accompaniment with classic beef in all forms, from medium-rare roast beef to braised short ribs. It's also great dolloped on toast points topped with smoked trout.

THREE SAUCES THAT'LL MAKE ANYTHING TASTE GOOD

Brooke believes sauces are like great accessories—they can dress up anything, adding a September-issue's worth of personality and panache to an otherwise boring ensemble. For all the plain chicken, simple pasta, and mixed green salad meals that are begging for a little decoration and a lot of extra flavor, we have a repertoire of simple sauces. Pesto in both its classic and more funky incarnations is refreshing, while romesco is smoky and brooding. And after you make our quick-and-easy marinara, you'll never buy jarred spaghetti sauce again. Make our sauces several times and commit them to memory (or at least commit them to the Documents section of your BlackBerry). You never want to be without these.

CALL IN THE SUBS: ALTERNATIVES TO PARMESAN CHEESE

Grana Padano, the economical alternative to Parmigiano-Reggiano, gives all the flavor and nutty, salty goodness without the brand-name price tag.

Pecorino (typically in the United States, Pecorino Romano), Parmesan's salty cousin, is made in Sardinia and around Rome. The sheep's milk cheese is made in the same style as Parmesan; however, it's a lot saltier given that it's made from sheep's milk, not cow's milk. Pecorino is typically less expensive than any form of Parmesan.

Classic Pesto and Variations

Genovese-style pesto—hailing from the namesake city in the Liguria region of Italy—is the classic, uncooked, warm-weather sauce to which all others must be compared. Brooke thinks she feels her taste buds smile when they register the sweetness of the basil, the nuttiness of the Parmesan and pine nuts, and the bite of the garlic.

makes approximately 2 cups

2 cups loosely packed fresh basil leaves

¼ cup pine nuts, toasted

1 cup grated Parmesan cheese

1 teaspoon minced garlic

¼ cup good-quality extra virgin olive oil,
    plus more as needed

1 lemon

kosher salt and freshly ground pepper to taste

Combine the basil, pine nuts, cheese, and garlic in a food processor or blender. Slowly drizzle in the olive oil through the top of the machine while it runs at high speed. The mixture should be well chopped but not a smooth puree. Transfer the mixture to a bowl and squeeze in fresh lemon juice to taste—begin with half a lemon. Taste. Season accordingly with more lemon, and salt and pepper. If the mixture is too thick, add more olive oil until it is smooth and fluid.

Spinach Pesto

From Goat Cheese, Pesto, and Sun-Dried Tomato Strata, page 260. Including fresh spinach in your pesto transforms the color, turning the puree a beautiful, vibrant green.

makes approximately 2 cups

SUBSTITUTE:

1 cup loosely packed spinach leaves

1 cup loosely packed fresh basil leaves

FOR:

2 cups loosely packed fresh basil leaves

DELETE:

¼ cup pine nuts, toasted

Proceed with the recipe for Classic Pesto with the above substitutions.

Mint Pesto

From Grilled Zucchini with Mint Pesto and Pecans, page 163.

makes approximately 2 cups

SUBSTITUTE:
2 cups loosely packed mint leaves

FOR:
2 cups loosely packed fresh basil leaves

DELETE:
¼ cup pine nuts, toasted

Proceed with the recipe for Classic Pesto with the above substitutions.

Parmesan-Pecan Pesto

From Sweet Potato and Brussels Sprout Salad with Parmesan-Pecan Pesto, page 302.

makes approximately 2 cups

SUBSTITUTE:
½ cup pecan pieces, toasted and roughly chopped

FOR:
¼ cup pine nuts, toasted

ADD AN ADDITIONAL:
¼ cup finely grated Parmesan cheese

Proceed with the recipe for Classic Pesto with the above substitutions.

Pesto Isn't Just for Pasta

- tossed with cooked shrimp, pasta, and fresh veggies for a perfect salad
- as a sandwich spread, especially with grilled chicken, mozzarella, roasted peppers, and prosciutto or salami
- as a sauce for roasted salmon
- as a dressing for green veggies, such as blanched green beans or asparagus

Romesco (Spanish Roasted Tomato and Sweet Pepper Sauce)

Romesco is a sauce that originated in the Catalonia region of Spain. It's brilliantly complex and smoky, letting the region show off its star local ingredients—specifically, almonds, tomatoes, and pimentón de la vera, or smoked Spanish paprika. The toasted and then pureed bread gives the sauce body, making it rich and satisfying even though there's no cream and not much oil involved.

serves 4 to 6

3 medium tomatoes

2 red bell peppers

¼ cup extra virgin olive oil, plus more for coating
    the peppers

¼ cup almonds (whole, sliced, or slivered)

2 cups 1-inch cubes bread (baguette or Italian loaf)

6 cloves garlic, crushed

½ cup diced onion

¼ teaspoon sriracha hot sauce

1 teaspoon smoked paprika

1½ teaspoons kosher salt

1 teaspoon sherry vinegar or red wine vinegar

TECHNIQUE TIP

Without a Broiler—The peppers can be roasted on the stovetop directly over the flame or on a hot grill until the skin is well charred. Roast the tomatoes in the oven at 450 degrees, keeping the temperature the same to toast the bread and almonds.

Preheat the broiler.

Cut the tomatoes in half horizontally and arrange on a baking tray cut side down. Rub the peppers with olive oil and place on the tray along with the tomatoes. Broil, turning the peppers every 5 minutes or so, until they are colored on all sides. When the skin is darkened and blistered (12 to 15 minutes), remove the peppers to a bowl and cover with a clean kitchen towel. Add the almonds and bread to the tray with the tomatoes and broil until the bread is well toasted.

While the tomatoes and peppers are roasting, combine the olive oil, garlic, and onion in a small saucepot or sauté pan. Heat over high heat until the mixture begins to bubble, then turn the heat to medium-low and continue to cook, stirring occasionally, until the onion is completely tender, about 15 minutes.

Peel the roasted peppers and discard the seeds. Remove the skins from the tomatoes. Place the roasted tomatoes and peppers, toasted bread, almonds, and onion mixture in a blender or food processor. Add the sriracha, smoked paprika, salt, and vinegar and process on high until smooth.

LIQUID LIFE-CHANGER

Romesco will change your snacking life. We've yet to find anything that isn't better when dipped into romesco for a snack (okay, Oreos weren't great, but you get the idea). So make a big batch, keep it in the fridge for up to 2 weeks, and get creative!

Fifteen-Minute Marinara

We're surprised that more people don't go into sugar shock after eating jarred spaghetti sauce. It's as if the red sauce execs threw out the corporate chefs and decided to rely on sugar instead of good-quality tomatoes, proper seasoning, and an ounce of judgment. We start out with a can of naturally sweet San Marzano tomatoes—grown, picked, and canned in southern Italy at the peak of freshness—and simmer them down with fresh garlic, onion, and a few herbs. The whole thing couldn't be more simple and it won't leave you feeling like you've topped your pasta with something better suited for dessert. Fresh basil finishes off the only marinara sauce that you'll ever need to know how to make.

serves 4

3 tablespoons extra virgin olive oil

1 small yellow onion, chopped

4 cloves garlic, chopped

kosher salt and freshly ground pepper

one 28-ounce can crushed San Marzano tomatoes

1 tablespoon dried oregano

1 teaspoon dried basil

½ cup water

pinch of granulated sugar

¼ cup fresh basil chiffonade

Heat the olive oil in a large nonstick skillet over medium-low heat. Add the onion and slowly cook until almost translucent. Add the garlic and season well with salt and pepper. (If you're not confident with your seasoning skills, add 1 teaspoon salt and a few grinds of pepper, then taste a bit of the onion. Continue seasoning with a pinch or two more salt as necessary.) Once the garlic is very aromatic—after about 2 minutes—stir in the tomatoes. Add the oregano and dried basil and allow the sauce to bubble over low heat for 10 minutes. After the sauce has thickened, add the water and stir. Let the sauce cook for 5 more minutes and remove from the heat. Add the sugar, stir, and taste. Continue seasoning the sauce with herbs, salt, pepper, and sugar until it is exactly to your liking. Finish the sauce with the fresh basil.

For perfect pasta, place 1 cup of finished sauce per person in a large sauté pan and warm over medium heat. Bring a large pot of salted water to a rapid boil. Add the pasta and cook until nearly tender, 8 to 10 minutes for dried pasta depending on the shape of the noodle. Transfer the pasta to the sauce along with ¼ to ½ cup of the pasta water. Allow the mixture to simmer for 2 to 3 minutes so the pasta is *just* tender. Remove to plates and top with lots of grated Parmesan cheese.

THREE (QUICK AND EASY) WAYS TO MAKE GRILLED/ ROASTED CHICKEN INTERESTING

Chicken is an easy protein to have hanging around the fridge for quick snacks and last-minute dinners. But, sometimes, we'll have a container of the cooked stuff hanging out in the fridge and think, "Now what?" It's not our style to be complacent about meals! We want to get excited about the favorite white meat! So this is our ode to quick and easy chicken and the three fantastic ways you can make it a meal worth remembering.

Five Flavor Boosters: Techniques

Harness your heat! Five ways your stovetop and oven heat transform a meal.

1. Searing—Get your cast-iron or nonstick skillet screaming hot and then sear your proteins for a good crust, or char.
2. Broiling—Use your oven's broiler to brown the tops of buttery casseroles and gratins and roast peppers and other veggies.
3. Sweating—Sauté onions, shallots, leeks, and garlic (all members of the onion family) without browning or adding color. The "sweating" will mellow them out, removing their sharp, sometimes harsh, flavor.
4. Caramelizing—Super slow cooking and browning all those brothers and sisters of the onion family will bring out their natural sweetness.
5. Toasting—On a baking sheet in the oven or in a sauté pan on the stovetop, you can toast nuts and spices to really bring out their natural aromas.

Master Recipe for Grilled/Roasted Boneless, Skinless Chicken Breasts

For instructions on roasting bone-in chicken, see Roasted Chicken for Salad, page 142.

4 boneless, skinless chicken breasts
2 tablespoons olive oil
1 teaspoon salt
a few grinds or ¼ teaspoon freshly ground pepper

OPTIONAL:

substitute 1 to 2 teaspoons seasoned salt from
     pages 61 to 63 for the salt and pepper
add about 1 teaspoon lemon zest, finely grated on a
     Microplane
add 2 to 3 teaspoons chopped fresh herbs, such as
     rosemary, thyme, parsley, tarragon, or basil
add 1 teaspoon chopped or finely grated garlic

In a large bowl, mix the chicken breasts with the olive oil, salt, pepper, and any optional seasoning. Cook the chicken on a hot grill, turning once, approximately 3 to 4 minutes per side. To cook on the stovetop, heat 2 tablespoons olive oil in a nonstick sauté pan over high heat and sear the chicken for 3 to 4 minutes on each side, until cooked through. Remove the cooked chicken to a rack to cool slightly before cutting.

CHICKEN PAILLARD

Paillard is the fancy name for what is sold in grocery stores as a chicken cutlet. It refers to a piece of boneless, skinless chicken breast that has been cut or pounded into an even thickness of ½ inch or less. Cook exactly as directed above, shortening the cooking time to 2 to 3 minutes per side.

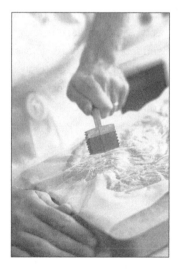

Spring Pasta Salad with Chicken and Feta

Tender asparagus, cool mint, sweet peas, and salty feta make this easy pasta salad refreshing and interesting. The addition of chicken stretches it, making it a real meal. When we were long-distance dating, and Brooke flew down to Birmingham to visit Jamie, this was our go-to lunch for lazy spring days in the park. It's delicious served hot or cold—or even after it's been warmed by the sun while sitting in the picnic basket—and it tastes even better the next day.

serves 6

1 pound penne pasta
olive oil as needed
1 bunch asparagus
2 cups sweet peas
1 bunch scallions, thinly sliced
juice of 1 lemon
2 tablespoons torn fresh mint leaves
1 cup crumbled feta cheese
kosher salt and freshly ground pepper to taste
4 cooked chicken breasts (page 89)

Bring a large pot of well-salted water to a boil. Add the pasta and cook until very tender. Be sure to taste before draining. The pasta should be slightly overdone. Because the pasta is going to be served cold, allowing it to cook a little longer will ensure tender pieces in the salad. Once the pasta is cooked, drain and lightly toss with 1 tablespoon olive oil. Spread out on a platter to cool in the refrigerator.

While the pasta is cooking, put another pot of well-salted water on to boil. Trim the bottom 1½ inches from the asparagus. When the water reaches a rolling boil, add the asparagus and cook until just tender, 2 to 3 minutes. Lift the asparagus from the water with tongs, place in a colander under cold running water, and remove to paper towels to dry. Next add the sweet peas to the boiling water. Cook for 1 minute, then drain and refresh with cold water. Leave in the sink to drain.

When the vegetables have cooled, chop the asparagus into 1-inch pieces and combine in a large bowl with the pasta, peas, scallions, lemon juice, mint, and feta. Add more olive oil as needed. Mix well and taste. Adjust the seasoning with more lemon or oil and salt and pepper as needed. Set aside for the flavors to combine.

To serve, slice the cooked chicken breasts and place on top of the pasta salad. To pack for a picnic, cool the chicken completely and toss with the chilled pasta salad.

Chicken Paillards with Marinated Mushrooms, Arugula, and Ricotta Salata

Roasted mushrooms and a dash of balsamic make everyday chicken sweet, sour, and super earthy.

serves 4

MARINADE
1 teaspoon dried oregano or marjoram
2 tablespoons extra virgin olive oil
2 tablespoons balsamic vinegar
4 branches fresh thyme

8 ounces crimini mushrooms, cut in half
8 ounces button mushrooms, cut into quarters

SALAD DRESSING
1 teaspoon fresh lemon juice
1 tablespoon balsamic vinegar
1 teaspoon Dijon mustard
3 tablespoons extra virgin olive oil

8 ounces (about 4 handfuls) fresh arugula or
    watercress
½ cup ricotta salata shaved into curls with a
    vegetable peeler
4 chicken paillards (page 89), seasoned with Italian
    Salt (page 62) and grilled, sautéed, or baked

For the marinade, combine the dried oregano, olive oil, vinegar, and thyme in a medium bowl. Add the mushrooms, mix well to combine, and set aside to marinate for a minimum of 30 minutes at room temperature or up to overnight in the refrigerator. To cook the mushrooms, spread them in a single layer on a hot grill and cook until tender, about 6 minutes, or spread the mushrooms on a baking sheet and roast in a 450-degree oven for 6 to 8 minutes. The mushrooms can also be cooked in olive oil in a large sauté pan over high heat until tender, 4 to 6 minutes. When the mushrooms are cooked, set aside to cool slightly.

For the salad dressing, combine the lemon juice, vinegar, and mustard in a medium bowl; whisk in the olive oil.

Add the cooked mushrooms, arugula, and cheese to the bowl with the salad dressing and toss well to combine. Place the grilled chicken in the center of each of 4 plates and pile the dressed salad on top of each piece.

Grilled Chicken Panzanella

Jamie loves making this bread salad when we have one too many baguettes left over from a big dinner party. He takes his cues from the Tuscans—the first thrifty chefs to come up with a juicy salad that features day-old bread—and mixes the ripe tomatoes and other veggies with the bread right from the start. This way, the vegetables' juices soften up the crusts, creating a succulent, toothsome salad.

serves 4 to 6

1 loaf leftover bread (Italian, French baguette, or sourdough loaf)
7 tablespoons extra virgin olive oil
2 cloves garlic, crushed
kosher salt and freshly ground pepper to taste
1 red onion
¼ cup red wine vinegar
1 large ripe tomato
2 tablespoons pitted black olives, halved
2 tablespoons torn fresh basil leaves
4 grilled chicken breasts (page 89), sliced
1 to 2 cups diced mozzarella cheese

Preheat the oven to 350 degrees.

Begin by trimming the dark crusts from the bread and cut the bread into ½- to 1-inch cubes. In a bowl, toss the cubes of bread with 4 tablespoons olive oil, garlic, and salt and and pepper. Mix well and spread on a baking sheet in a single layer. Toast in the oven until golden brown, about 7 minutes.

Next cut the red onion in half through the root. Lay one of the halved onions flat on the cutting board, trim away the root and stem ends, and slice lengthwise as thinly as possible. Keep the other half of the onion tightly wrapped in the refrigerator and save for another use. In a small bowl, mix the sliced onion with the vinegar. Season with salt and pepper and mix well. Set aside to marinate for at least 15 minutes.

While the onion is marinating, remove the core from the tomato and coarsely chop. Scrape the chopped tomato and all of its juices into a large bowl. Pour off the excess vinegar from the onion and add the onion to the tomato along with the olives and basil. Stir gently until well combined.

Remove the bread from the oven and cool slightly before adding to the tomato mixture. Stir together, adding the grilled chicken, cheese, and the remaining olive oil. Season to taste with salt and pepper.

Try spicing up your panzanella by adding or substituting the following ingredients:

roasted peppers (yellow or red) / cucumbers / variety of olives / cherry tomatoes / cornbread / tender lettuces, such as arugula or baby spinach / roasted corn kernels / toasted pepitas

TECHNIQUE TIP

How to Slice an Onion—Cutting onions into julienne (thin) strips instead of half-moon shapes gives you more even pieces and consistent flavor and no huge onion chunks (and the bad breath that goes with them!).

Seafood Succotash

Classic succotash is a thrifty cook's favorite side dish made simply from a combination of corn and lima beans. But since we're familiar with this Southern staple, we decided to up the ante and add sweet chunks of shrimp, crab, and scallops. To make the dish rich and bright, we finish it off with butter and lots of lemon juice and fresh dill.

serves 6

4 tablespoons (½ stick) unsalted butter

1 shallot, minced

1 cup sweet corn, cut from the cob or frozen kernels

kosher salt and freshly ground pepper to taste

1 cup okra, sliced ½ inch thick

2 cups cooked butter beans, lima beans, or black-
    eyed peas, liquid reserved, or canned

1 cup cherry tomatoes, halved

1½ tablespoons chopped fresh dill

½ to 1 pound lobster, shrimp, crabmeat, and/or
    scallops, cooked and cut into bite-size pieces
    (optional)

½ lemon, juiced

Tabasco or other hot sauce

TECHNIQUE TIP

Precook seafood by poaching, sautéing, grilling, or baking. But leave it a little underdone (think medium-rare) so it can finish cooking in the succotash without becoming tough. Remember that crabmeat is already steamed when you buy it, so it does not require any precooking.

In a large sauté pan, melt 2 tablespoons of the butter over medium heat and add the shallot. Cook gently, without browning, for 2 to 3 minutes. Add the corn and sauté for 3 to 4 minutes, still over medium heat. If the pan seems dry, add ¼ cup water. Season well with salt and pepper. Add the okra, butter beans, and 1 cup of the bean cooking liquid (you can make up the difference with water if you need to). Bring this mixture to a simmer and cook until the okra is tender, about 3 minutes more. To finish, stir in the tomatoes, dill, seafood, lemon juice, hot sauce, and remaining 2 tablespoons butter. Taste for seasoning and add salt, pepper, or more lemon as needed.

Canned beans are an acceptable substitute for fresh cooked beans. Be sure to rinse them well before adding to the pan and use chicken stock, vegetable broth, or water in place of the beans' canning liquid.

WHAT IS SUCCOTASH?

Though many regions of the South claim succotash as their own, its origin can be traced to Native Americans who taught early settlers how to make the corn-centric dish. Some even say that succotash was on the table at the first Thanksgiving. Why do we love it? It's a catchall buttery ragout of vegetables that includes beans and, when you venture to a kitchen south of the Mason-Dixon, it often showcases okra. By adding shredded pork or seafood, this traditional side dish effortlessly becomes a meal.

Grilled Snapper and Green Tomatoes with Pecan Sauce

Our good friend Colleen Duffley is the photographer and creative mastermind behind Studio B, in Alys Beach, Florida. She envisioned her whitewashed, blue-tiled gallery space and Moroccan-themed garden as the twenty-first century's answer to the Parisian salon (step aside, Gertrude and Alice!). Painters, sculptors—and, yes, cooks!—travel down to the Caribbean-clear water and sugar-white sand of the Gulf Coast to strut their stuff and share their métier with Colleen and her very cool group of friends and arts patrons. Our summer dinner at the Studio featured this grilled snapper with green tomatoes and pecan sauce. Our thought was that great fish deserves to be prepared simply—but we also wanted to impress and have a little fun with our garnish. While we were tempted to fry the green tomatoes, Jamie simply sliced them and then devised a savory/sweet pecan sauce that's like nothing you've ever tasted. Crunchy pecans, sweet molasses, and bright lemon are the perfect complement for tart green tomatoes and smoky grilled fish.

serves 4

Pecan Sauce

juice and grated zest of 1 lemon
1 teaspoon molasses
½ cup extra virgin olive oil
1 teaspoon kosher salt
1 cup pecans, toasted and chopped
¼ cup chopped fresh parsley

Combine the lemon juice, zest, and molasses in a small bowl; whisk in the olive oil and set aside. Shortly before serving, stir in the salt, pecans, and parsley.

Grilled Snapper and Green Tomatoes

4 boneless red snapper fillets (substitute grouper, striped bass, or other mild white fish)
extra virgin olive oil as needed
kosher salt
2 medium green tomatoes, sliced ¼ to ½ inch thick

Preheat a grill, grill pan, or broiler to high.

Brush each of the snapper fillets with olive oil, season with salt, and place over the hottest part of the grill. Cook for 2 to 3 minutes per side and remove to a platter.

Brush the green tomato slices with oil and season with salt only. Grill the tomato slices until tender but not mushy, about 2 minutes per side. Arrange the tomato slices on top of the fish on the platter. Spoon the pecan sauce over the fish and tomatoes, saving some to pass on the side. Serve immediately.

Crabcakes

Any good crabcake is about crab, not bread or fillers. So this recipe isn't as fancy or jazzed up as some you might find in other books. We definitely adhere to the less-is-more mentality and prefer to let the succulent, sweet crabmeat do its thing.

makes 4 large cakes

CRABCAKES
1 pound lump crabmeat

4 tablespoons (½ stick) unsalted butter

¼ cup thinly sliced scallions

1 tablespoon minced shallot

¼ teaspoon cayenne

1 large egg, beaten

1 cup coarse breadcrumbs (fresh are best)

2 tablespoons thinly sliced fresh chives

1 lemon, zest grated and juiced

kosher salt and freshly ground pepper

BREADING
1 large egg

2 tablespoons milk

breadcrumbs as needed

vegetable or canola oil for frying

For the crabcakes, pick through the crabmeat to remove any pieces of shell or cartilage. Refrigerate the picked meat in a large covered bowl. Combine the butter, scallions, and shallot in a small sauté pan over high heat. When the mixture begins to sizzle, turn off the heat and stir in the cayenne. Cool slightly and add to the crabmeat along with the egg, breadcrumbs, chives, and zest and juice of the lemon. Gently stir the mixture together and season to taste with salt and pepper. Form the mixture into 4 even-size cakes.

For the breading, beat together the egg and milk in a medium bowl. Dip each of the cakes into the egg mixture, then roll in breadcrumbs until coated on all sides. Transfer to a large plate and refrigerate until ready to cook.

Preheat the oven to 350 degrees.

Pour the oil into a large, heavy-bottomed pan to a depth of ¼ to ½ inch and place the pan over medium-high heat. When the oil is hot, brown the cakes 2 at a time on each side. Transfer to the oven and bake until hot in the center, about 4 minutes. Serve immediately with one of the mayonnaise sauces that follow or Greta's Spicy Avocado Crema (page 60) on the side.

TECHNIQUE TIP

Party Time—Slice 'n Bake Crabcakes for Your Next Soiree: Make the crab mixture just as directed above. Lay a piece of plastic wrap on the countertop and arrange the crab on the plastic in a log shape about 1 inch in diameter. (It should look like a long, thin roll of slice 'n bake cookies.) Roll into a tight cylinder with the plastic and freeze until very firm, 30 to 60 minutes. Cut the log into ½-inch slices, then dip each slice in the egg mixture and roll in breadcrumbs. Place on a baking sheet and bake at 425 degrees for 7 minutes or fry in 350-degree oil until golden brown.

Mayonnaise Sauces

We're required to love mayo—we're Southern. But that doesn't mean our fridge is stocked with jars of the stuff. This basic mayonnaise is the fresher and tastier replacement for the jarred mixture that survives for years on supermarket shelves. The fresh kind is an essential part of any good cook's repertoire. Once you feel comfortable making this basic sauce, you'll have thousands of sauces at your fingertips.

When making your own mayo, you have to know that—strange as it may seem—it is the oil that thickens the sauce. As you slowly whisk the oil into the egg yolks, the sauce should begin to thicken. If half the oil has been added and the sauce is still very fluid, it's likely that it is broken. "Broken" refers to the emulsion, meaning that the liquid in the egg yolk has separated from the oil. This usually happens because the oil was added too fast or the whisking wasn't rapid or vigorous enough. There's only one way to fix a broken mayonnaise—start over. The broken emulsion can be gradually whisked into two fresh egg yolks in a clean bowl with a clean whisk. Extra egg yolks will make the mayo a little richer, but you won't need any additional oil or to make any other changes to the recipe.

Basic Mayonnaise

makes 1 cup

2 large egg yolks
1 tablespoon fresh lemon juice
pinch of kosher salt
1 cup canola oil
water as needed

In a mixing bowl, combine the egg yolks, lemon juice, and salt. Whisk briefly.

Gradually whisk in the oil in a slow, steady stream. As the mixture thickens, add water to thin as necessary. Adjust the final consistency of the mayonnaise by adding more oil to thicken or water to thin.

Aioli

Add 2 finely minced garlic cloves (or grated on a Microplane) to the egg yolks before whisking in the oil.

Homemade Tartar Sauce

Tartar sauce was invented to be eaten with seafood, fried seafood specifically. Though man can't live on fried seafood alone (we know many who have tried), this sauce is equally exciting on grilled or broiled fish, seafood sandwiches, and, of course, crabcakes. But the most creative/delicious use we found for tartar sauce is to dress up leftover braised meat—short ribs, lamb shanks, and so on—for a cold lunch salad with fresh greens.

makes 1½ cups

1 cup mayonnaise
1 tablespoon chopped capers
2 tablespoons chopped cornichon or pickle
1 tablespoon whole-grain mustard
2 tablespoons chopped fresh parsley, chives,
      chervil, or tarragon (or a combination)
1 teaspoon fresh lemon juice, or to taste
salt and freshly ground pepper to taste
Tabasco sauce to taste

Mix together the mayonnaise, capers, cornichon, mustard, herb, and lemon juice. Season to taste with salt, pepper, more lemon juice if needed, and Tabasco.

Spicy Garlic Mayo

This version of aioli kicked up with some hot sauce is the ultimate sandwich spread. The key to keeping it from being too garlicky is letting the grated garlic sit with the lemon juice to help mellow the raw garlic flavor. It's also been known to win over crowds as a dip for all things fried (including crabcakes).

makes 1 cup

1 clove garlic, finely grated
½ lemon, juiced
1 cup mayonnaise
1 teaspoon Dijon mustard
sriracha hot sauce to taste

Stir together the garlic and lemon juice in a small bowl and let stand for 5 minutes. Whisk in the mayo, mustard, and hot sauce.

BIG FLAVOR FAST

Try adding any of these to your homemade mayo:

- roasted garlic puree
- chopped fresh chives, basil, chervil, tarragon, dill, parsley, or a combo
- Dijon mustard and honey
- citrus juice and grated zest

Fish Cookery 101—Heat and Skin

Heat is the most important part of the fish-cooking equation. Whether grilling, searing, or broiling, fish should be cooked over high heat. There are, of course, exceptions (that is, poaching), but those are for another time. Cooking fish over high heat creates the "sear" or browning on the outside that gives great flavor and texture and ensures that the fish will not stick to the cooking surface or tear.

In restaurants, we say "presentation side first," meaning the "pretty side" of anything to be cooked (fish or meat) goes face down into the pan because the first side to hit the pan or grill gets the best coloring. Picking the right side might seem tricky at first, but think of it this way—if the skin is left on, it should be cooked golden or crisp or it is likely to become a slimy, unappealing mess. If the skin is removed, the red-colored blood line is exposed and turns shades that may range from rust to gray when cooked, so the opposite side should be cooked to golden perfection.

Now, how to cook fish. Starting with a very hot and well-oiled pan or grill, season the skin side with salt and pepper. Dusting with flour is helpful in drying the skin and making it crisp, but too much flour will result in black, burned pieces. Carefully lay the fish in the pan, letting it fall away from you so hot oil does not splash. Immediately press the fish with the back of a spatula (gently!) to ensure that it is in full contact with the pan and the fillet remains flat. Cook over high to medium-high heat for 3 to 4 minutes. When the edges of the fish are browned, turn the fish and cook for approximately 2 minutes more. The fish should be slightly translucent in the center when you remove it from the pan.

Remember, the fish will continue to cook after it is removed from the heat. Allow the fish to rest for 2 minutes before serving. If cooking fish without the skin, all the same rules apply. However, the side of the fillet that was once against the bone should be cooked first.

Wild Salmon with Sautéed Green Peas

When Brooke is slammed with column deadlines, book edits, a fussy baby, and needs an omega-3-loaded protein fix, she reaches for salmon. She mixes together a teaspoon of Dijon mustard and a tablespoon of wild honey and slathers the mixture on a fillet of salmon that bakes for ten minutes inside a 425-degree oven. But then she feels a little guilty. Why should this buttery, silken fish act as just an "old standby"? Jamie challenged himself to come up with a polished dish that features classic salmon accompaniments like Dijon mustard and sweet peas. In the end, he developed a standout everyday dinner that keeps his girls happy.

serves 4

1 tablespoon extra virgin olive oil

4 portions wild salmon fillet, about 6 ounces each

kosher salt and freshly ground pepper to taste

1 cup cream

2 tablespoons Dijon mustard

½ lemon, juiced

2 tablespoons chopped fresh chives or tarragon

Preheat the oven to 200 degrees.

Place a nonstick skillet over high heat. Add a thin layer of oil to cover the bottom of the pan, approximately 1 tablespoon. Season the salmon with salt and pepper and sear in the hot oil for 2 to 3 minutes per side. Remove the salmon to a warmed ovenproof plate or tray and place in the oven. Hold in the oven while you prepare the sauce.

Drain the excess fat from the pan and wipe lightly with a paper towel. Pour in the cream and bring to a boil. Cook until the cream is reduced by half. Whisk in the mustard, lemon juice, and herbs. Season to taste with salt and pepper. Pour over the salmon and serve with sautéed peas.

Green Peas

4 tablespoons (½ stick) unsalted butter

1 shallot, finely minced

3 cloves garlic, chopped

1 head romaine lettuce, finely sliced

4 cups frozen green peas (petits pois)

½ cup water or chicken broth

kosher salt and freshly ground pepper

Melt the butter in a medium pot. Add the shallot and garlic and cook over medium-high heat until tender and aromatic but not browned. Add the lettuce and stir occasionally until wilted, about 2 minutes. Stir in the peas and water and bring the mixture to a simmer. Taste the liquid and adjust the seasoning with salt and pepper. Cook for about 2 minutes more; the liquid should be reduced and the peas tender.

TECHNIQUE TIP

Searing fish gives them a beautiful golden crust. For successful searing, heat the oil until smoking and pat the fish dry with a paper towel immediately before putting it in the pan. Make sure the fish isn't stuck to the pan before turning. If the fish sticks to the pan, it's not ready to turn yet, so don't pry. Let the fish continue to cook until you can shake the pan and the fish moves freely before turning.

Pork Chops with Bourbon and Prunes

Nothing is as satisfying as a good, thick pork chop for dinner on a chilly winter's night. We brown ours and then simmer them down with sweet prunes and a drop of bourbon. To get the sauce smooth—and decadent—we finish it with a few spoonfuls of cream. Nestle the chops on a bed of fluffy white rice to help sop up the sauce. This is Brooke's absolute favorite cool-weather, weeknight meal (though it's special enough to make for Saturday night friends).

serves 4

4 pork chops or loin medallions (¾ inch thick)
kosher salt and freshly ground pepper
ground cumin
1 medium yellow onion, sliced
1 cup pitted prunes, chopped

RICE
2 cups chicken broth
kosher salt
1 cup long-grain rice

3 tablespoons canola oil
2 tablespoons unsalted butter
½ cup bourbon
1 cup chicken broth
¼ cup cream
kosher salt and freshly ground pepper to taste

Season the pork with salt and pepper, then sprinkle lightly with cumin. Leave the pork to absorb the seasoning while you slice the onion, chop the prunes, and get the rice cooking.

To cook the rice, bring the chicken broth with a pinch of salt to a boil. Once the liquid is boiling, add the rice and stir through one time. Place a cover on the rice pot and turn the heat to its lowest setting. Leave the rice to cook undisturbed until you can tilt the pot on its side and see no more liquid, about 13 minutes. Remove the rice from the heat, fluff with a spatula, and cover with the lid to steam for 2 minutes before spooning onto a platter.

To cook the seasoned pork, heat the oil in a cast-iron skillet or large sauté pan over high heat. Add the pork and brown well on both sides, 2 to 3 minutes per side. Remove the pork from the pan (it will not be fully cooked) and set aside. Discard the oil remaining in the pan. Add the butter and onion to the pan and reduce the heat. Cook the onion until lightly browned, about 5 minutes. Remove the pan from the heat and stir in the prunes and bourbon. Carefully return the pan to the heat and simmer until reduced by half. Return the pork to the pan, add the chicken broth, and simmer, covered, about 8 minutes more.

Remove the pork from the pan and place on top of the plated rice. Add the cream to the remaining liquid in the pan. Bring the mixture to a boil and cook for 2 to 4 minutes, until thickened. Taste and adjust the seasoning of the sauce with salt and pepper, then pour the mixture over the pork and rice.

Ground Chicken and Green Curry Vegetable Roast

We make this side-dish-turned-dinner at the end of summer just when the seasons meet. Corn, eggplant, and warm weather are on their way out as broccoli and cool weather make their way in. Adding green curry and basil to the fresh veggies gives them the spice they need to come together. Cucumbers and tomatoes do their part by adding some crisp freshness. If you can't find prepared green curry sauce, a mixture of fresh curry paste (Mae Ploy is excellent) and coconut milk can be substituted.

serves 4

CURRY VS. CURRY

In the wide world of all things spicy, there are two types of curry. Indian-style curries are based on blends of different dried spices or masalas (the proper name of Indian spice blends). The yellow stuff we know as curry powder is a completely different story of British invention and relatively unknown in India. Thai-style curries are based on pastes made of ground fresh chiles, ginger, lemongrass, garlic, and herbs. Fresh curry pastes can be found in the specialty aisle of most well-stocked supermarkets.

GARNISH

1 cup cherry tomatoes, split

2 Kirby cucumbers, seeded and sliced

½ lime, juiced

2 teaspoons extra virgin olive oil

2 teaspoons chopped fresh basil

kosher salt and freshly ground pepper to taste

2 Japanese eggplants (about 8 ounces), diced

2 heads broccoli (about 8 ounces), trimmed into florets

3 ears corn, kernels cut from cobs

2 cloves garlic, thinly sliced

2 teaspoons kosher salt, plus more as needed

2 tablespoons extra virgin olive oil

1 pound ground chicken

freshly ground pepper to taste

1 cup green curry sauce (see sidebar below)

lime juice to taste

3 tablespoons chopped Thai basil (or regular basil if unavailable)

CALL IN THE SUBS

Green curry sauce is available at Trader Joe's, Whole Foods, and most specialty food stores. If you can't find it, whisk together 1 tablespoon curry paste and 1 cup coconut milk.

Preheat the oven to 425 degrees.

For the garnish, place the cherry tomatoes and cucumbers in a small bowl. Season with the lime juice, olive oil, basil, salt, and pepper. Mix thoroughly and set aside.

Combine the diced eggplant, broccoli, corn kernels, garlic, salt, and olive oil in a large bowl and mix thoroughly. Spread the vegetables in a single layer on a baking sheet and roast in the oven until tender and slightly charred.

Lightly season the ground chicken with salt and pepper. Brown the chicken in a skillet over medium-high heat. Reduce the heat to low and add the green curry sauce. Bring to a simmer and adjust the seasoning to taste with salt, pepper, and lime juice.

When the vegetables are finished roasting, add them to the skillet and mix well. Return the mixture to a simmer and stir in the basil. Divide among 4 plates and garnish with the chopped tomatoes and cucumbers.

TECHNIQUE TIP

On the Double—A two-burner attack gets dinner on the table in a hurry. Veggies roast in the oven for about 12 minutes while the chicken is browning and simmering on the stovetop for about 10 minutes. Minus chopping time, dinner is ready in about 15 minutes!

Whole-Wheat Pappardelle with Butternut Squash and Blue Cheese

One gusty, freezing January night, the baby was giving us a lot of grief. The whipping wind outside of our apartment windows and Parker's little tantrum forced us to raid the veggie bowl, the pantry, and the refrigerator in hopes we could find the makings for dinner. Fifteen minutes later, we both cradled bowls filled with ribbons of warm pasta lightly coated with blue cheese and studded with butternut squash.

serves 2

2 tablespoons extra virgin olive oil

1 medium yellow onion, diced

1 cup diced peeled butternut squash

¾ cup chicken stock

8 ounces whole-wheat pappardelle (whole-wheat fettuccine is a nice substitution)

½ cup blue cheese crumbles (about 4 ounces)

2 to 3 tablespoons chopped fresh parsley

½ cup toasted walnuts

Bring a large pot of salted water to a boil.

Heat the olive oil in a large sauté pan over medium-high heat. Add the onion and cook until softened but not browned. Toss in the butternut squash and cook for 3 to 4 minutes more before adding the chicken stock.

While the squash is cooking, drop the pasta into the boiling water. Cook until tender but not completely softened (al dente). Scoop the pasta from the boiling water directly into the sauté pan; you should transfer about ¼ cup of the pasta water along with the pasta. Bring this mixture to a simmer and mix well. After a minute of simmering, remove the pan from the heat and mix in the blue cheese, parsley, and toasted walnuts. If the pasta seems dry, add a few tablespoons of the cooking water before serving.

TECHNIQUE TIP

When sautéing and trying to avoid browning, as in this recipe, adding a small amount of water (¼ cup or so) can actually speed cooking and prevent browning. Especially after the butternut squash is added, a little water keeps the squash from sticking to the pan.

Bar-B-Qued Shrimp

How simple is this? Brooke's mother passed down a version of this recipe from one of her Gulf Coast Junior League cookbooks. The "barbecue" part is a little bit of a mystery—there's no grill and there aren't any five-alarm spices involved—but we're not going to hold that against the simplest and most satisfying summer dinner in this cookbook. As the seasoned shrimp hang out on the baking sheet, they really flavor the melted butter with their salty, unctuous goodness. That's why it's important to ask your fish guy for "head-on" shrimp—the flavor's in the head, not the tail. And don't necessarily go for the biggest critters with the smallest "count" (the bigger the shrimp, the fewer that can be purchased in a pound, thus, the smaller "count" per pound). Our favorite shrimp are midsize (26/30) and from the Gulf of Mexico.

serves 4

3 pounds fresh shell-on shrimp, heads on if possible

1 cup (2 sticks) unsalted butter

2 tablespoons Ultimate Grill Salt or Creole Seasoning
    (page 61 or 63)

1 lemon, juiced

2 tablespoons chopped fresh parsley

1 baguette, warmed in the oven

Preheat the oven to 425 degrees.

Place the shrimp in a colander and rinse under cold water. Leave to drain well.

Place a large roasting pan on top of the stove over medium heat. Melt the butter in the pan, then add the seasoned salt and the lemon juice. Stir with a wooden spoon until the butter comes to a boil. Add the shrimp and mix with a wooden spoon to coat with the butter mixture. Transfer the roasting pan to the oven and cook for 5 minutes. Remove the pan from the oven, stir well, and return to the oven. Continue to cook until the shrimp are cooked through, about 5 minutes more. Remove the pan from the oven and let rest for 5 minutes. Stir in the parsley just before serving, with the baguettes on the side.

The buttery juices in the bottom of the pan are the best part, so divide the juices into small bowls and set them around the dinner table.

TECHNIQUE TIP

Just tear the baguette into chunks and place in the center of the table. Everyone will be more than happy to rip into their own hunk of bread to sop up the juices.

EVERYDAY DESSERTS

There are times when you just want a little nibble of something sweet. Nothing over the top. Well, the flavor needs to be extraordinary—because the smaller the bite, the sharper and more focused the flavors need to be—but the prep work and grocery shopping should be easy. For our Everyday Desserts, no fancy gadgets are required (Brooke's never liked candy thermometers or double boilers), and we embrace the beauty of one-stop shopping. The fresh fruit desserts can be made after a quick trip to the farmstand and with fridge and pantry staples such as flour, sugar, butter, nuts, and a spice or two. The chocolate concoctions don't require more than a quick trip down the baking aisle. Our hope is that you can pull together these desserts on the fly, pulling a warm pan of goodness out of the oven somewhere between your afterwork yoga session and dinner at seven.

Strawberry Layer Cake

For our daughter's first birthday, we knew we had to make a spectacular cake. But what kind? She's a Taurus, an April baby, and that means strawberry season. So we quickly edited our yellow-cake-with-chocolate-buttercream plans and figured out how to best showcase the season's sweetest, juiciest berries. Whipped cream cheese icing perfumed with orange zest fills in between the three layers and then cascades down the sides, making it a gorgeous but effortlessly casual cake.

makes one 3-layer cake or 30 cupcakes

YELLOW CAKE

1 cup (2 sticks) unsalted butter, at room temperature, plus more for the pans

3 cups cake flour, sifted, plus more for the pans

2 tablespoons baking powder

½ teaspoon baking soda

½ teaspoon kosher salt

2 cups granulated sugar

4 large eggs

2 teaspoons vanilla extract

1 cup whole milk

Preheat the oven to 350 degrees.

Butter and flour three 9-inch cake pans or line a 12-cup muffin pan with muffin cups.

In a medium bowl, combine the flour, baking powder, baking soda, and salt. Stir with a dry whisk or fork to thoroughly combine.

In a large bowl, beat the butter and sugar with an electric mixer until light and fluffy. Add the eggs one at a time, beating well after each addition. Add the vanilla and beat again to combine.

Continue by adding half the flour mixture and then half the milk, beating well after each addition. Add the remaining flour and then the remaining milk, beating until smooth and creamy.

Divide the batter among the cake pans or fill the muffin cups two-thirds full, being sure not to overfill them. For cake layers, bake until a toothpick inserted into the center comes out clean, 25 to 30 minutes. For cupcakes, bake until the tops are golden, the edges are a bit brown, and a toothpick inserted into the center cupcake comes out clean, about 20 minutes. Cool in the pans for 10 minutes. Remove from the pans and finish cooling on racks. Repeat to bake as many more cupcakes as you can.

Lemon-Dressed Strawberries

It doesn't take much to dress up strawberries when they're in season between May and July. But to gild the lily—and to give 'em a bit of zing—we toss the strawberries with fresh lemon juice and a touch of sugar.

1 pint ripe strawberries, rinsed, dried, and hulled
grated zest and juice of 1 lemon
2 teaspoons granulated sugar

Cut the strawberries into quarters. Transfer the strawberries to a medium bowl and toss with the lemon zest, lemon juice, and sugar. Allow the strawberries to macerate (a fancy word for "marinate") for 15 minutes.

Cream Cheese Icing with Orange Zest

Our cream cheese icing seems lighter because we add a touch of orange zest. The citrus freshens everything up, begging you to eat just one more forkful.

8 tablespoons (1 stick) unsalted butter, at room temperature
¼ cup whole milk
1 teaspoon vanilla extract
1 teaspoon lemon juice
grated zest of 1 orange
8 ounces cream cheese, at room temperature
3 cups powdered sugar

In a large bowl, beat together the butter, milk, vanilla, lemon juice, orange zest, and cream cheese with an electric mixer. With the mixer on low speed, add the powdered sugar 1 cup at a time and continue beating until smooth and creamy.

To assemble the cake, place one of the three cake layers in the center of a large platter. Spread about one-quarter of the icing on the layer. Invert the next cake layer onto the icing so that the rounded top rests atop the icing. Spread with one-quarter of the icing. Top with the final layer, rounded side down, and pour over the remaining icing. With a butter knife or small plastic spatula, smooth the top of the cake while letting the excess icing drip down the sides of the cake. Spoon the macerated strawberries in the center of the top layer.

For the cupcakes, spread a generous amount of the icing on each cake, then top each with a spoonful of the macerated strawberries.

Brooke's Best Lemon Squares

Brooke's good friend Lauren Solimando-Kovary is whippet-thin (the guys call her "Stems" because of her long, beautiful legs), but she'll definitely make room for dessert—it just has to be a worthy dessert. The parties that she and her husband, Ed, throw at their home in the Hamptons always feature a buffet of luscious treats that put Magnolia Bakery to shame. So when she told us that her grandma Helen Solimando had the hands-down best lemon square recipe, we listened. With a few tiny tweaks, we created the ultimate lemon custard that is equal measures puckery and sweet. The crust, for its part, is light and buttery. For looks and practical purposes, cut your squares small. Once you set a plate of these down, they're gone!

makes 12 squares

1 cup all-purpose flour

¼ cup powdered sugar, plus more for decoration

8 tablespoons (1 stick) unsalted butter, cold

1 cup granulated sugar

1 tablespoon cornstarch

½ teaspoon baking powder

2 large eggs

⅛ teaspoon kosher salt

2 tablespoons (well packed) finely grated lemon zest

2 tablespoons fresh lemon juice

Preheat the oven to 350 degrees.

Combine the flour and powdered sugar. Add the butter and, with your fingers, mix together the ingredients until a coarse, crumblike texture is achieved. Be careful not to overmix.

Evenly press the mixture into an ungreased 8-inch square baking pan. Bake for 20 minutes.

While the crust is baking, combine the granulated sugar, cornstarch, and baking powder. Add the eggs, salt, and lemon zest and juice and beat with an electric mixer for about 3 minutes.

Pour the egg mixture over the hot crust.

Bake for 25 minutes. Remove from the oven when the top is slightly golden. Allow to cool completely on a baking rack. Transfer to the refrigerator and chill for at least 1 hour before serving. Cut into 12 lemon squares. Sift a tablespoon or two of powdered sugar over the top. Serve slightly chilled.

Cornmeal and Summer Berry Cobbler

This is one of those "mix, pour, and bake" desserts that make you look like an oh-so-brilliant-yet-rustic cook. The fresh fruit–studded batter is just sweet enough—the kind of simple ending that you want after a lazy, warm-weather meal.

serves 6

4 cups mixed berries—blueberries, blackberries,
    strawberries, and/or raspberries

grated zest and juice of 1 lemon

1 tablespoon cornstarch

¼ cup powdered sugar, plus more for dusting

6 tablespoons (¾ stick) unsalted butter

½ cup whole milk

2 large eggs

1 cup self-rising flour

¼ cup cornmeal

½ teaspoon salt

¾ cup granulated sugar

Preheat the oven to 350 degrees.

In a medium bowl, toss together the berries, lemon zest and juice, cornstarch, and powdered sugar; set aside to marinate.

Melt the butter in a small saucepan. Add the milk and remove from the heat, then stir in the eggs.

In a large bowl, combine the flour, cornmeal, salt, and granulated sugar. Pour the butter mixture into the cornmeal mixture and stir with a wooden spoon until there are no lumps. Pour the marinated fruit into a 1-quart gratin dish or into six 8-ounce ramekins, adding any of the juices that have collected in the bottom of the bowl. Pour the batter over the fruit, adding enough to fill the dish(es) , but not to completely cover the fruit.

Place the dish(es) on a baking sheet and bake until puffed and golden brown, about 30 minutes. Dust with powdered sugar and serve immediately.

WHAT IS CORNMEAL?

Cornmeal is a coarse flour made from dried corn. "Regular" flour is made from dried wheat.

STONE-GROUND VS. REGULAR CORNMEAL

Stone-ground cornmeal is—surprise!—ground between two stones. The big flavor difference enters the picture because the hull and the germ of the corn kernel are left in, giving the cornmeal more texture and "corn" flavor. If we have the option, we buy stone-ground.

TECHNIQUE TIP

Baking this cobbler on a baking sheet keeps all those bubbly juices from burning on the bottom of the oven. To make cleanup even easier, line the pan with aluminum foil and there's no scrubbing required.

Milkshakes with Spiced Pecans

Jamie has a thing for milkshakes. Brooke enjoys a sip now and again, but she'd much rather run away with a pan of brownies than a tall glass of vanilla. Finally, after three years of dating and six months as marrieds, Jamie made Brooke one of his milkshakes. His secret for achieving the perfect consistency is heavy cream and a little ice. Adding a shot of bourbon definitely helped him prove his point!

serves 2

2 cups ice cream—vanilla, coffee, or chocolate

½ cup cream

2 or 3 large ice cubes

1 teaspoon vanilla extract

½ cup bourbon (optional)

1 cup fresh or frozen fruit, such as strawberries or
    peaches (optional)

Combine all the ingredients in a blender and process until smooth. For a thinner shake, add more cream; or add more ice to thicken.

ANCHO POWDER

Dark red, smoky, and just a little spicy, ancho chiles are the base ingredient for dark chili powder and many Mexican dishes such as mole. Here they add an unforgettable kick to spiced pecans.

Palmetto Bluff Spiced Pecans

Jamie likes to take full credit for these pecans. The fact that he first tasted them on his honeymoon and merely guessed the secret ingredient, ancho powder, doesn't bother him at all. You'll love how the egg wash gives the nuts an amazing crunch.

makes 2 cups

1 egg white

1 teaspoon ground dried ancho chile (optional)

½ teaspoon ground cinnamon

1 scrape nutmeg

3 tablespoons granulated sugar

1 teaspoon kosher salt

2 cups pecans

Preheat the oven to 325 degrees.

Whisk the egg white in a medium bowl until frothy. Add the remaining ingredients except the pecans and whisk a moment more. The mixture should be foamy. Stir in the pecans and turn out onto a baking sheet lined with parchment paper. Toast until golden brown and crisp, about 30 minutes. Remove and cool on the baking sheet.

Serve milkshakes on a platter with these pecans scattered around the base of the glasses or let a few pecans float on top of each shake.

Pecan/Walnut Crumble for Year-Round Desserts

Once you master this topping—and, really, how hard is it to crumble bits of butter and flour between your fingers?—a delicious dessert will be at the ready, any time of year. Our crumble is a multitasker that pulls double duty by helping to coat a wintry mixture of apples and pears (we call that a "streusel") as well as ripe, juicy summer peaches (that's a "crisp"). No matter what you call it, this'll definitely help you solve your last-minute dessert woes.

Combine all the ingredients in a food processor and pulse until the mixture resembles little pebbles. Without a food processor, combine all the ingredients in a large bowl and work between your fingers until the mixture resembles little pebbles. Refrigerate or store, tightly covered, in the freezer for up to 6 months.

makes approximately 4 cups,
enough for 2 baked crumbles

8 tablespoons (1 stick) unsalted butter, cold, cut into
     small pieces
¼ cup granulated sugar
¼ cup brown sugar
½ cup chopped pecans or walnuts
½ cup all-purpose flour
1 teaspoon ground cinnamon
½ teaspoon kosher salt

Milkshake Combos

Peach Milkshake—Vanilla ice cream, fresh/frozen peaches, vanilla extract (with or without bourbon!)
Strawberry—Vanilla or strawberry ice cream, fresh/frozen strawberries, and vanilla extract
Coffee—Coffee ice cream, vanilla extract, and bourbon
Chocolate Bourbon—Chocolate ice cream, 1 banana, 2 teaspoons cocoa powder, and bourbon

Apple and Pear Gratin with Pecan/Walnut Streusel

The word "streusel" means "mixture" in German. We take this to mean that with every successful diet plan, you need to "mix it up" a little. So we came up with a dessert that focuses on baked fruit with just enough topping to satisfy your sweet tooth. This is a snap to assemble.

serves 6

4 Golden Delicious, Honeycrisp, or Rome apples

4 Bosc pears

2 lemons, zest grated and juiced

1 cup medium-dry red wine

½ recipe Pecan/Walnut Crumble (recipe precedes)

Preheat the oven to 375 degrees.

Remove the stems from the fruit; cut in half and scoop out the seeds and cores. Cut a small slice from the back of each half so it will sit flat in the baking pan, with its core facing up. Toss with the lemon zest and juice. Arrange the fruit in a single layer in a 13- x 9-inch baking dish or 3-quart gratin dish and pour the red wine around the base. Fill the scooped cores with the crumble mixture and scatter more over the surface of the fruit. Bake on the center rack of the oven until the crumble is browned, 20 to 25 minutes.

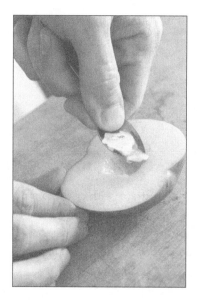

Peach Crisp

Think of this as the lazy man's pie—and we mean that in a good way. If you're not yet comfortable with your crust-making abilities, our peach crisp is just as delicious as—maybe even better than—a deep-dish pie. The salty, buttery, and crunchy crumble topping beats out a thin layer of pastry dough any day. Summertime peaches are the best for this recipe, but if you have a hankering for this crisp in the wintertime, use frozen sliced peaches.

serves 6

3 tablespoons cornstarch

8 peaches, pitted and sliced

½ teaspoon grated lime zest

juice of 1 lime

4 tablespoons (½ stick) unsalted butter

½ cup brown sugar

1 recipe Pecan/Walnut Crumble (page 111)

Preheat the oven to 350 degrees.

In a large bowl, sprinkle the cornstarch over the cut peaches; add the lime zest and juice and mix gently until the juice is absorbed. In a large sauté pan, melt the butter over medium heat Add the brown sugar and cook until melted and bubbly. Stir in the peaches—being careful not to break them—and warm through. Put the peaches in a13- x 9-inch baking dish or 3-quart gratin dish and scatter the crumble topping generously over the top. Bake until bubbly and well browned on the top, about 15 minutes.

MAKE AHEAD

When peaches hit their peak in summer, make a double or triple batch of the crumble and keep it in the freezer for up to a month to have a brilliant dessert ready in a hurry.

Hungarian Shortbread with Raspberry Jam

Shortbread can be tricky to handle because of all the butter. But if you freeze the dough and then grate it with a box grater into the pan, it's no muss, no fuss, and you get an amazingly tender crumb. Next comes the sweet raspberry jam and then, finally, one last layer of grated dough. When all is said and done and the oven timer dings, you have a melt-in-your-mouth rustic, fruit-filled dessert.

serves 10 to 12 as a light dessert

1 pound (4 sticks) unsalted butter

4½ cups all-purpose flour, plus more for dusting

1½ cups granulated sugar

1 tablespoon baking powder

1 teaspoon salt

4 large egg yolks

1 large egg

1¼ cups raspberry jam (or any other flavor), at room
    temperature

powdered sugar for dusting

Cut the butter into small cubes and place in the freezer to chill. Combine the flour, granulated sugar, baking powder, and salt in the bowl of a food processor. Add the butter to the dry ingredients and pulse until the mixture has the texture of coarse meal. Transfer the mixture to a large bowl. Add the egg yolks and egg and stir with a wooden spoon until a ball forms. Transfer the dough to a floured workspace and knead lightly until smooth. Divide the dough in half, wrap each tightly in plastic wrap, and freeze until very firm, at least 1 hour.

Preheat the oven to 350 degrees.

When the dough is frozen, unwrap one ball of dough and grate on a box grater. Spread the grated dough in a single layer on the bottom of a 13- x 9-inch baking dish. Press lightly to form an even layer. Spread the raspberry jam over the dough. Remove the second ball of dough from the freezer, unwrap, and grate. Spread the grated dough over the raspberry jam and press lightly to form an even the layer.

Bake until firm and golden brown on the top, about 25 minutes. Cool completely and dust with powdered sugar before cutting.

___

THE SPICE OF LIFE

Have fun with this recipe, mixing up the flavors. We love making seasonal variations with Fig Chutney (page 257) or good strawberry jam.

Chocolate Chip Blondies

We load up our blondies with so many chocolate chips, we should probably call them "brunettes." Our chocolaty wonders turn out soft and chewy every time because we melt the butter before whipping it with the sugar and we bake them as "bar cookies" not individual drop-and-bakes. If you're tired of temperamental, rock-hard chocolate chip cookies, give our moist and melty blondies a try.

serves 6 to 8

¾ cup (1½ sticks) unsalted butter, plus more for
    the pan
1½ cups all-purpose flour, plus more for the pan
1 cup packed brown sugar
½ cup granulated sugar
1 large egg, lightly beaten
1 teaspoon vanilla extract
1 teaspoon baking powder
½ teaspoon kosher salt
1 cup semisweet chocolate chips

Preheat the oven to 350 degrees.

Lightly butter and flour an 8-inch square baking pan and set aside.

Melt the butter in a small saucepot. Combine the sugars in a large bowl. Add the melted butter and beat with an electric mixer until smooth and lightened in color, about 3 minutes. Beat in the egg and vanilla.

Combine the flour, baking powder, and salt in a separate bowl and mix well. Add half of the flour mixture to the sugar mixture and stir with a large spoon or spatula to combine. Stir in the remaining flour mixture and the chocolate chips.

Spread the batter in the baking pan and smooth the surface. Bake until golden brown on top and a toothpick inserted in the center comes out clean, 30 to 40 minutes. Cool before cutting.

How to Separate Egg Yolks

There are several methods for separating eggs (the yolk from the white), but our favorite doesn't require any silly gadgets or leave you with sticky fingers. Holding the egg in one hand, tap it firmly on a countertop to crack the egg around its middle. Turn the egg so that the cracked side is facing up, then hold the egg in both hands, placing one thumb on each side of the crack. Pull the egg apart at the crack by rotating your thumbs out. This will turn the shells so each half has its broken side facing up. The yolk should fall neatly into one side of the broken egg. Carefully transfer the remaining egg back-and-forth between the shells until all of the white has fallen into the bowl. Drop the yolk into a separate bowl and repeat the process. Unused egg whites can be frozen indefinitely or used for a healthy breakfast within a few days.

Tarte Tatin

Who needs a fusty pineapple upside-down cake when you can have an elegant apple tart (that so happens to be served upside down)? While tarte tatin is the stuff of legend—and inspires very intimidating visions of Julia Child—it's really easy to make. Instead of wringing your hands over the perfect crust, all you really need is to focus on sautéing the apples to a deep golden brown and arranging them in a pretty pattern on the bottom of an ovenproof pan. Then lay your dough over the apples, tuck the dough between the fruit and the pan, and pop the whole thing in the oven. To serve the tart, you'll invert it onto a plate, so any crust snafus will be hidden—and forgotten—when friends taste the rich caramelized apples.

serves 6 to 8

CRUST

1½ cups all-purpose flour, plus more for dusting

2 tablespoons granulated sugar

1 teaspoon kosher salt

8 tablespoons (1 stick) unsalted butter, cold, diced

1 large egg

APPLES

3 Golden Delicious, Honeycrisp, Jonagold,
   or Granny Smith apples, peeled and cored

1 lemon, zest grated and juiced

½ cup granulated sugar

4 tablespoons (½ stick) unsalted butter

½ cup brown sugar

For the crust, put the flour, sugar, and salt in a food processor and pulse to combine. Add the butter and continue pulsing until the mixture resembles coarse meal. Add the egg and let the processor run for 2 to 5 seconds. Do not overmix. The mixture should just begin to gather into a dough. Turn the mixture out onto a floured surface and knead quickly until a dough forms. Wrap tightly in plastic wrap and rest in the refrigerator.

Preheat the oven to 375 degrees.

Cut the apples into ¼-inch slices and toss in a large bowl with the lemon zest, juice, and granulated sugar. Set aside for 20 to 30 minutes.

Strain the juices that have collected in the bottom of the bowl of apples. Combine the juices from the apples and the butter in a 9-inch cast-iron skillet or nonstick pan. Bring the mixture to a boil and reduce until just a few tablespoons remain. Stir in the brown sugar and cook until the mixture becomes very thick and bubbly, approximately 5 minutes more. Add the apples and sauté until just softened, about 3 minutes. Take the pan off the heat and arrange the cooked apples in concentric circles in a slightly overlapping single layer.

Roll the dough into a circle approximately 1 inch larger than the pan. Lay the dough over the apples and tuck the extra between the apples and the sides of the pan. Cut a few steam holes in the top of the dough. Bake until the pastry has browned and crisped, about 20 minutes. Let the tart sit for 10 to 15 minutes before unmolding. Unmold the tart by inverting it onto a serving dish (so the pastry is on the bottom) and serve warm or cold with whipped cream or vanilla ice cream.

New Baby Banana Pudding

Brooke gave birth . . . and then she went to Magnolia Bakery. We're not kidding. Our newborn daughter, Parker Lee, came home from the hospital, rested for two days, and then found herself at the corner of Bleecker Street and West 11th inhaling the smell of warm butter and eggs, chocolate and sugar. But Brooke wasn't interested in the famous cupcakes. She brushed past them to make a beeline for the banana pudding, that bowl of creamy, Nilla comfort that'd get her through the next four feedings (and the middle of the night). To keep both his girls happy, Jamie quickly came up with his own version of the recipe. By pureeing overripe bananas into the milk, he created over-the-top "banana-y" flavor and a pudding texture that's a bit softer than the standard.

serves 8

2 overripe bananas

2 cups whole milk

2 teaspoons vanilla extract

2 large eggs

2 large egg yolks

¾ cup granulated sugar

¼ cup cornstarch, plus 1 tablespoon

1 teaspoon kosher salt

2 tablespoons butter, at room temperature

Nilla wafers as needed

Chop the overripe bananas and combine with the milk and vanilla in a medium saucepot. Bring to a simmer and turn off the heat. Cover with a lid and set aside for 10 minutes.

Combine the eggs, egg yolks, sugar, cornstarch, and salt in a large bowl or the workbowl of an electric mixer; beat until smooth. Slowly add the hot milk and bananas while the mixer is running. Return the mixture to the saucepot and whisk constantly over high heat until it begins to simmer and thicken. Move the thickened mixture back to the mixing bowl, add the butter, and continue beating on high until cooled.

Spoon one-third of the pudding into a bowl or trifle dish. Add a layer of wafers, then another one-third of the pudding. Continue layering in this manner. Refrigerate for at least 3 hours before serving.

THE NEXT LEVEL

As you layer the pudding and wafers, add even more slices of fresh bananas to kick up that "banana-y" flavor. Or for an adult treat, whisk in ½ cup banana liqueur after cooking the pudding (in the same step as the butter).

Crostata Two Ways

Our freeform tarts (think easy, rustic pie but without the pie pan) showcase good butter, even better fall produce, and heavenly frangipane. Make the crostata year-round by substituting spring and summer stone fruits such as nectarines and peaches for the figs and plums.

makes two 10- to 12-inch crostate

1½ cups all-purpose flour, plus more for dusting

1 tablespoon granulated sugar

¼ teaspoon kosher salt

8 tablespoons (1 stick) unsalted butter, cold,
    cut into small cubes

3 tablespoons ice water

1 recipe Frangipane (recipe follows)

1 recipe Fig Filling (recipe follows) *or*

1 recipe Plum Filling (recipe follows)

1 large egg, beaten

Combine the flour, sugar, and salt in a large bowl. Add the chilled butter and quickly work into the dry ingredients with your fingers, leaving the butter in small chunks. Add the ice water and stir with a wooden spoon until the mixture gathers into a ball. Transfer to a floured surface and knead lightly so the dough just comes together. Divide into 2 balls. Wrap the dough in plastic wrap, then press each ball into a disc. Refrigerate for at least 30 minutes and up to 2 days.

Preheat the oven to 375 degrees.

Roll the dough into a large circle—don't worry if the circle isn't perfect. Transfer the circle to a baking sheet lined with parchment paper or aluminum foil. Spread one-third of the frangipane on the dough, leaving a 2-inch border. Arrange your fruit (figs or plums) on top of the frangipane, still making sure to leave the 2-inch border of dough. Fold the edges of the dough over the fruit toward the center. The dough should come in approximately 2 inches from the edges; the fruit will be mainly uncovered. Ball up a piece of paper towel and dip it into the small bowl of beaten egg. Brush the folded edges of the crust with the egg wash. Repeat the process with the second ball of dough (if, in fact, you are making two crostate—one with plum filling and one with fig).

Bake until the crust is golden and the fruit has softened, 40 to 50 minutes. After the crostata has cooled on the pan for 5 minutes, remove to a baking rack and allow to cool for 20 minutes. Serve warm. (Though we've never turned down a room-temperature dessert!)

Frangipane

Heaven is homemade frangipane, an almond pastry cream that lends itself particularly well to simple tarts like ours. It serves as a sweet, delicately flavored base for the fresh fruit.

makes enough for 3 crostate

1 cup slivered almonds
½ cup granulated sugar
pinch of kosher salt
8 tablespoons (1 stick) unsalted butter, at room
  temperature
1 large egg
⅛ teaspoon almond extract (optional)

Add the almonds, sugar, and salt to the bowl of a food processor and pulse until finely chopped. Remove the mixture to a medium bowl and add the softened butter. Beat with a handheld electric mixer on high until the butter is nicely whipped, about 2 minutes. Add the egg and almond extract, if using, and continue beating on high until the mixture is light and fluffy. Store extra frangipane in a tightly sealed plastic container. Keeps for 10 days.

Fig Filling

makes filling for one 10- to 12-inch crostata

1 teaspoon finely grated lemon zest
1 teaspoon fresh lemon juice
¼ teaspoon kosher salt
2 tablespoons honey
½ teaspoon fresh thyme leaves
¾ pound Black Mission figs, stems removed,
  quartered

In a medium bowl, whisk together the lemon zest, lemon juice, salt, honey, and thyme. Add the figs and toss gently to coat.

Plum Filling

makes filling for one 10- to 12-inch crostata

3 plums, pitted, cut into 8 slices each
1 small lemon, zest grated and juiced
1 tablespoon cornstarch
⅓ cup light brown sugar
1 teaspoon ground cinnamon

In a medium bowl, combine the plums, lemon zest, lemon juice, cornstarch, brown sugar, and cinnamon. Stir and allow the plums to macerate for at least 20 minutes.

Cheesecake Parfaits with Fresh Strawberries

Brooke has a fetish for martini glasses—she thinks that anything tastes better when it's in a fun glass. Jamie remembered that when he was trying to come up with a quick, foolproof dessert. So instead of the usual time-intensive cheesecake that's baked in a water bath, he created layers of cheesecake and spiced, baked crust that look fabulous in Brooke's favorite cocktail glass. His final flourish is a hill of minted strawberries.

serves 6

CRUST

1 package graham crackers (9 pieces)

½ teaspoon kosher salt

2 tablespoons granulated sugar

¼ teaspoon ground ginger

¼ teaspoon ground cinnamon

6 tablespoons (¾ stick) unsalted butter, melted

PARFAIT

8 ounces cream cheese, at room temperature

2 tablespoons orange juice

5 tablespoons granulated sugar

2 cups cream

1 teaspoon vanilla extract

about 1 quart fresh strawberries

1 tablespoon chopped fresh mint

TECHNIQUE TIP

The Easy Way Out—If the clock is ticking and the girls are on their way, skip the baked graham cracker crumbles and simply top the parfaits with plain crushed crackers.

Preheat the oven to 350 degrees.

For the crust, grind the graham crackers into crumbs in a food processor. Combine the crumbs in a bowl with the salt, sugar, and spices. Add the melted butter and mix well until moistened. Press the crumbs into a lightly greased 13- x 9-inch baking pan, forming an even layer on the bottom. Bake the crust until lightly browned and firm, about 10 minutes. Remove and cool on a rack. Crumble into large chunks, then store in the freezer until ready to assemble, up to 4 weeks.

For the parfait, combine the cream cheese, orange juice, and 4 tablespoons of the sugar in a bowl. Mash with a whisk and whip until smooth.

In a separate, well-chilled bowl, combine the cream and vanilla. Beat until soft peaks form. Add the remaining 1 tablespoon sugar and whip to firm peaks. Whisk one-third of the whipped cream into the cream cheese mixture. Finish by folding in the final two-thirds in two separate batches.

Spoon the cream cheese mixture into six wine or martini glasses to fill approximately halfway. Refrigerate until ready to serve.

Just before serving, cut the strawberries into quarters, toss with the mint, and place a large spoonful in each glass. Top with the graham cracker crumbles.

SOUPS AND SANDWICHES

Back in the day, soups and sandwiches were a Ladies-Who-Lunch thing. Remember when your mom would order a chicken salad sandwich and a bowl of something brothy and discuss tomato plants with her girlfriends? Well, we do, and we also remember vowing that our midday eating ritual would be different—it'd be less light and froufrou and more substantial. But when we actually became adults and got stuck with hectic work schedules, we discovered the silent virtues of good, honest protein between two slivers of bread.

Both sandwiches and soups are well-rounded meals that don't try too hard. Whether the ingredients are stacked, chopped, or pureed, you can feel good about fresh ingredients that aren't too fussed with. The same can be said for a really good soup. And soups that can be made on Sunday night and reheated at work throughout the week just make good, common (delicious!) sense. There's nothing froufrou about leftovers like these, is there?

The key here is to use your noggin and think ahead. When you make a grocery store run on Saturday afternoon, make a list of sandwich fixings you need to have on hand for at least two of our recipes. Most of our soups taste better the next day (or the day after that), so Sunday's batch of Roasted Butternut Squash Soup should take you to midweek. Then, at the appointed hour, all you do is heat, ladle, slice, and serve . . . and watch your coworkers drool.

Our soup and sandwich lunches serve as a little bright spot in our busy weeks. Here are a few of our favorite combos:

- Cucumber and Buttermilk Soup (page 123) with Brooke's Ultimate Grilled Cheese Sandwiches (page 132)
- French Onion Soup (page 129) with Chicken Salad sandwich (page 142)
- Chilled Tomato Soup (page 122) with The Provençal (page 133)
- Roasted Butternut Squash Soup (page 128) with The Spaniard (page 130)

Origins of Gazpacho

Gazpacho was invented about the same time as the wheel. Okay, it wasn't that long ago. But food historians say that a version of today's chilled soup—using stale bread, vinegar, and olive oil—is one of the ancestral soups of the Western world. There's even a mention of it in the Bible's Book of Ruth. While the Moors brought it to Spain between the eighth and twelfth centuries, the gazpacho that we know and love—the one that showcases juicy, vine-ripened tomatoes—can be credited to the specific region of Andalusia, in the southernmost province of Spain. Of course, they had to wait until tomatoes were brought back from the New World in the sixteenth century, before they could work the recipe into its modern-day form.

Chilled Tomato Soup

This is Jamie's more elegant version of Spanish gazpacho. You could just as easily drink it from a mug as you could eat it from a bowl. But we definitely prefer to sit down and make a meal out of it. We dress it up with fresh Gulf crabmeat, peppers, and basil. Suddenly we have a beautiful summer meal. Think of this as a cold soup with the virtues of a salad.

serves 4 in bowls or 8 in cups

10 ripe red tomatoes
5 Kirby cucumbers
2 shallots
1 red bell pepper
¼ cup fresh basil leaves
1 tablespoon red wine vinegar, plus more to taste
kosher salt and freshly ground pepper
good-quality olive oil for garnish

Roughly chop the tomatoes, cucumbers, shallots, bell pepper, and basil; toss together in a large bowl with the vinegar and a healthy pinch of salt and pepper. Refrigerate for 1 hour or up to overnight. Remove the vegetable mixture from the fridge and, working in batches, pulse in a food processor or blender until the mixture is smooth. Transfer to a chilled container. Season to taste with salt, pepper, and vinegar. Store tightly covered in the refrigerator until ready to serve. Garnish each bowl of soup with a drizzle of good-quality olive oil. Keeps up to 5 days.

GARNISH (OPTIONAL)
4 to 8 ounces jumbo lump crabmeat (about 1 ounce per person), shells and cartilage removed
1 cup finely diced cucumber
1 small red bell pepper, finely diced
2 tablespoons chopped fresh basil leaves
1 tablespoon red wine vinegar
kosher salt and freshly ground pepper to taste

Combine all the ingredients in a bowl and season to taste. Place a small ring mold in the center of a chilled soup bowl and pack full of the crabmeat mixture, making it compact by pressing with the back of a spoon. Pour in the soup and carefully remove the ring mold. For a more casual presentation, fill each bowl or cup with soup and place a large spoonful of the garnish in the center of each.

Cucumber and Buttermilk Soup

As adults, we don't really find ourselves drinking tall glasses of milk with our meals. We prefer water or wine. But when you pair this cool, refreshing soup with one of our grilled cheeses—or even with grilled fish—you feel like a kid again, slugging down cold milk on a scorching summer day. It doesn't get any more refreshing than the flavors of buttermilk, cucumber, and dill.

serves 4 in bowls or 8 in cups

2 pounds Kirby cucumbers

1 tablespoon chopped fresh dill

1½ teaspoons chopped fresh mint leaves

1 clove garlic, crushed

1 shallot, minced

1½ tablespoons white wine vinegar, plus more to taste

2 teaspoons kosher salt, plus more to taste

several grinds pepper, plus more to taste

1½ cups buttermilk

Cut the cucumbers in half, remove the seeds with a spoon, and slice ¼ to ½ inch thick. Combine the cucumbers with the dill, mint, garlic, shallot, and vinegar in a stainless-steel, glass, or plastic bowl. Season with the salt and pepper. Mix well and refrigerate for at least 1 hour.

Puree the mixture in a blender or food processor until well chopped but not perfectly smooth. The soup should have a good bit of texture. Stir in 1 cup of the buttermilk, then add the remaining ½ cup to adjust the consistency if needed. Season to taste with salt, pepper, and vinegar. Serve very cold.

COOK LIKE A PRO

Kirby Cucumbers—These small, crunchy, and super flavorful cucumbers hit their peak in late spring and summer. We've found that Kirbys are the best variety for this soup—without them the flavor tends to fall a little flat. They don't have to be peeled as long as you thoroughly wash them. We think their skin gives the soup a nice color—but you can peel them if you like.

Health Benefits of Buttermilk

How can a liquid that leads with the word "butter" be good for you? And how can it also be low in fat? First of all, it's called "buttermilk" because almost all the fat has been removed to make butter. Buttermilk is supereasy for your body to digest and it's high in potassium, vitamin B12, riboflavin, and phosphorus. The health benefits are a boon, but the flavor—both buttery and tangy—is what makes this milk our liquid of choice for muffins, pancakes, and even soups.

Zucchini and Corn Soup au Pistou

Our light, brothy soup makes the most of gorgeous zucchini and corn at their peak (June through August). But this soup is unique—and pretty enough to serve at a luncheon—because of the pistou (pees-TOO). Just think of pistou as pesto without the nuts (in the Provençal dialect, pistou means "pounded"). A little garlic, basil, and olive oil make quite a difference!

serves 6 to 8

SOUP

4 ears corn, shucked and silk threads removed

about 2 tablespoons extra virgin olive oil

8 ounces pancetta or bacon, cut into ½-inch pieces

1 yellow onion, diced

2 cloves garlic, crushed

kosher salt

one 10-ounce can chopped tomatoes

6 to 8 basil stems (from the pistou), tied into a bundle

one 2-inch-square piece Parmesan rind (optional)

4 cups chicken stock or water

freshly ground pepper to taste

3 medium zucchini, diced

PISTOU

1 cup packed basil leaves

1 clove garlic, coarsely chopped

3 tablespoons finely grated Parmesan cheese

¾ cup olive oil

For the soup, cut the corn from the cobs with a sharp chef's knife. Work over a bowl so you don't lose any of the goodness.

Place a large, heavy-bottomed saucepot over medium-high heat. Add about 2 tablespoons olive oil and the pancetta and cook, stirring frequently, until lightly browned. Stir in the onion, garlic, and a pinch of salt. Sauté until the onion is translucent and fragrant.

Turn the heat to high and scrape the corn into the pot. Cook, stirring constantly, until nearly dry. Add the tomatoes, basil stems, and Parmesan rind if using. Cook for 2 minutes. Add the chicken stock, bring to a boil, and season to taste with salt and pepper. Reduce the heat and simmer for 10 minutes. Stir in the zucchini and simmer until tender. Remove the basil stems and Parmesan rind before serving.

For the pistou, place all the ingredients in a blender or food processor and blend until well chopped but not smooth. Keep covered in the refrigerator, up to 10 days.

Spoon the soup into bowls and garnish with large spoonfuls of pistou. Serve with a crusty baguette.

LAZY NIGHT?

The pistou element of this dish is so fun—and gives you serious bragging rights—but some nights you're just too tired. Fine. We get it. When we're feeling a bit lazy and don't want to drag out the Cuisinart, we skip the pistou recipe too. Just top the soup with a healthy dose of good olive oil and torn basil leaves and sprinkle a generous amount of Parmesan cheese on everything. Yummy and easy.

Shrimp and Beer Summer Chowder

Summer in the city isn't so bad. The streets are quiet, the waterfront parks are beautiful, and you can nab a reservation at any restaurant in town. But a couple of years ago, we wanted to pretend that we were lounging on the beach in Montauk, taking in the salty ocean breezes instead of roasting on the patio of Brooke's SoHo studio on Thompson Street. Several beers in, Jamie began tossing corn, bacon, and shrimp into a saucepot, trying to figure out the best way to change our perspective and to use his warm-weather stash of light beer. The result was a mellow, slightly smoky, sweet chowder that kind of tastes like a good summer day.

serves 4 as a first course

2 cups heavy cream

1 cup chicken stock

1 pound medium (26/30) shrimp, peeled, deveined, and cut into thirds, shells reserved

2 branches thyme

1 bay leaf

8 to 10 slices bacon, chopped

2 cloves garlic, minced

1 red bell pepper, peeled (see page 76) and diced

1 green bell pepper, peeled (see page 76) and diced

1 small yellow onion, diced

2 teaspoons paprika

pinch of cayenne

1½ cups corn kernels, fresh or frozen

½ can beer

kosher salt and freshly ground pepper to taste

Good hot sauce to taste

Sherry vinegar or lemon juice to taste

Place the cream, chicken stock, shrimp shells, thyme, and bay leaf in a small saucepot over medium heat and reduce by one third.

In a medium saucepot, sauté the chopped bacon over medium heat until rendered and brown. Add the garlic, bell peppers, onion, paprika, and cayenne; turn the heat to high. Cook the vegetables until tender and very aromatic. Add the corn and sauté for 3 minutes more. Pour in the beer and reduce by half. Pour the reduced cream into the pot through a strainer and discard the solids. Stir well and cook for a few minutes more at a low simmer to allow the flavors to come together. Season to taste with salt and pepper and add hot sauce and sherry vinegar as well. Moments before serving, stir the shrimp into the soup and simmer for 3 minutes more. Ladle immediately into warmed bowls.

Cauliflower Soup with Mussels

On this side of the Atlantic, we always see cream of broccoli soup on the menu, but in Paris, it's all about cauliflower. No surprise because the vegetable blends up to make a supersmooth puree, and its flavor is a little more interesting and elegant than you can hope for with broccoli. In this recipe, we combine regional French products—mussels (from Brittany), cauliflower (from Normandy)—for one fabulous dinner in a bowl.

serves 4 in bowls or 8 in cups

2 tablespoons unsalted butter

2 leeks, sliced and rinsed

4 cloves garlic

1 bay leaf

3 branches thyme

1 cup white wine

30 mussels, debearded and scrubbed

2 heads cauliflower, florets and stems chopped

2 teaspoons kosher salt

4 cups water or chicken stock, or as needed

1 cup cream

Melt the butter in a large pot over medium heat. Add the leeks, garlic, bay leaf, and thyme and cook until tender. Deglaze with the wine and bring the mixture to a boil. Add the cleaned mussels, cover the pot, and cook until the mussels are just opened, 3 to 5 minutes. Remove the mussels to a bowl, leaving the liquid and vegetables behind.

Simmer until the liquid is reduced by three-quarters. Add the cauliflower and salt. Pour in enough water or chicken stock so that the cauliflower is ½ inch from being covered. Cook at a low boil until tender, about 20 minutes.

Remove the bay leaf and thyme branches. Empty the pot into a blender, working in batches, and puree until smooth. Return the puree to the pot over medium heat. Gradually add the cream (you may not need it all) to adjust the consistency and stir in the liquid collected in the bottom of the bowl of mussels.

Divide the cooked mussels among warmed bowls and fill with the soup.

GARNISH
1 baguette, thinly sliced
melted butter

Preheat the oven to 400 degrees.

Brush the slices of bread with the melted butter and place in the oven on a cooling rack. Bake until toasted to a deep brown. Serve on a plate along with the soup.

Working with Mussels

As soon as you get your catch home, check to see that they are alive. Live mussels should be tightly closed. If they are not, run them under cold water and gently push the shells together with your fingers. If they still won't close, throw them away (unless you're looking for a way to get a few days off work). Store the mussels (and all other shellfish) in the coldest part of your fridge. Keep them covered with damp paper towels or newspaper, never covered in water. Under ice is ideal, but be sure there is a way for the water to drip away as it melts (think mussels and ice in a colander with a bowl underneath to catch the drips).

Mussels are the easiest of all to clean, since they're the only bivalve that doesn't live on the ocean floor. A quick rinse takes care of the shells. Then there's the "beard," the tough fibers mussels use to hold on to the rope, pier, or barge they live on; just pinch these hairs between your fingers and give 'em a yank.

Roasted Butternut Squash Soup

We only had six people at our wedding reception, so we were allowed to go a little crazy with the food—like, ten courses crazy. As we made our way through the exquisite menu that Jamie dreamed up for that special dinner in Palmetto Bluff Resort's wine cellar, we all agreed that this simple soup was our favorite. (And, oh, my lord, why don't we garnish with fried sage leaves more often?) Turns out, the soup is all about sautéing, pureeing, and, Brooke's personal favorite recipe phrase, "unattended cook time." Even though we commemorated one of the most special days of our lives with this soup, it's just as good enjoyed from a thermos at your desk.

serves 4 to 6

2 tablespoons olive oil

pinch of red pepper flakes

½ teaspoon fennel seeds

½ teaspoon ground coriander

1 medium yellow onion, chopped

6 cloves garlic, sliced

2 cups chopped peeled carrots

kosher salt to taste

1 medium butternut squash (about 1½ pounds),
      peeled, seeded, and chopped (about 4 cups)

2 Bosc or Bartlett pears, cored and chopped

½ cup white wine

3 cups chicken stock

1 cup cream

freshly ground pepper to taste

Heat the olive oil in a wide, heavy-bottomed pot over medium heat. Add the red pepper flakes, fennel seeds, coriander, onion, garlic, and carrots. Season with salt and cook over medium heat until tender but not browned, 5 to 7 minutes. Stir in the squash and pears and increase the heat to high. Cook, stirring, until the vegetables begin to brown. Add the white wine and scrape any brown bits from the bottom of the pot. Continue cooking until the wine is reduced by half. Add the stock and bring to a boil. Reduce the heat and simmer until the squash is tender enough to be crushed against the side of the pot with the back of a spoon.

Place a colander over a large bowl and pour the mixture into the colander to separate the liquid and solids. Working in batches, place all of the solids in a blender or food processor. Begin pureeing the solids, gradually adding the liquid until the mixture runs smooth, then return the mixture to the pot and stir in the cream, adding just enough to make the soup silky and pourable. Bring the soup to a simmer and season to taste with salt and pepper.

THE NEXT LEVEL

Fried sage makes a killer garnish, especially for any dish that includes pears. Here their texture and aroma go a long way to enhance an already fabulous soup. Here's how you do it: Pour ½ inch canola or vegetable oil into a small to medium sauté pan, add fresh sage leaves (1 per person), and turn the heat to high. After a few moments, the leaves will begin to bubble rapidly. When the bubbling slows, remove the leaves to paper towels to drain and cool. When cooled, the leaves should be very crisp. Cut 1 Bartlett or Bosc pear into a fine dice, discarding the core. Float the crisp sage leaves and diced pear on top of the hot soup.

French Onion Soup

We're from the same hometown down South, so the blustery winters in New York have never been easy for us. Jamie tries to make Brooke feel better by preparing warm soups. Nothing does the trick like this one. By thinly slicing onions and then slowly caramelizing them in our Dutch oven, the apartment is soon filled with the most delicious aroma, both sweet and earthy. We might be crazy for leaving the South for frozen New York City life, but at least we're able to enjoy each other and the comfort of a good meal.

serves 4

4 tablespoons (½ stick) unsalted butter
3 yellow onions, thinly sliced
kosher salt
4 cloves garlic, finely minced
¼ cup brandy
5 cups veal stock or beef broth
2 branches fresh thyme
1 bay leaf
freshly ground pepper

CROUTONS
4 slices baguette or Italian loaf, toasted
½ to 1 cup Gruyère or fontina cheese, grated

Heat the butter in a large, heavy-bottomed pot until melted and the foam subsides. Add the onions and stir frequently until the sizzling in the pot stops. Turn the heat to low and cook the onions, stirring occasionally, until caramelized.

Properly caramelizing onions takes about 45 minutes and must be done over low heat. The onions should be added to a very hot pot, then the temperature reduced. The onions do not require constant attention; just stir every 5 minutes or so.

After 20 to 25 minutes of cooking, the onions should be tender and lightly brown. Continue cooking until the onions darken and a heavy fond (tasty brown bits on the bottom of the pot) develops.

Salt the onions generously (about 2 teaspoons); this will release the excess moisture from the onions and loosen the fond from the pot. As the onions pick up the fond, they will continue to darken. When the bottom of the pot is clean, turn the heat to high and wait for it to begin sizzling. Add the garlic and cook for 30 seconds. Deglaze with the brandy and reduce until dry. Add the stock, thyme, and bay leaf and bring the mixture to a simmer. Season to taste with salt and pepper and simmer 10 to 15 minutes more, allowing the flavors to develop. Remove the bay leaf and thyme and divide the soup among heated bowls.

Place the 4 slices of toasted bread on a baking pan. Top each slice of bread with a generous amount of grated cheese. Place the pan on the top shelf of the oven, directly below the broiler, until the cheese is fully melted. Float a cheese-topped crouton in each soup bowl.

The Spaniard

We don't think you'll find a bocadillo *like this on any menus in Madrid. But when we walk into Despaña, our favorite Spanish specialty food shop on the edge of SoHo and Little Italy, all these ingredients nearly jump off the shelves and into our basket, begging to be made into something delicious. This sandwich has it all—a little sweet, a little smoky, a touch of salty, and a lot of cheese. There's nothing not to like. In fact, this is a sandwich to LOVE!*

makes 4 sandwiches

1 jar piquillo peppers, drained
1 tablespoon sherry vinegar
½ teaspoon smoked paprika
2 tablespoons quince or fig paste
2 ounces cream cheese, at room temperature
8 slices white bread
4 ounces Manchego or Garrotxa cheese, thinly sliced
    or grated
4 ounces serrano ham, thinly sliced
olive oil as needed

Dress the peppers with the vinegar and paprika. Set aside. Blend the quince or fig paste with the cream cheese until smooth.

Spread an even layer of the cream cheese mixture on 2 slices of bread. Cover each slice with the cheese. Arrange the ham and peppers on top of the cheese and press the 2 sides of the sandwich together.

Brush the outside of the bread generously with olive oil. Heat a cast-iron skillet or nonstick pan over medium heat. Add the sandwich to the pan, press lightly with a spatula, and leave to cook until golden brown on one side, about 3 minutes. Flip the sandwich and brown on the second side, another 2 to 3 minutes. Remove the sandwich from the pan and cool slightly before cutting. Alternatively, toast in the oven on a baking sheet at 425 degrees.

Repeat the process with the remaining ingredients.

PICK A PEPPER

Piquillo peppers are a variety of chile that grows in northern Spain. They're harvested in fall to winter, roasted over an open fire, peeled, seeded, and packed into jars or tins. Smoky and sweet after roasting, jarred piquillos may seem more like roasted red bell peppers, which are easily substituted for piquillos in this recipe. Piquillo peppers stuffed with meat or cheese are a mainstay at most Spanish tapas restaurants.

¿Que Es Serrano?

Serrano ham or *jamón serrano* is a Spanish dry-cured ham. You might be more familiar with its Italian cousin, prosciutto. While prosciutto and serrano are not exactly the same, the process by which they are made is very similar. To begin curing, serrano hams are packed in sea salt before being hung to dry for a minimum of one year. The biggest differences between serrano and prosciutto come from the breed of pig used, its feed, and the environmental factors of where it is cured. Until recently, serrano hams were not widely available to American consumers, one of the reasons for prosciutto's greater popularity.

¿No serrano? No problem! Substitute sliced prosciutto, and if you're feeling spicy, sprinkle it with a bit of paprika and black pepper before assembling the sandwich.

Brooke's Ultimate Grilled Cheese Sandwiches

There were two non-negotiables during Brooke's pregnancy: carbs and cheese. We found that the easiest, thriftiest, and most satisfying way to marry these two ingredients was with the grilled cheese. During nine months of intensive "research," we learned three fundamentals for turning out the perfect oozy, melty sandwich. You must grate the cheese (not slice it), you must use a blend of cheeses (never just one—and don't even entertain the idea of "American" cheese), and you can only reach grilled sandwich nirvana if you whip a soft cheese—such as cream cheese—into the mix. After many intense grilled cheese practicals (like lab practicals in high school science), we eventually began to throw in a few "extras" for fun. Learn how to make Brooke's Ultimate and then graduate to the next level with The Provençal (page 133) and The Spaniard (page 130).

makes 4 sandwiches

1 tablespoon mayonnaise

2 tablespoons cream cheese, at room temperature

¼ teaspoon garlic powder

¼ teaspoon paprika

1 cup grated Cheddar cheese

1 cup grated provolone cheese

8 slices bread (white or wheat)

softened butter as needed

Blend together the mayonnaise, cream cheese, garlic powder, and paprika in a medium bowl. Fold in the grated cheeses. Store the mixture in the refrigerator if not using immediately. Keeps for 1 week.

Spread about ¼ cup of the cheese mixture between 2 slices of bread and press the slices together. Spread the softened butter on the outside of the bread. Heat a cast-iron skillet or nonstick pan over medium heat. Add the sandwich to the pan, press lightly with a spatula, and leave to cook until golden brown on one side, about 3 minutes. Flip the sandwich and brown on the second side, another 2 to 3 minutes. Remove the sandwich from the pan and cool slightly before cutting. Alternatively, toast in the oven on a baking sheet at 425 degrees. Repeat with the remaining cheese and bread.

TECHNIQUE TIP

Cooking a perfect grilled cheese requires the perfect temperature. Too high a heat will burn the bread before the cheese inside reaches full, melty goodness. Too low a heat creates bread that's dry and pale rather than buttery, crisp, and golden brown.

MAKE AHEAD

Serving a Crowd?—Assemble all of the sandwiches ahead of time. When ready to serve, preheat the oven to 250 degrees and place an ovenproof tray inside. Fry your sandwiches one or two at a time and transfer them to the oven as they brown. Keep your sandwiches warm until the last one is cooked.

The Provençal

Sometimes, when two cultures collide, the results are unforgettable, like Sly Stallone vs. the Russian in Rocky IV. *But here we're taking the ingredients and the simplicity native to the Provençal kitchen—sweet red peppers, sun-ripened tomatoes, and zucchini—and smashing them into that stalwart of Americana, the grilled cheese sandwich. Olive oil and those herb-roasted vegetables blend beautifully with goat cheese, then get all gooey between crisp, buttered slices of sourdough.*

makes 6 sandwiches

1 red bell pepper, peeled (see page 76) and cut
    into ½-inch-wide strips
1 zucchini, sliced lengthwise and cut into
    2- to 3-inch lengths
1 beefsteak tomato, sliced
¼ cup olive oil, plus more as needed
1 tablespoon herbes de Provence (see sidebar)
1 teaspoon kosher salt
¼ teaspoon freshly ground pepper
12 ounces goat cheese, at room temperature
12 slices sourdough or white bread
fresh basil leaves

Preheat the oven to 375 degrees.

Toss the vegetables in a large bowl with the ¼ cup olive oil, herbes de Provence, salt, and pepper. Spread in a single layer on a baking sheet and roast in the oven for 15 minutes.

Spread approximately 1 ounce goat cheese on each of the slices of bread. Place some of the roasted vegetables on top of each piece of bread. Add 1 or 2 basil leaves, then press 2 slices together to make 6 sandwiches.

Brush the outside of one sandwich generously with olive oil. Heat a cast-iron skillet or nonstick pan over medium heat. Add the sandwich to the pan, press lightly with a spatula, and leave to cook until golden brown on one side, about 3 minutes. Flip the sandwich and brown on the second side, another 2 to 3 minutes. Remove the sandwich from the pan and cool slightly before cutting. Alternatively, toast in the oven on a baking sheet at 425 degrees. Repeat with the remaining cheese, vegetables, and bread.

HERBES DE PROVENCE

Before spice companies threw a fancy label on these summer herbs, good Provençal housewives snipped them from their gardens, dried them on the wall, and kept them in a jar next to the stove while the leafless plants rested throughout the winter. This mixture of dried herbs has as many different formulations as there are people who make it, though the usual suspects are thyme, rosemary, and savory. Some mixes include the iconic herb and flower of Provence—lavender—which can be overly floral for this purpose. If you don't have herbes de Provence in your spice cabinet, substitute dried thyme or an "Italian herb blend." Herbes de Provence is well suited for seasoning meats, especially lamb, potatoes, or summer vegetables before roasting.

Chicken and Mushroom Burgers

Beef burger joints are the new, big thing in Manhattan—especially (and appropriately) in the meatpacking district. And, really, we just don't get it. We think the beef boys aren't worth making unless you have an outdoor grill or some amazing state-of-the-art flattop. But the patty thing—the blend of a high-quality protein with fresh basil, garlic, and a curveball ingredient like wine-soaked mushrooms—can't be beat. Our chicken and mushroom burger fulfills the amazing duty of being healthful and a meal you can really sink your teeth into.

makes 4 burgers

2 tablespoons olive oil, plus more as needed

2 cloves garlic, sliced

1 shallot, minced

8 ounces fresh mushrooms, roughly chopped

½ cup white wine or chicken stock

1 pound ground chicken

6 tablespoons dry breadcrumbs

2 large eggs, beaten

2 tablespoons chopped fresh basil

1 teaspoon kosher salt

freshly ground pepper to taste

1 beefsteak tomato

grated Parmesan cheese

4 burger rolls

softened butter to spread on the rolls

Dijon mustard

lettuce leaves (optional)

Heat the olive oil in a large sauté pan. Add the garlic and shallot and cook over medium heat until softened. Add the mushrooms and wine or stock and simmer until the pan is completely dry. Continue cooking until the mushrooms are lightly browned. Set aside to cool.

Combine the cooled mushroom mixture, ground chicken, breadcrumbs, eggs, basil, salt, and pepper in a bowl. Blend well and form into 4 patties. Cook the patties in a sauté pan with a small amount of oil in the pan approximately 5 minutes per side over medium to medium-high heat. Or cook on the grill, or roast in a 425-degree oven, until cooked through, about 12 minutes.

Cut the tomato into 4 thick slices, cover with grated Parmesan, and place on a baking sheet. Split the 4 rolls, spread with softened butter, and arrange, cut side up, on the baking sheet with the tomatoes. Broil until the buns are toasted and the cheese is slightly melted.

Spread one side of the toasted buns with Dijon mustard before assembling the burgers, adding lettuce if desired.

THE NEXT LEVEL

An extra pat of butter added once the wine evaporates will really help the mushrooms brown and kick the flavor into overdrive.

If you can get your hands on truffled Dijon mustard (we sneaked ours back in our luggage after our last trip to Paris), spread a thin layer on your burger bun and then close your eyes—you're officially in burger heaven.

Italian Sausage Pitas with Feta and Watercress

Jamie's never met a street fair he didn't like. The deep fryers churning out french fries and elephant ears, the greased-up griddles, and trays of freshly squeezed lemonade make him a little giddy. But his all-time favorite street food is an Italian sausage and pepper sandwich. So he decided to do a slightly more healthful riff on the Little Italy sandwich staple by making his own sausage (page 136) and pairing it with light, clean flavors like mint, watercress, and a salty dose of feta. This is a sandwich you could eat on the street or enjoy at your dinner table with a glass of red.

serves 4

½ red onion, very thinly sliced

1 tablespoon red wine vinegar

6 links Italian sausage (hot or sweet)

1 bunch watercress, tough stems removed

5 ounces feta cheese, crumbled

2 tablespoons torn fresh mint leaves

2 tablespoons olive oil

kosher salt and freshly ground pepper to taste

4 pitas with pockets

Combine the onion and red wine vinegar in a large bowl. Set aside to marinate for 15 minutes while you prepare the remaining ingredients.

Pierce the sausages all over with the tip of a knife and place on a grill or in a preheated 350-degree oven to cook through. While the sausages are cooking, add the watercress, feta, mint, and olive oil to the marinated onion. Mix well and season to taste with salt and pepper.

Warm the pitas on the grill or in the oven; cut away the top one-quarter of each pita, leaving a large pocket to be stuffed.

When the sausages are cooked and cool enough to handle, cut into ½- to 1-inch-thick slices and toss in the bowl with the other ingredients. Divide the mixture into quarters and stuff in the pitas.

HOMEMADE SAUSAGE—SAVE A BUCK, AND A GUT

It's no secret that Jamie loves pork, especially when it comes in the form of sausage. But there is one thing that he doesn't always like—buying sausage. Often a recipe calls for a small amount of sausage as a filling or as the base of a dish. And while he can always find a use for the leftovers, the fact is, Brooke isn't a huge fan of having a freezer full of ground, spiced pork products. Our compromise? "Making" sausage at home. Don't worry, it's not nearly as messy as it sounds. With Jamie's special spice blends, an exact quantity of ground meat, and a quick stir—voilà! Sausage is made. Okay, fine, it's not technically sausage—it's actually 10 to 15 percent leaner than typical store-bought sausage—but it perfectly fits the flavor profile and is an excellent, healthful substitute in any recipe.

All of the following sausage recipes yield 1 pound. The sausage should be fully cooked, with no pink left. Each mixture can be stored, refrigerated, for up to 3 days. The recipes can be halved.

Italian Sausage

1 pound ground pork
1½ teaspoons kosher salt
½ teaspoon freshly ground pepper
2 teaspoons fennel seeds
2 tablespoons finely grated garlic, or 2 teaspoons garlic powder
2 teaspoons paprika
1 teaspoon red pepper flakes
½ teaspoon dried oregano or marjoram

Combine all the ingredients in a bowl and blend well.

SERVING SUGGESTIONS

Form into patties and grill or bake for Italian Sausage Pitas with Feta and Watercress (page 135).
Sauté in large crumbles to top Simple Breakfast Focaccia (page 33).
Sauté in large crumbles with dark greens, such as spinach or broccoli rabe, and add a hearty pasta—orecchiette or rigatoni.

Fresh Chorizo

SPICE MIXTURE

2 tablespoons chili powder

2 teaspoons onion powder

3 cloves garlic, chopped, or 1 teaspoon
    granulated garlic

⅛ teaspoon ground cinnamon

½ teaspoon ground cumin

1 teaspoon paprika

1 teaspoon dried oregano

½ teaspoon cayenne

2 teaspoons kosher salt

1 teaspoon freshly ground pepper

1 tablespoon olive oil

Combine all the ingredients in a bowl and blend well.
Store, tightly covered, in the refrigerator.

SAUSAGE

12 ounces ground pork and 4 ounces ground beef,
    or 1 pound ground pork

¼ cup spice mixture

2 tablespoons water

In a medium bowl, blend the meat, spice mixture, and
water until smooth and slightly tacky. Form into patties
or links or cook crumbled.

SERVING SUGGESTIONS

Form into small balls and place on a skewer with
    fresh shrimp for Shrimp and Chorizo Skewers
    with Roasted Garlic–White Bean Dip (page 183).
Cook in crumbles as the base for a really great pot
    of chili.
Sauté in crumbles with onions and sweet peppers;
    add to scrambled eggs for a spicy, filling break-
    fast.

Merguez

HARISSA SPICE PASTE
6 tablespoons sriracha hot sauce
2 tablespoons ground cumin
2 tablespoons ground coriander
1 tablespoon ground caraway seeds
2 tablespoons grated garlic
3 tablespoons paprika
1 tablespoon ground turmeric
2 teaspoons cayenne
¼ teaspoon ground cinnamon
6 tablespoons olive oil

Blend all the ingredients into a paste. Store, tightly covered, in the refrigerator.

SAUSAGE
1 pound ground lamb
1½ tablespoons harissa spice paste
2 teaspoons kosher salt

In a medium bowl, blend the meat, spice paste, and salt until smooth and slightly tacky. Form into patties or links or cook crumbled.

SERVING SUGGESTIONS

These spicy lamb sausages are great when formed into patties and grilled or sautéed. They can also be substituted for Italian sausage in Italian Sausage Pitas with Feta and Watercress (page 135).

Breakfast Sausage

SPICE MIXTURE
1 tablespoon dried sage
2 teaspoons dried marjoram
1 teaspoon dried thyme
½ teaspoon cayenne
2 teaspoons brown sugar
1½ teaspoons kosher salt
½ teaspoon freshly ground pepper
½ teaspoon grated garlic

Combine all the ingredients in a bowl and mix well. Store, tightly covered, in the refrigerator.

SAUSAGE
1 pound ground pork
5 tablespoons spice mixture
¼ cup water

In a medium bowl, blend the meat, spice mixture, and water until smooth and slightly tacky. Form into patties or links or cook crumbled.

SERVING SUGGESTIONS

Form into patties and sauté along with your eggs in the morning.
Sauté in crumbles, then add diced zucchini and beaten eggs to make a frittata (see page 32).
Use to make Sawmill Gravy (page 31).

A MOVEABLE FEAST

The way we live now, meals can't always be enjoyed at the table—or even while snuggling on the couch with a TV tray. We snack on our feet, munch midday meals on the go, and eat dinners on planes, trains, and in automobiles as we commute from one gig to the next. Life as go-getting newlyweds is tough, isn't it?

While pack 'n go meals aren't always romantic, we're here to make sure that they're dang good. We do hearty salads, the perfect wrap, and Apricot and Oatmeal Cookies that are so irresistible, you'll start nibbling on them with your morning coffee.

When we created our roster of recipes, we heeded a few Southern Mother warnings. How could we forget their intimidating tales about the perils of overheated mayonnaise and improperly cooked proteins? Our salads go light on mayo and, instead, get a healthy dose of olive oil. Sliced avocado, fresh corn, and fava beans ensure that we get our daily serving of something healthful that just so happens to taste like a million bucks.

The best thing about your Moveable Feast is that it's low-key, one thousand times better for you than any fast-food option, and a snap to put together. Just follow our few simple tips and tricks to make your next meal on the road a feast.

TIPS FOR YOUR MOVEABLE FEAST

- **PACK UP**—Start from the bottom of your mini insulated cooler bag and work your way up. First, place an ice pack or frozen gel pack on the bottom of your bag. (Don't even think about using loose ice. You'll end up with a puddle of slush and floating tortilla chips at the end of the day.) Then place your most temperature-sensitive proteins—such as our chicken salad or Southwestern turkey wraps—directly on top of the ice pack. Cheese and fruit could go next, while "crunchables," such as chips, cookies, and crackers, should rest on top.

- **ROOM TEMP**—Don't plan on eating a bowl of spaghetti Bolognese or an ice cream sandwich on your commute home. Really, anything that needs to be served piping hot or ice cold should be eliminated from your menu line-up. But don't worry—our room-temp food rocks!

- **LOW-MAINTENANCE EATS/EDIBLE UTENSILS**—Veggies, crackers, and chips should be pretty much the only "utensils" you need for your feast. Sure, keep forks and spoons handy for the pasta and chicken salads, but just about everything else can be served (or scooped) with tortilla chips or good, rustic potato chips.

- **QUANTITIES**—You don't want to be wasteful and you don't want leftovers. Pack 'n go foods are meant to be eaten that day. Plan your quantities wisely.

Grilled Corn and Andouille Salad with Charred Tomato and Scallion Vinaigrette

Jamie loves the word "charred," because it lets him burn things in the name of good food. But really, who said you could only char steak? A crispy, slightly burned exterior coupled with tender flesh works just as well for summer-ripe vegetables as it does for a rib-eye. We decided to fire up all the veggies on the outdoor grill to give them a gorgeous smoky flavor. Then we blended up the charred tomatoes and scallions to create a thick, full-flavored sauce for sausage and corn. After a little time at the grill and the blender, you have a hearty, totally unique, mayonnaise-less salad that can withstand high temps at the beach and help calm flaring tempers on your cross-country road trip.

serves 6

4 ears yellow or bicolor corn

2 bunches scallions

4 Roma or plum tomatoes, cut in half through the stem

¾ cup olive oil, plus more as needed

1 tablespoon kosher salt, plus more to taste

1 teaspoon freshly ground pepper, plus more to taste

8 ounces andouille sausage

¼ cup red wine vinegar, plus more as needed

shaved Parmesan or Pecorino cheese for garnish

THE NEXT LEVEL

Make It a Meal—By using a little extra dressing and tossing this salad with some cooked pasta, like penne, you've got the perfect dish for your next picnic.

Shuck the corn and remove all the silk threads. Trim the roots from the scallions; thinly slice the dark green tops and reserve for garnish. Combine the corn, trimmed scallions, and halved tomatoes in a bowl and toss with ¼ cup of the olive oil, the salt, and pepper. Toss well to thoroughly coat the vegetables. Place all of the vegetables on a hot grill and cook until charred on all sides, 8 to 10 minutes. The tomato skins should split and become very dark. Remove all the vegetables to a platter or bowl to catch the juices and let stand until cool enough to handle. If you don't have a grill, spread the vegetables in a single layer on a baking pan and cook on the top rack underneath the broiler or on the center rack at 500 degrees.

Split the andouille sausage lengthwise and grill until well marked and heated through. Or sear the sausage on the cut side in a lightly oiled cast-iron skillet or nonstick pan.

Remove the skins from the tomatoes and squeeze out the seeds. Place the tomatoes, scallions, any vegetable juices, the vinegar, and salt and pepper to taste in a food processor. Puree until mostly smooth, then drizzle in the remaining ½ cup olive oil with the machine still running. Taste and adjust the seasoning with salt and pepper. Add more olive oil if the dressing is too acidic or more vinegar if it's too bland.

Cut the corn from the cobs and chop the grilled andouille. Toss the corn and sausage in a bowl and add enough of the pureed dressing to coat. Mix well and season again. Garnish with the scallion tops and shaved cheese.

Fava Beans with Lemon and Pecorino

FEEL THE BURN

Charring or lightly burning vegetables can be done on a grill, underneath a broiler set to high, or in a preheated 500-degree oven. Proper charring gives veggies a pleasant smoky flavor and draws out their natural sweetness. The key to charring is to stop cooking as soon as the exterior turns black. Too much heat and your veggies could turn into charcoal bricks.

CALL IN THE SUBS

Andouille sausage is a heavily spiced and smoked sausage made from coarsely ground or hand-chopped pork. Its origins can be traced to the original French colonies of the Louisiana territory. Now synonymous with Cajun cooking, andouille sausage is widely available in the United States, though any smoked sausage can be substituted in this recipe or the sausage can be left out altogether for a vegetarian option.

There's nothing fancy about this salad. Really, its light, lemony flavors are so simple, you'll wonder, "Why didn't I think of that?" Pull out a container of this during your next spring picnic or even on your dinnertime work commute. It smells and looks so delicious and vibrant, your seatmate might ask for a bite.

serves 4 as a side

2 cups shelled fava beans
1 teaspoon grated lemon zest
½ teaspoon coarse sea salt
2 tablespoons extra virgin olive oil
¼ cup finely grated Pecorino cheese

Bring a large pot of salted water to a boil. Drop the fava beans into the boiling water and cook for 2 minutes. Drain and refresh immediately under cold water. Drain well and pat dry with paper towels. Toss with the lemon zest, salt, olive oil, and cheese.

CALL IN THE SUBS

If fava beans are out of season or you just can't do that much shelling, substitute shelled edamame, available in the freezer section of most grocery stores. Blanch in boiling water and refresh just as directed above.

Chicken Salad Three Ways

Chicken salad should really be the fifth basic food group. It's easy to make, inexpensive, and serves so many different purposes—light lunch, quick snack, down-home party food (stuffed inside a homegrown tomato)—that we had to dedicate a couple of pages to it. It's one of those things we always have in the fridge, and it is typically the first thing we pack in the cooler before heading out the door. To make sure that we don't get bored with it, we'll change it up every now and then. These three are our favorite versions, always in heavy rotation (kind of like Jack Johnson, the Gypsy Kings, and Jason Mraz).

serves 4

Roasted Chicken for Salad

2 bone-in, skin-on chicken breasts (1½ to 2 pounds)
extra virgin olive oil
kosher salt and freshly ground pepper

Preheat the oven to 375 degrees.

Place the chicken on a baking pan and pat dry with paper towels. Rub the skin and bone sides with olive oil and season generously with salt and pepper. Place the pan on the center rack of the oven. Cook to an internal temperature of 160 degrees or until, when you cut into the breast, the juices run clear, about 20 minutes. When cooked through, remove from the oven and cool completely on the baking pan.

Remove the skin and pull all of the chicken meat from the bones, tearing it into bite-size pieces. Combine all of the ingredients for one of the dressings below in a bowl, add the chicken, and mix well. Add salt and pepper to taste.

Chicken salad can also be made with boneless, skinless breasts that have been roasted or grilled. Or it can be made from a roasted whole chicken whose meat has been pulled from the bones. Recipes for dressing are written for a maximum of two pounds meat but can be doubled or tripled.

Dressings

For each dressing, combine all the ingredients in a large bowl. Add the cooked chicken and mix well. The flavor will always improve as the salad sits.

French

This "French" take on chicken salad is Jamie's favorite. Fresh tarragon, shallots, and Dijon mustard give it that classic French flavor profile. But with mayo and sour cream in the mix to smooth things out, it starts to taste more like potato salad's meaty cousin.

½ teaspoon chopped fresh tarragon leaves
1 teaspoon white wine vinegar
¼ teaspoon minced shallot
2 tablespoons mayonnaise
1 tablespoon sour cream

½ teaspoon Dijon mustard

½ teaspoon kosher salt

freshly ground pepper to taste

Curry

What midafternoon snack dreams are made of! The curry powder and lime juice create a bright and spicy dressing, while the cashews and dried cranberries add crunch and a hint of sweetness. We make a batch of curried chicken salad, stick it in the fridge, and usually eat the entire thing on whole-wheat crackers within two days.

1 tablespoon fresh lime or lemon juice

½ teaspoon curry powder

2 tablespoons mayonnaise

3 tablespoons chopped cashews

2 tablespoons dried cranberries

1 teaspoon chopped fresh cilantro

½ teaspoon kosher salt

2 teaspoons Major Grey's mango chutney
    (optional but, oh, so good)

freshly ground pepper to taste

Thai

Traditionally, green papaya salad is served as a cooling foil for the standard hot and spicy southeast Asian fare. For us, this picnic-perfect entrée is a coolant for our steamy summer days. Tart green papaya, crisp cucumbers, and fresh cilantro keep things light, while the sriracha lends just the right kick.

½ green papaya, coarsely grated (about 2 cups)

3 scallions, thinly sliced

¼ cup roasted salted peanuts, chopped

1 teaspoon grated lime zest

1 tablespoon fresh lime juice

1 cup sliced seeded cucumbers

1 tablespoon chopped fresh cilantro

1 cup grated carrots

1 tablespoon fish sauce or soy sauce

1 to 2 teaspoons sriracha hot sauce

kosher salt and freshly ground pepper to taste

granulated sugar to taste

SKINNY CHICKEN VS. FAT CHICKEN

Many people think that to prepare the most healthful meal, they need to buy boneless, skinless chicken breasts. The truth is that roasting bone-in, skin-on breasts will leave you with the juiciest, most flavorful meat. After cooking the chicken with its best parts still intact, wait for it to cool and then remove the skin with your fingers. You won't have all the calories of the skin, but you'll be left with all the flavor.

Avocado Salad with Oranges, Fennel, and Mint

Sweet, salty, crunchy—this is a salad for your sophisticated friends. (Don't have any? It's up to you to convert them!) The usual potato salad and cold noodles are rejected in favor of a southern Mediterranean mingling of marinated fennel (whose anise flavor tastes a little bit like licorice—but in a good way), citrus, olives, and mint. Ripe avocado brings the right level of creaminess to the mixture and plays off the oranges in the most wonderful way.

serves 4

1 fennel bulb, thinly sliced

1 shallot, minced

2 tablespoons red wine vinegar

kosher salt and freshly ground pepper to taste

1 orange

¼ cup Niçoise olives, pitted and chopped

⅓ cup extra virgin olive oil

2 tablespoons chopped fresh mint leaves

2 ripe avocados

a few dashes of Tabasco sauce

8 ounces cow's milk feta cheese, cubed
 or crumbled (optional)

CHEF'S TIP

It's important to slice the fennel as thinly as possible so it can soften while it marinates in the vinegar.

Trim the green tops from the fennel bulb and cut it into quarters through the core. Slice the fennel lengthwise as thinly as possible with a sharp knife or mandoline. In a large bowl, combine the fennel, shallot, and vinegar. Season with salt and pepper. Set aside to allow the fennel to soften.

Cut the orange into supremes (page 14) over a small bowl to catch the juice and squeeze the extra juice from the pulp. Add the juice to the bowl of fennel and shallot. Stir in the olives, oil, and mint. Cut the avocados in half and remove the pits. Scoop the flesh from the skin and cut into ¼-inch-thick slices. Add the avocados, Tabasco, and orange to the fennel, season well with salt and pepper, and stir gently to combine with a spatula or wooden spoon. Add the feta cheese, if using. Taste and adjust the seasoning.

CHEESE PLEASE

Brooke is a confessed cheese-aholic. While some of her sheep, cow, and goat's milk decisions are unwise, the addition of feta to this salad just makes sense. Along with the avocado, the cheese makes the dish buttery and satisfying enough so that it could be a light meal on its own.

Black Bean and Roasted Green Chile Turkey Wraps

Black beans, cans of green chiles, and really good turkey are all you need to make a killer Southwestern wrap. Jamie would give up his cheffy foods (foie gras, duck, sweetbreads) and eat these for a week straight if Brooke would let him. These wraps are the natural midday evolution of Jamie's ALL-TIME favorite one-handed meal, the breakfast burrito.

makes 4 wraps (and a whole lotta delicious, juicy leftover turkey)

one 3- to 5-pound bone-in turkey breast, removed from the fridge 1 hour before cooking
2 tablespoons extra virgin olive oil
kosher salt and freshly ground pepper
one 16-ounce can black beans
½ teaspoon ground cumin
one 6-ounce can roasted green chiles, well drained
½ cup Basic Mayonnaise or Aioli (page 96)
2 tablespoons chopped fresh cilantro
four 10-inch whole-wheat flour tortillas
1 cup shredded lettuce
1 cup grated Monterey Jack or Cheddar cheese

LEFTOVERS

Yes, a whole turkey breast is more than you need for this recipe, but what's everyone's favorite part about Thanksgiving? The leftovers! You can substitute turkey for the chicken in any of the recipes beginning on page 88 or slice it thin for a killer sandwich on toasted 7-grain bread with Romesco (page 86).

Preheat the oven to 350 degrees.

Place the turkey breast in a baking pan, pat dry, and rub the skin with 1 tablespoon of the olive oil. Season liberally with salt and pepper. Roast on the center rack of the oven until a thermometer inserted in the center reads 155 degrees, or when you pierce the breast, the juices run clear. Cook time, depending on weight, will be from 60 to 90 minutes. Leave the turkey to rest for at least 15 minutes before slicing.

Drain the black beans. Place the black beans in a medium bowl. Add 1 tablespoon olive oil and the cumin. Mash the beans into a chunky paste with a whisk or wooden spoon. Season to taste with salt and pepper.

Finely chop the green chiles. Mix with the mayonnaise and cilantro.

Warm the tortillas and slice the cooked turkey breast. Spread the black beans down the center of the tortillas; top with sliced turkey, shredded lettuce, cheese, and the chile-mayo mixture. Roll up the tortillas and wrap in aluminum foil if not serving immediately. Heat—still wrapped in aluminum foil—in a 350-degree oven for 10 minutes before serving, or enjoy cold.

TURKEY TIME

Figuring out the cook time for your turkey breast is pretty darn easy. In a 350-degree oven, allow 20 minutes per pound. That means a 3-pounder needs to cook for 1 hour, a 4-pounder for 1 hour 20 minutes, and a 5-pounder for 1 hour 40 minutes. And you thought you were bad at math. . . .

Oven-Dried Tomato Spread

This spread is outrageously delicious and can go with you everywhere from the subway to the airport. All that's required for this savory snack is cream cheese, tomatoes, and a little patience. Slow-roasting the tomatoes is how the dip gets its deep, intense flavor. Prepare yourself for the "secret ingredient" question because everyone who tastes this is going to want to know how a few simple things can taste that good.

makes 1 cup

2 medium-size ripe tomatoes or 4 Roma tomatoes
kosher salt and freshly ground pepper to taste
8 ounces cream cheese, at room temperature
¼ teaspoon garlic powder
¼ teaspoon chopped fresh thyme, plus whole
    leaves for garnish
carrots, celery, and/or pita chips

Preheat the oven to 275 degrees.

Slice the tomatoes crosswise ¼ to ½ inch thick. Arrange the tomatoes in a single layer on an aluminum-foil-lined baking sheet. Season lightly with salt and pepper. Bake until dry on the surface and very firm but not browned, 45 to 60 minutes. Cool completely. Remove the skins from the tomato slices.

Combine the tomatoes, cream cheese, garlic powder, and thyme in a food processor and blend until smooth. Garnish with fresh thyme leaves and serve with carrot or celery sticks and/or pita chips.

PLAN AHEAD

Whip It Good—If you planned ahead and allowed your cream cheese to sit out and soften for several hours, it's not necessary to break out the food processor for this super-simple dip. To combine all the ingredients, all you need is a medium bowl, a wooden or metal spoon, and a little biceps action. Blending everything by hand couldn't be simpler.

Apricot and Oatmeal Cookies

Brooke loves dried apricots, instead of raisins, on her bowl of oatmeal, so she thought they'd be just as delicious in her oatmeal cookies. Boy, was she right! The zing from the lemon zest really sets these apart and so does their petite shape, making them a lighter, more refreshing cookie than you'd expect. Because these aren't meant to look like those huge discs at the corner coffee shop, make sure to use a small teaspoon—not an ice cream scooper!—when portioning out the dough.

makes about 2 dozen cookies

¾ cup (1½ sticks) unsalted butter, at room
    temperature
1 cup packed light brown sugar
finely grated zest of 1 lemon or orange
½ teaspoon ground cinnamon
¼ teaspoon kosher salt
1 large egg
½ teaspoon vanilla extract
1 cup all-purpose flour
¾ teaspoon baking powder
2 cups old-fashioned rolled oats (not the instant
    or quick-cooking variety)
1 cup dried apricots, chopped

Preheat the oven to 350 degrees.

Combine the butter, brown sugar, zest, cinnamon, and salt in a bowl. Beat with an electric mixer until light and fluffy, 3 to 4 minutes. Add the egg and beat well. Add the vanilla and continue mixing to incorporate fully.

Combine the flour, baking powder, oats, and apricots in another bowl and mix well. Add half the oat mixture to the butter mixture and stir together with a wooden spoon or spatula. Add the remaining oat mixture and fold to incorporate it fully.

Lightly grease a baking sheet. Drop small spoonfuls of the batter onto the pan 1 to 1½ inches apart. Bake until the edges are golden brown and the centers are firm, 17 to 20 minutes.

BAKE YOUR COOKIE DOUGH, REFRIGERATE IT TOO!

We often make this dough and store it in the refrigerator. Our reasons are twofold: First, the raw cookie is one of the most knock-your-fuzzy-slippers-off things you ever tasted. And, second, we like to drop a couple of spoonfuls of the chilled dough on a cookie sheet every morning and have freshly baked cookies with our coffee. When baking from cold dough, extend the cooking time 4 to 5 minutes. The dough will keep in the fridge up to 12 days or tightly wrapped in the freezer up to 3 months.

Blueberry Pancakes
with Maple Sauce
(page 26)

Simple Breakfast Focaccia with
Spinach, Butternut Squash,
and Fontina (page 33)

Warm Tomato Salad
with Bacon Vinaigrette
and Goat Cheese (page 201)

Brooke's Ultimate Grilled Cheese
Sandwich (page 132)

Arugula, Peach, and Feta Salad
(page 160)

Cauliflower Soup
with Mussels
(page 126)

Blue Cheese, Apple, and Walnut Spread (page 46)

Chocolate-Guinness and Butterscotch Pudding (page 196)

Hungarian Shortbread with Raspberry Jam (page 114)

Blue Cheese Crackers with Fig Chutney, Mushroom Topping, and Tomato Topping (pages 254, 255, and 257)

The Smackdown and White Wine Margarita (page 262)

Ratatouille Crostini (page 49)

Avocado Salad (page 144)

Seared Tuna and
Crispy Artichokes
(page 172)

Whole-Wheat Pappardelle
with Butternut Squash
and Blue Cheese
(page 103)

Strawberry Layer
Cake (page 106)

FIXIN'S, OR SECOND THOUGHTS

Up North, they're called "side dishes." Down South, they're "fixin's." They crowd the table alongside plates of crispy fried chicken, bowls of steaming gumbo, or that huge platter of sticky ribs. But if you stand back and watch, you might notice something funny. These "others"—these second thoughts—often get more attention than the stars of the show.

When we're in New York, we head to the Union Square Greenmarket or to Chelsea Market's Manhattan Fruit Exchange to select the freshest seasonal produce we can find. We try to buy our greens, corn, broccoli, apples, peaches, and everything else from New York farmers or farms just a state away. Then, just like the truckers, farmers, doctors, and housewives do for lunchtime south of the Mason-Dixon, we cook up a vegetable plate. There are always four distinct vegetables, a pitcher of iced tea, and a slab of cornbread to top things off. And just like that, the fixin's become a yummy meal of their own.

Thrifty Table

Pretty Platters: Serve family-style (instead of individually plating each course for your guests), allowing the large platters of pasta, veggies, fish, and meat to be the ultimate table decor.

Cooking Peas and Beans: A Little Love and Attention Go a Long Way

Cooking peas and beans, whether they're dried or fresh, is a lot like that first year together—a little love and attention, and a lot of patience, go a long way. A delicious batch of peas or beans starts out with a good aromatic base. When cooking field peas (black-eyed peas, butter beans, and so on), sweat onions and garlic first until completely tender, then add the peas, fresh or dried, and sauté 2 to 3 minutes more before adding the cooking liquid. Fresh peas benefit from having whole branches of fresh thyme and a bay leaf added to the cooking liquid. When cooking dried beans (especially chickpeas and black beans), start by sweating garlic with minced onion or scallion. Then add ground dried spices (cumin, coriander, smoked paprika, curry, and so on) and cook until the spices are very aromatic, about 1 minute. Stir in the dried beans, sauté 2 to 3 minutes more, and add the cooking liquid.

Dried beans DO NOT have to be soaked before cooking. Soaking can speed the cooking process, make the beans less likely to break—and make it so that you're less likely to break wind (soaking beans is known to remove some of the enzymes in beans that wreak havoc on your digestive system). However, soaking dried beans is not required for proper cooking. If you do soak beans, always discard the soaking liquid and rinse the beans before cooking. When adding your cooking liquid (usually water—in our opinion, stock is a waste) to the beans, add only enough to cover the beans by about 1 inch. Bring the pot to a simmer—never let beans boil!—and leave to cook. As the beans cook, water will be absorbed. After 15 minutes or so of simmering, the beans will no longer be covered by water. Pour more water into the pot so the beans are once again covered by 1 inch. Continue this process until the beans are completely tender. Gradually adding water to the pot allows the natural starches released by the beans to remain concentrated in the cooking liquid, giving a creamier pot of cooked beans.

APPROXIMATE SIMMERING TIMES FOR BEANS
Fresh—30 to 45 minutes
Dried, soaked—45 to 60 minutes
Dried, not soaked—75 to 90 minutes

QUICK TIPS FOR COOKING BEANS
Add salt at the end of cooking. Once the beans are tender, taste the cooking liquid and season accordingly. The flavor will improve as they sit.

Acid slows the softening of beans, so don't add any until the beans are completely tender. What's classified as an acid? Well, it can take many forms—vinegar, tomatoes, wine, even molasses for baked beans. Molasses also has high levels of sugar and calcium, which slow the softening of dried beans.

Field Pea Puree Crostini

Field peas are the humble, earthy, slightly sweet offerings of the warm months. We love them so much, we had to come up with a way to make them into something we could pass at our warm-weather parties. Turns out, all these little guys require is a quick puree and a dash of lemon juice. This is the perfect spread for rounds of toasted baguette.

makes 3 cups

½ cup minced yellow onion

4 cloves garlic, sliced

2 branches fresh thyme

½ cup extra virgin olive oil

4 cups fresh, frozen, or dried field peas, cooked, or two 15.5-ounce cans black-eyed peas or lima beans, drained

2 tablespoons fresh lemon juice

2 tablespoons chopped fresh herbs, such as parsley, chives, basil, or dill

1 baguette, sliced, drizzled with olive oil, and toasted

Parmesan cheese, sliced into curls with a vegetable peeler

CALL IN THE SUBS

Although fresh beans make the best puree by far, we were surprised by how much we liked this recipe when made from canned field peas. Be sure you buy only the best quality, though.

In a large sauté pan over medium heat, combine the onion, garlic, thyme, and ¼ cup of the olive oil and cook for 5 minutes. Reduce the heat and stir as necessary to keep the onion from browning. Add the peas and bring the mixture to a simmer, adding a few tablespoons of water or a few tablespoons of the beans' cooking liquid as needed (do not use the liquid from canned beans, for it has too much starch). Puree the cooked peas with an immersion blender in the sauté pan, or transfer to a food processor and try not to puree too much; ideally you will leave some of the beans whole. Stir in the remaining ¼ cup olive oil, the lemon juice, and herbs.

Spread spoonfuls of the puree on slices of the toasted baguette and top with curls of Parmesan cheese.

WHAT'S A FIELD PEA?

Field peas, specifically "southern field peas," include hundreds of different varieties of peas that can be divided into four main groups: field peas, Crowder peas, cream peas, and black-eyed peas. They were originally brought over from the Niger River Basin of West Africa and have been grown in the New World since colonial times. Their popularity down South can be attributed to the fact that they can withstand droughts and thrive in a number of different soils.

Eggplant and Tomato Gratin

Wouldn't you rather tell your friends that you're serving them a gratin (pronounced gra-TAN) than a casserole? But the truth is, despite the fancy name, this is simple French home-cooking that requires very few ingredients and even fewer skills. You'll know this dish is perfectly baked when the edges of the custard are golden brown, looking more like a sweet sponge cake than a savory side dish. Every time we serve this gratin, its rustic flavors outshine the main dish.

serves 6

2 large or 3 medium Italian eggplants, sliced into
    rounds ¼ to ½ inch thick
5 tablespoons extra virgin olive oil
salt and freshly ground pepper
1 large yellow onion, diced
4 cloves garlic, minced
4 beefsteak tomatoes, cored and diced, or
    one 28-ounce can chopped peeled tomatoes
    (preferably San Marzano)

A LITTLE OF THIS, A LITTLE OF THAT

Goat cheese typically comes packaged in 5- or 6-ounce logs. Our recipe calls for 8 ounces. What to do? Throw in a ¼ cup—or 2 ounces—finely grated Parmesan cheese to make up the difference. The saltiness and nuttiness of the Parmesan has a great way of cozying up to the roasted eggplant and tomato sauce.

GOAT CHEESE CUSTARD

1 cup whole milk
8 ounces goat cheese, at room temperature
2 large eggs
2 large egg yolks
kosher salt and freshly ground pepper

3 tablespoons fresh basil chiffonade

Preheat the oven to 350 degrees.

On a cookie sheet, arrange the eggplant slices in a single layer and drizzle with 3 tablespoons of the olive oil. Season with salt and pepper. Bake until just tender, 15 to 20 minutes. Allow the eggplant to cool slightly.

In a large sauté pan, heat the remaining 2 tablespoons olive oil over medium heat. Add the onion and cook until tender but not colored. Add the garlic and cook until aromatic, less than 1 minute. Stir in the tomatoes and turn the heat up to high. Simmer, stirring occasionally, until nearly dry. Season to taste with salt and pepper; set aside until ready to assemble.

For the custard, whisk together the milk, goat cheese, eggs, and egg yolks in a medium bowl. The goat cheese will still be in small chunks—don't stress! This is fine. Season with salt and pepper.

To assemble the gratin, spoon half of the tomato mixture over the bottom of a 2-quart oval gratin dish or 2-quart square glass baking dish and spread it into an even layer. Arrange half of the eggplant slices on top, slightly overlapping. Spread the remaining tomato mixture over the eggplant. Scatter the basil over the tomatoes and pour over half of the custard. Tap the dish on the counter to release any air bubbles. Layer the remaining eggplant on top and cover with the remaining custard.

Bake in a 350-degree oven until the custard is set and golden brown on top, about 45 minutes.

MAKE AHEAD

Like casseroles, gratins are made for convenience. You can make everything ahead, layer it in your gratin dish, cover, and refrigerate for up to 12 hours. An hour before you want to serve dinner, pop it in the oven. Before you know it, a bubbling, golden wonder will be ready to eat.

GRATINS VS. CASSEROLES

The word "gratin" comes from the French *gratin,* meaning "to brown." In a gratin, the ingredients are topped with a browned crust that often includes breadcrumbs, grated cheese, egg, and/or butter. A gratin dish is a shallow, ovenproof container. Casseroles are, well, the stuff you grew up on—clear glass pans filled with some variety of meat, cheese, noodles, and probably some vegetable from a can.

Custard Confusion

Custard. What's it all about? Talking custard can be a bit confusing because the word itself can refer to two different things—boiled custard (see New Baby Banana Pudding, page 117) and baked custard (see Eggplant and Tomato Gratin, page 152).

To break it down as simply as possible, baked custards like flan and crème brûlée are, well, baked. While boiled custards, like pudding and crema Catalana, are cooked on the stovetop and must be stirred constantly to prevent curdling. However they are formed, custards are rich and luxurious thanks to the eggs that help them thicken. They require the proportion of egg yolk to be equal to—or greater than—that of whole egg because egg yolk has the power to turn the liquid solid. Egg whites can thicken too, but the amount of water an egg white adds vs. its thickening power doesn't make it very effective.

Baked custards can be made of anything, sweet or savory, by following these simple steps:

1. **Create the liquid to be thickened.** The liquid is usually cream- or milk-based and can be flavored with herbs, spices, or fruit or vegetable puree.
2. **Measure the amount of the flavored liquid.**
3. **Add 1 large egg and 1 large egg yolk for each cup of liquid.** Blend well.
4. **Bake at 325 degrees until just set.** The time will vary depending on the size and amount of custard being baked.

This basic ratio will help you with everything from crème brûlée (where the flavored liquid is whole milk with vanilla) to red pepper flan (where the flavored liquid is roasted red peppers pureed with cream). So go ahead—get creative!

Wilted Cabbage and Goat Cheese Salad

Cabbage is often mistreated. As coleslaw, it's usually dressed with too much mayo. And when it's made into sauerkraut, it's loaded with vinegar and pickling spices. Here Jamie shows it the respect and affection it deserves by pickling it with a light hand and warming it through on the stovetop. Then he studs it with creamy goat cheese. This typically serves four, but Brooke's been known to eat the entire recipe by herself for dinner.

serves 4

1 medium head red cabbage

¼ cup red wine vinegar

2 teaspoons kosher salt, plus more as needed

2 tablespoons granulated sugar

½ teaspoon freshly ground pepper, plus more as needed

2 cloves garlic, chopped

1 apple, peeled, cored, and grated

8 ounces sliced bacon, chopped

1 cup minced onion

6 ounces goat cheese, at room temperature

Cut the cabbage in half through the stem and remove the core. Slice as thinly as possible. Combine the cabbage with the vinegar, salt, sugar, pepper, garlic, and apple; mix thoroughly. Cover and leave to marinate for 30 minutes at room temperature or overnight in the refrigerator.

After marinating the cabbage, place a large saucepot over medium-high heat, add the bacon, and brown it. When the fat is well rendered and the bacon is slightly crisp, add the onion and cook until tender and translucent. Turn the heat to high. When the pan begins to sizzle, add the cabbage along with its marinade. Stir rapidly to begin wilting the cabbage. After a minute or 2 of stirring, reduce the heat to medium and cover the pot. Leave the cabbage to cook for 20 to 30 minutes, until tender. As the cabbage simmers, lift the lid occasionally to stir and make sure the cabbage isn't browning or sticking to the bottom of the pot. Reduce the heat if necessary. Taste and adjust the seasoning with salt and pepper.

Divide the cabbage among 4 plates and scatter pieces of the goat cheese around the piles of cabbage.

TECHNIQUE TIP

If the cabbage begins to stick to the bottom of the pan or begins to brown, add ½ cup water to the pot.

TO WARM IS TO WILT

Wilting (aka sautéing) helps to soften the texture of the cabbage, making it more tender and easier to eat. Cooked cabbage is also more mild in flavor. Think of it like marinating for coleslaw, only faster.

Roasting Revealed

Want to whip up a fast and healthful meal? It's as easy as chopping up some fresh veggies, tossing them with a few seasonings, and letting the oven do the rest.

So while your oven is working overtime—the superhigh temperature concentrating and creating new flavors—you might as well grab your Scrabble board and a bottle of Morellino di Scansano, because roasting is the most effective and flavorful cooking method that requires approximately zero attention.

SIMPLE ROASTING RULES

- A little oil or butter helps the vegetables color.
- Never forget the kosher salt and freshly ground pepper.
- Try to cut all the veggies into a similar size so they cook evenly, though it's okay to make different shapes to keep it interesting.

METHOD

- Cut the items to be roasted into bite-size pieces and combine in a bowl.
- Season with salt, pepper, herbs, and/or spices.
- Add some form of fat (oil or butter)—just enough to coat.
- Spread the items in a single layer in a pan with low sides. Don't crowd!
- Get it into a hot oven. Dense, slow-cooking vegetables (think root vegetables like butternut squash) should cook at 400 to 425 degrees for 20 to 25 minutes. Tender, quick-cooking vegetables (spring and summer veggies like squash and corn) can be cooked at 400 to 450 degrees for 8 to 12 minutes. Always roast vegetables until they are tender enough to be pierced with a knife.

SOME FAVORITE COMBINATIONS

- diced butternut squash tossed with branches of thyme, coriander, and garlic cloves (page 157)
- eggplant, corn, and broccoli with fresh basil (page 101)
- Brussels sprouts, halved and tossed with olive oil and garlic cloves; after roasting, add shaved Parmesan cheese and toasted pine nuts
- potatoes roasted with fresh rosemary, chopped garlic, white wine, and olives
- carrots dressed with honey, lime zest, coriander seeds, and ground ginger before cooking (page 158)
- sweet potatoes and/or parsnips roasted with fresh sage leaves; finish with a drizzle of balsamic vinegar
- cauliflower roasted with curry powder, olive oil, and garlic cloves
- fennel cut into wedges and sliced red onions; serve with olives tossed with fennel seeds, orange zest, and olive oil

Coriander-Roasted Butternut Squash Salad with Arugula and Parmesan

We decided to combine Brooke's all-time favorite flavors and ingredients and make them into a cold-weather salad. Sweet butternut squash, spicy arugula, and nutty Parmigiano Reggiano combine beautifully to give this salad some heft. The flavors are hearty, yet the salad itself feels light, making this the perfect "compromise dinner."

serves 4

1 medium butternut squash, peeled, seeded, and cut into ½- to ¾-inch dice (about 5 cups)

4 or 5 branches fresh thyme

4 cloves garlic, crushed

1½ teaspoons ground coriander

3 tablespoons extra virgin olive oil, plus more for the dressing

3 strips lemon zest

1 tablespoon kosher salt, plus more to taste

4 cups loosely packed arugula

juice of ½ lemon

freshly ground pepper

Parmesan cheese for shaving

Preheat the oven to 425 degrees.

Place a baking sheet lined with aluminum foil in the oven to preheat. In a large bowl, combine the butternut squash, thyme, garlic, coriander, olive oil, lemon zest, and salt; mix thoroughly. Spread in a single layer on the preheated baking sheet, being sure not to overcrowd the sheet. Roast until the squash is tender and browned around the edges, 20 to 25 minutes. Remove from the oven and cool slightly on the baking sheet.

Divide the warm squash evenly among 4 plates. Dress the arugula with the lemon juice, 2 to 3 tablespoons olive oil, and salt and pepper to taste and place a pile on top of the squash. Add a generous amount of Parmesan shavings.

TECHNIQUE TIP

Preheating the roasting pan is not required but doing so ensures that the cubes of butternut squash will be well browned and a little crisp without overcooking or becoming mushy. Browning vegetables creates texture and gives the vegetable more flavor.

Roasted Carrots with Lime and Coriander

A few summers ago, a Broadway producer (and big foodie) invited us to stay with him at his Hudson Valley weekend home. Riding along in his station wagon down a narrow, rutted lane, we had no idea what lay before us. Finally, the overhanging tree limbs cleared, and we saw two elegant, modernist, glass cabins perched on the bank of a lake. Even more impressive was his lush, acres-long garden bursting with fragrant herbs, lettuces, fruits, and vegetables. The next day, while Brooke floated on the lake in an inner tube, Jamie dug up carrots and sampled herbs. For dinner, alongside our stuffed chicken and onion flatbread, Jamie roasted the carrots with the garden's fresh cilantro and local honey from the town's farmers' market. Inspiration and instinct made for an unforgettable meal.

serves 4

1 clove garlic, crushed

½ teaspoon crushed coriander seeds

¼ teaspoon ground ginger

1 tablespoon honey

2 tablespoons extra virgin olive oil

1 lime, zest grated and juiced

1 teaspoon kosher salt

freshly ground pepper to taste

4 to 6 multicolor carrots, peeled and cut into
    bite-size pieces (about 3 cups)

2 tablespoons chopped fresh cilantro

Preheat the oven to 375 degrees.

Put the garlic, coriander, and ginger in a bowl and whisk in the honey, olive oil, and the lime juice. Season to taste with salt and pepper. Toss the carrots with the dressing and spread on an aluminum-foil-lined baking pan in a single layer. Roast until easily pierced with the tip of a knife, approximately 20 minutes. Remove from the oven and toss the roasted carrots with their juices from the roasting pan with the cilantro and the lime zest.

Sweet-and-Sour Apples

A delicious way to revisit the big day is through the food you enjoyed at your wedding lunch or dinner. (Better yet if your wedding was followed by a cocktail-only reception!) Along with our Roasted Butternut Squash Soup (page 128), one of the most memorable plates at our candlelit wedding dinner was slow-roasted pork with sweet-and-sour apples. The apples hang out with just enough vinegar and rosemary to make them a bit tart and "herby"—the perfect partner for tender meats.

serves 4

2 tablespoons unsalted butter

¼ cup brown sugar

4 apples (preferably Golden Delicious), peeled, cored, and diced

½ cup cider vinegar

1 whole branch rosemary

1 lemon, zest grated and juiced

Melt the butter in a sauté pan over medium heat. Stir in the sugar and cook until melted and bubbling, about 4 minutes. Add the apples and toss well to coat with the sugar and butter. Stir in the vinegar and rosemary. Bring the mixture to a simmer and cook until the apples are just tender and the mixture is well thickened, about 5 minutes more. Remove the rosemary from the pan and season to taste with a bit of the lemon zest and juice.

TECHNIQUE TIP

Cooking with Whole Herbs—When using whole herbs, as in this recipe, you can add the herbs' flavor to a dish without overwhelming it. Simmering a whole branch of rosemary with the apples allows the rosemary to scent the apples, but keeping it on the stem makes it easy to remove so the flavor remains very delicate.

Arugula, Peach, and Feta Salad with Shaved Corn Vinaigrette

This is our first date—re-created as a salad. Jamie convinced Brooke to accompany him to Birmingham's Pepper Place farmers' market (in July, when it was hot as Hades!) to pick through bins of peaches, corn, and fresh greens for his restaurant menu. As the chef de cuisine at Highlands Bar & Grill, it was his job to squeeze his way through the summertime produce . . . and he figured he might as well take his crush along with him. Five years, two wedding rings, and one baby later, this salad still makes us smile. It brings back wonderful memories of that first morning and reminds us of how unlikely ingredients can really sing together.

serves 4

1 sweet onion, such as Vidalia

⅓ cup extra virgin olive oil, plus more for the grill

2 ears sweet yellow or silver corn, shucked
    and silk threads removed

pinch of red pepper flakes

1 teaspoon ground coriander

3 tablespoons white wine vinegar

pinch of granulated sugar

2 peaches, slightly firm

4 ounces (approximately 4 cups loosely packed)
    arugula or watercress

¼ cup crumbled feta cheese

3 tablespoons coarsely chopped smoked
    or toasted almonds (optional)

Slice the onion, keeping the layers together in full rounds. Lightly oil a hot grill or cast-iron skillet and place the onion slices on the heated surface. Cook one side until completely blackened and charred. Turn and char the other side. When all the onion is cooked, cool them completely, roughly chop, and reserve.

Remove the corn from the cobs by shaving it into small pieces with a vegetable peeler. Place the corn and any of its juices in a small bowl. Add the red pepper flakes, coriander, vinegar, and sugar. Mix well and set aside to allow the flavors to combine, 10 to 15 minutes. Whisk in the olive oil and add the onion.

Cut the peaches in half, remove the pits, and cut into thin wedges, 10 to 12 pieces each.

Toss the arugula and peaches with the shaved corn dressing in a large bowl. Garnish with the feta cheese and the smoked almonds, if using.

COOK LIKE A PRO

"Tender" Lettuces (aka those-delicate-green-things-that-turn-mushy-and-slimy-way-too-fast)—Greens like arugula, watercress, microgreens, and herbs are best when tossed with dressing just moments before serving. The longer the greens are left to mingle with acidic vinegar or lemon and heavy oil, the more they will break down, looking wilted and becoming soft.

PEACHES

When it comes to peaches and their juicy, drip-down-your-chin goodness, nothing beats local. Locally grown peaches are allowed to ripen on the tree since they spend less time in trucks traveling to market. Whether we're in New York or down South, we always seek out our favorite peaches from New Jersey; Chilton County, Alabama; or Georgia.

SWEET ONIONS—WELL, RELATIVELY

Don't expect to crunch into one of these onions like an apple—that's a move we've never embraced. Compared to standard yellow or red onions, sweet onions are much milder (but still nowhere near a Red Delicious). That's because they're grown in rich, low-sulphur soil and have a much higher water content. As a result, they shed the pungent aroma and tear-causing components that those other onions possess—especially when raw. The most famous varieties are named for the areas in which they're grown, like Walla Walla, Washington; Vidalia, Georgia; Maui, Hawaii; and Texas.

Fried Okra

At Highlands Bar & Grill, Jamie learned that the best way to sell an entrée was to list fried okra as the side dish. A hill of the golden-fried, tender pod cut into bite-size pieces made just about any dish a sellout!

Okra as needed (breading will coat up to 2 pounds)
Buttermilk as needed
Canola oil for frying

BREADING
2 cups cornmeal
1 cup all-purpose flour
1 teaspoon kosher salt, plus more as needed
½ teaspoon freshly ground pepper
pinch of cayenne

TECHNIQUE TIP

As with all things fried, okra is best served hot. To enjoy your okra at its best, set up your frying pot and corn-meal breading and drain the okra. Then when the rest of dinner is ready, you can fry up batches of okra and serve them hot.

Begin with small tender pieces of okra: cut the larger pieces into ½-inch slices and leave the smaller pods whole. Place the okra in a large bowl and pour in buttermilk until just covered. As they would say back home, "leave that be" for about 1 hour.

While the okra is marinating, make your breading mixture by whisking together all the ingredients in a large bowl.

Fill a medium saucepot three-quarters full with canola oil and heat it on top of the stove until it reaches 375 degrees; adjust the heat to maintain this temperature. Drain the buttermilk from the okra and toss the okra with the cornmeal mixture until all pieces are well coated. Shake off the excess and carefully drop into the hot oil in batches (1 to 2 cups at a time). Cook until golden brown and remove to paper towels to drain. Season immediately with salt and serve hot.

O-WHAT?

You might not have grown up like us, passing bowls of fried okra around the dinner table and throwing pods into every soup and stew that was bubbling on the stovetop. Don't worry—you can make up for lost time. When cooked properly, okra, the flowering plant that hails from the Ethiopian highlands and is part of the same family as hibiscus, cotton, and cocoa, happens to cook up into a succulent, two-bite morsel with tender flesh and a pleasant seedy interior. Every part of the okra pod is meant to be eaten. So throw your head back, pop a pod, and enjoy!

Grilled Zucchini with Mint Pesto and Pecans

Mint has such a will to grow that even Brooke can't kill it. When we were living together in her SoHo studio apartment, Brooke tried to plant herbs on her postage-stamp-size back patio. Everything died—except the mint. We had no choice but to make as many mint-centric dishes as possible. Example one:

serves 6

4 medium zucchini

1 tablespoon extra virgin olive oil, plus more
    for brushing

½ teaspoon kosher salt, plus more to taste

freshly ground pepper

1 cup pecan halves, chopped

1 teaspoon finely grated lemon zest

¼ teaspoon cayenne

1 recipe Mint Pesto (page 85)

¼ cup grated Parmesan cheese

Trim the ends from the zucchini and cut the zucchini crosswise into 2- to 3-inch sections. Slice the pieces lengthwise ¼ to ½ inch thick. Brush each piece with olive oil and season with salt and pepper.

Cook the zucchini slices on a hot grill or under the broiler until just tender, 1 to 2 minutes per side. While the zucchini is cooking, combine the pecans with the 1 tablespoon olive oil, lemon zest, cayenne, and the ½ teaspoon salt. Wrap the mixture in an aluminum foil packet and grill or broil so the pecans can toast while the zucchini cooks.

Arrange the cooked zucchini on a platter and drizzle with the Mint Pesto while the zucchini is still warm. Open the foil and garnish with the pecan mixture and Parmesan.

TECHNIQUE TIP

Drizzling the zucchini with the pesto while it's still warm from the grill will help the vegetables absorb the flavor and make the sauce more fragrant.

STIRRING THE POT

Ah, the mystery and grandeur of risotto. For home cooks, risotto can be one of the more intimidating dishes to prepare, but, when it's done right, one of the most exhilarating to serve. There are no shortcuts to a great bowl of risotto, but there is a way to make your time in the kitchen easier. Just know that every risotto is made from the same formula. After you practice a few times with our recipes here, you'll be ready to color outside the lines and create a new risotto with your favorite ingredients.

THE FORMULA

INGREDIENTS

Aromatics—shallots, onions, leeks, and/or garlic

Rice—short-grain rice (see note on page 167)

Wine—for flavor (optional)

Liquid—chicken stock, vegetable broth, or water if you must

Main Ingredient—Whatever you want to flavor the risotto with. The main ingredient may need to be precooked, such as sautéed mushrooms or blanched asparagus or sweet peas.

Butter and Cheese—to be stirred in at the last moment, because they always make things better

METHOD

Begin by sweating the aromatics in a small amount of fat. Butter or olive oil is fine.

When the aromatics begin to smell sweet, add the rice and stir well to coat with the fat. Continue cooking and stirring until the rice begins to sizzle.

Deglaze with the wine. Cook until the wine is completely evaporated.

Make your first addition of stock (be sure to preheat it). Add just enough stock to cover the rice completely. Bring the mixture to a simmer while constantly stirring. When the mixture is very thick and the stock is reduced by over half, add enough stock to return it to its first level. The more you stir, the creamier the risotto will be.

When the rice is two-thirds cooked, either spread it out on a parchment-paper-lined baking sheet to cool quickly or add the main ingredient to the pot if serving right away.

If reheating, 5 to 10 minutes before serving, bring a small amount of stock and butter to a boil in a large pot. Add the cold risotto at once and stir rapidly to reheat. Fold in the main ingredient, continuing to stir and cook. Adjust the consistency and doneness by adding stock as needed.

Remove the pot from the heat. Add butter and cheese to taste and beat the mixture rapidly with a wooden spoon.

Wild Mushroom Risotto

THE ULTIMATE RISOTTO TRICK

One of the most intimidating things about this creamy Italian rice dish is the time it can take to prepare it. And that's why most home cooks keep it off the menu. Great risotto takes time. So, then, how do restaurants consistently churn out bowls of perfect risotto, every five minutes, for hours on end? There's a trick, of course, and it's one chefs use every time they serve risotto to diners.

During dinner parties, while Brooke is filling guests' glasses, Jamie may prefer to hide out in the kitchen, stirring risotto with one hand and updating sports scores with the other. But that's just poor hosting. So here's how a home cook can make like a high-flying restaurant chef:

- Make an entire pot of risotto but cook it about two-thirds of the way, so the rice is softened but still a bit crunchy.
- Spread all of the risotto in a thin layer on a large baking sheet to cool the rice as quickly as possible.
- When ready to serve, heat 1 to 2 cups stock and a large spoonful of butter in a clean pot. When it is boiling, add the cold risotto and stir until heated through and creamy.
- Finish the risotto as directed in the recipe (garnishes, butter, cheese, and so on).

This is a great year-round risotto. To make it seasonal, add cubes of butternut squash in the fall, sweet peas in the spring, or diced zucchini in the summer.

serves 4

3 tablespoons freshly grated Parmesan, plus more for garnish
1 tablespoon finely chopped fresh parsley
4 ounces assorted mushrooms, such as black trumpet, hedgehog, yellowfoot, crimini, and/or shiitake, cut into bite-size pieces
2 tablespoons olive oil
kosher salt and freshly ground pepper
6 cups homemade or low-sodium chicken broth
4 tablespoons (½ stick) unsalted butter
½ cup finely chopped leeks, spring onion, or yellow onion (rinsed if using leeks or spring onions)
1½ cups Arborio, Carnaroli, or Vialone Nano rice
1½ cups dry white wine
hot sauce

Before cooking the rice, grate the Parmesan, chop the parsley, and cut the mushrooms. Place a large sauté pan over high heat and add 2 tablespoons olive oil. When the oil begins to shimmer, add the mushrooms and cook until tender. Season to taste with salt and pepper (reserve any pan juices) and set aside.

Bring the broth to a simmer in a small saucepan.

Melt 2 tablespoons of the butter in a large, heavy-bottomed saucepan over medium heat. Add the leeks and sauté, stirring occasionally, until tender but not browned, 3 to 4 minutes. Add the rice and continue to cook until the rice begins to sizzle, 1 to 2 minutes. Add the wine and 1 teaspoon salt. Stir constantly with a wooden spoon or rubber spatula until the wine is completely absorbed.

Add 2 scant cups of the simmering broth to the rice and cook, stirring constantly, over medium heat until the broth is absorbed. Continue simmering the risotto and adding broth, 1 to 2 cups at a time, stirring constantly and allowing each addition to reduce by half before adding the next. Cook until the rice is just tender and creamy but still has a little bite, 20 to 25 minutes (there will be leftover broth).

Stir in the sautéed mushrooms, Parmesan cheese, and remaining 2 tablespoons butter, then taste. Add salt, pepper, and/or hot sauce as needed. When the risotto is seasoned to your satisfaction, stir in the parsley. Divide among 4 bowls and top with a sprinkling of Parmesan. Pour 1 tablespoon of the leftover chicken stock or mushroom juice over the rice in each bowl to moisten the edges.

CHEF'S TIP

Mushrooms are always a welcome addition in any season. Their earthy depth provides a sturdy foundation from which you can build your dish. In the spring, the damp northwestern United States is producing black trumpet, hedgehog, and yellowfoot mushrooms. If you can't find these, crimini mushrooms (baby portabellas) and shiitakes are readily available in most grocery stores. If you're really in a pinch, dried mushrooms (we prefer porcini) are great and pack tons of flavor. Follow the directions on the package for rehydrating and try to include some of that soaking liquid in your chicken broth.

Romaine Lettuce Risotto

Romaine lettuce gives a wonderful delicate flavor and great texture to the rice. This makes a perfect light dinner or a very satisfying lunch.

serves 4

1 head romaine lettuce

6 cups chicken broth

4 tablespoons (½ stick) unsalted butter

1 tablespoon minced garlic

1½ cups Arborio, Carnaroli, or Vialone Nano rice

kosher salt and freshly ground pepper

1 cup dry white wine

¼ cup grated Parmesan cheese

COOK LIKE A PRO

The Big Three—Carnaroli, Arborio, and Vialone Nano are the varieties of short-grain rice most commonly used for making risotto. All three are native to northern Italy. Short-grain rice has more starch, which means beautiful, creamy risotto.

Remove the dark green outer leaves of the lettuce, slice thinly, and set aside for garnish. Coarsely chop the remaining lettuce to cook in the rice.

Pour the chicken broth into a small saucepot and bring to a simmer.

Place a separate, large saucepot over medium-high heat, add 2 tablespoons of the butter, and melt it. Add the garlic and rice; sauté until aromatic. Stir in the lettuce and a pinch of salt and cook until wilted. Continue cooking until the pan is dry. Add the white wine and cook until dry again. Pour in enough stock to completely cover the rice. Maintain a simmer in the pot while stirring constantly. When the stock is reduced by half, add enough to again just cover the rice. Continue cooking in this manner until the rice is tender, about 20 minutes or after 3 or 4 additions of stock. Be sure to taste the cooking liquid as you go, adding salt and pepper as needed.

When the rice is tender, stir in the Parmesan cheese and the remaining 2 tablespoons butter. Beat vigorously with a spoon until smooth and very creamy. Stir in the thinly sliced outer lettuce leaves and serve immediately.

Sweet Pepper and Corn Risotto

Ours is a delicious summer risotto—with a little spice. The flavors of sweet pepper and corn go so well with a main dish of grilled meats or fish. Or do like Brooke and stir into the risotto pieces of shrimp, crab, or scallops to make it an unforgettable meal.

serves 4

2 ears corn, kernels cut from the cobs, cobs
    reserved

6 cups chicken broth

kosher salt to taste

4 tablespoons (½ stick) unsalted butter

3 cloves garlic, minced

1 red bell pepper, finely chopped

1 teaspoon chili powder

1½ cups Arborio, Carnaroli, or Vialone Nano rice

1 cup dry white wine

freshly ground pepper to taste

¼ cup grated Parmesan cheese

2 tablespoons chopped fresh herbs, such as
    chives or cilantro (optional)

Cut the corn cobs into pieces and place in a large pot. Add the chicken broth and a pinch of salt, bring the mixture to a simmer, and hold while you prepare the risotto.

Place a second pot over medium-high heat and melt 2 tablespoons of the butter in it. Add the garlic, bell pepper, and corn kernels; sauté until tender but not browned, about 5 minutes. Stir in the chili powder, rice, and a pinch of salt and cook until the rice begins to sizzle, about 2 minutes. Add the white wine and cook until the pot is dry. Pour in enough stock to completely cover the rice. Maintain a simmer in the pot while stirring constantly. When the stock is reduced by half, add enough to again just cover the rice. Continue cooking in this manner until the rice is tender, about 20 minutes or after 3 or 4 additions of stock. Be sure to taste the cooking liquid as you go, adding salt and pepper as needed.

When the rice is tender, stir in the Parmesan cheese and the remaining 2 tablespoons butter. Beat vigorously with a spoon until the risotto is smooth and very creamy. Stir in the herbs and serve immediately.

THE LIGHTER SIDE

There are a few times a year (the holidays, football season, after summer vacation) when our jeans get a little tight and we feel a bit puffy. We know that we need to lighten things up a bit, but we're not ready for drastic measures or any sort of cleanse involving lemon juice and cayenne pepper. By simply incorporating more light dishes into our weekly eating, we can get back to feeling good and fit in no time.

The plan here is to go easy on the meat and amp up the seafood, to get more vegetables into meals, and not forget about fruit. This isn't a diet—so don't consider it one. Think of these dishes as taking your digestive system for a week at the spa.

Five Flavor Boosters: Big Flavor, Few Calories

These ingredients are not for the faint of heart, but they add big punch to food in a hurry without adding fat or calories. Stir in any of these at the last moment for a real taste-bud boost.

1. Anchovies—Add to tomato- or olive-oil-based sauces, especially with garlic, lemon, olives, or parsley.
2. Capers—Add to anything with tomatoes (fresh or cooked); especially great with fish; pair well with lemon, olive oil, and fresh herbs.
3. Fresh chiles—Add heat to any dish, most common in Latin and Southeast Asian dishes.
4. Chopped herbs—Especially cilantro, basil, tarragon, marjoram, and oregano; give a lift to any dish when stirred in or tossed through at the last moment. Heating herbs releases more of their aroma, though the heat can slightly change the flavor.
5. Fresh ginger, grated—Especially good in dishes that include cilantro, garlic, lime, scallions, and/or basil. In its raw state it can add heat or "bite." Cook briefly for full flavor and aroma.

West Indies Crab Salad

When Brooke was growing up, her family prepared West Indies salad exclusively for visiting dignitaries, like Brooke's chic aunt who drove over from New Orleans. A salad made from premium lump crabmeat was too extravagant for us kids, so it was reserved for wowing guests and impressing family members. But now that we're in charge, we want to see this make more frequent appearances.

serves 4

DRESSING
1 tablespoon fresh lime juice
1 tablespoon fresh orange juice
1 tablespoon red wine vinegar
1 jalapeño, finely minced
1 tablespoon finely minced shallot
2 tablespoons extra virgin olive oil

SALAD
1 cup long-grain rice
1 pound fresh lump crabmeat
kosher salt and freshly ground pepper
1 head green-leaf lettuce
2 tablespoons chopped fresh parsley
1 tablespoon extra virgin olive oil

For the dressing, whisk together all the ingredients in a bowl. Set aside 15 minutes for flavors to develop.

For the salad, bring a pot of salted water to a boil. Add the rice, stir well, and cook at a rapid boil until tender, about 8 minutes; be sure to taste. Pour the rice through a colander and rinse with cold water. Leave the rice in the colander to drain, about 15 minutes.

(These first two steps can be done up to 24 hours in advance.)

Pick through the crabmeat, discarding any shell or cartilage. Mix the crabmeat and dressing and season to taste with salt and pepper. Cover and refrigerate until ready to serve.

Shred the lettuce and divide among 4 plates. Add the parsley and olive oil to the rice and mix thoroughly. Place a pile of rice in the center of each bed of lettuce. Top with the crab mixture and drizzle any remaining dressing around the lettuce.

Optional Garnishes: cherry tomatoes, diced sweet peppers, sliced cucumbers.

TECHNIQUE TIP

Don't Shred on Me—When picking through the crabmeat to remove shell and cartilage, keep the crabmeat in as large pieces as possible. Break the pieces in half to look for cartilage but avoid shredding the meat.

TECHNIQUE TIP

Cooking rice the same way you would pasta—by boiling and then draining it—is an easy way to ensure tender rice without worrying about clumping or sticking.

Rigatoni with Escarole, Pine Nuts, and Goat Cheese

Brooke makes this rigatoni when both she and the baby are screaming for a quick, comforting dinner (that happens to be healthful). Simmering escarole, rigatoni, and goat cheese together for a few minutes with a little pasta water makes a sauce that coats the pasta like a cream sauce, without the calories. A sprinkling of red pepper flakes adds some exciting heat.

serves 4

2 heads escarole

4 cloves garlic, grated on a Microplane

5 tablespoons extra virgin olive oil

½ teaspoon red pepper flakes

¼ cup pine nuts

kosher salt and freshly ground pepper

1 pound rigatoni

4 ounces goat cheese

juice of ½ lemon

TIP

Dinner in a Hurry—You'll wait about as long for your pot of water to boil as it will take for the entire dish to cook!

Trim the darkest green ends of the leaves from the heads of escarole (about ½ inch off the top) and discard any wilted or bruised outer leaves. Roughly chop the remaining escarole, discarding the cores. Wash the escarole and set aside to drain.

Bring a pot of salted water to a boil for the pasta.

Place the garlic in a wide-bottomed pot with 4 tablespoons of the olive oil, the red pepper flakes, and the pine nuts. Turn the heat under the pot to medium. When the garlic begins to sizzle and smell sweet, add all of the escarole at once with a pinch of salt and a few grinds of fresh pepper. Stir occasionally as the escarole begins to wilt.

While the escarole is cooking, drop the pasta into the boiling water to cook, stirring occasionally to prevent sticking. Boil until the pasta is softened but still a bit crunchy, 7 to 9 minutes. Transfer it to the pot of escarole and stir well. Scoop 1 cup of the pasta cooking water into the pot as well. Bring the entire mixture to a simmer. Stir in three-quarters of the goat cheese and blend until completely dissolved. Cook until the mixture is slightly thickened and the pasta is tender, about 2 minutes.

Remove the pot from the heat and stir in the lemon juice and the remaining 1 tablespoon olive oil. Season to taste and divide among 4 plates. Garnish with the remaining goat cheese.

Seared Tuna, Crispy Artichokes, Capers, and Marjoram

This dish tastes a little bit like sunshine. We think the use of warm-weather ingredients like baby artichokes and capers, as well as the irresistible brown butter, has a way of warming us through like a day on the Gulf. This is a healthful, full-flavored fish dish that you'll come back to again and again.

serves 4

four 6-ounce tuna steaks
kosher salt and freshly ground pepper
2 tablespoons olive oil or canola oil
1 lemon, zest removed with a vegetable peeler
4 tablespoons (½ stick) unsalted butter
3 tablespoons brined capers, drained
½ lemon, juiced
1 tablespoon chopped fresh marjoram

CRISPY ARTICHOKES
6 baby artichokes, cleaned
1½ cups all-purpose flour
olive oil
kosher salt

Pat the tuna steaks dry and season liberally with salt and pepper. Place a sauté pan over high heat, add the oil, and heat until smoking. Carefully lay the tuna in the hot pan and sear on each side until well browned, about 2 minutes per side. Remove the tuna from the pan and place on a rack to rest.

Discard the remaining oil from the pan and add the lemon zest and butter. Place the pan back over medium heat and allow the butter to melt completely. When the foaming subsides, watch the butter carefully as it begins to turn brown. Add the capers and fry until popped and crisp. Squeeze in the juice of ½ lemon, remove from the heat, and stir in the marjoram. Set aside to cool.

Slice the cleaned artichokes lengthwise as thinly as possible. Place in a bowl and toss with the flour. Pour olive oil to a depth of 1 inch into a sauté pan and place over high heat. When a small amount of flour sprinkled into the oil sizzles immediately, thoroughly shake all of the excess flour from the artichokes and drop them into the hot oil in batches. Cook until golden brown and crisped, about 2 minutes per batch. Remove with a slotted spoon to a paper-towel-lined plate. Season with salt immediately.

Cut the tuna in half on the bias and place in the center of each plate. Place a small pile of artichokes on top of the tuna, then spoon the caper sauce over the tuna and artichokes.

Pablo Neruda Ate Capers Here

Remember the beautiful little gem of a movie *Il Postino*? In it, Pablo Neruda, the famous Chilean poet, is exiled to a tiny Mediterranean island. He whiles away his days writing, teaching the beauties of poetry to his postman, and eating simple, sunny meals. The island of Salina, the backdrop for the movie, is famous for its caper harvesting. Its twin volcanoes provide the island with extraordinarily fertile soil for the flowering caper plants, and the small "salt lakes," or *salinas*, provide the salt necessary for preserving what are considered the world's best capers.

Cleaning Artichokes

A rule of thumb with artichokes: green = tough. The first step in preparing artichoke hearts is to squeeze juice from 1/2 lemon into a bowl of water so the cleaned artichokes may be placed in the water to prevent browning. Then, with a sharp knife, cut off the top one-quarter of the artichoke. Working quickly, pull back and rip off all of the green leaves, so only the yellow (or VERY pale green) leaves attached to the heart remain. Finally, use a vegetable peeler to peel the green fibrous parts of the stem, exposing the lighter-colored tender stem beneath. Drop the cleaned artichoke into the lemon water and begin the process again with the next artichoke.

 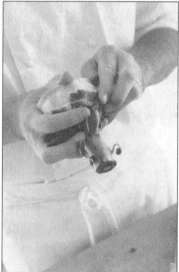 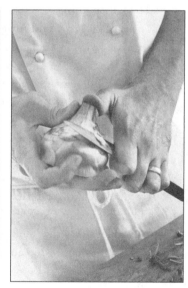

Curing Fish

The vocabulary for raw and cured fish can vary greatly. Carpaccio (pronounced car-PA-chee-o) is a raw, Italian preparation of thin slices of seafood. The raw slices typically lie flat, fanned out on the plate, while sauces or garnishes are placed on top. Crudo (pronounced CROO-doe), literally meaning "raw" in both Italian and Spanish, and sushi fall into the completely raw category as well. Ceviches, found in Latin and Caribbean cuisines, are a bit different. They're made with fish or shellfish and are "cooked" or cured by the acid in the citrus juices that comprise their marinades.

Yet, there are other preparations that fully cure fish, a practice that dates back thousands of years as a method to preserve fish and avoid spoilage. This type of curing is done by conventional means—with salt. Lox and smoked fish, like salmon, trout, and whitefish, are all cured with a salt-sugar mixture or a brine. Whether you're serving carpaccio, sushi, ceviche, or full-on lox, there are three rules for raw or uncooked seafood:

1. **Fresh fish**
2. **Fresh fish**
3. **Fresh fish**

. . . Get the picture?

Great fresh seafood should be very firm, be a little tacky to the touch, and smell like the sea. There should be no fish smell at all. And its colors should be crisp—especially the brightly colored blood line. If anything looks dull, it might be a little old, which is okay (but not ideal) for cooking but won't pass the test for raw. Always store your seafood in the coldest part of your refrigerator. If possible, keep it on ice in a colander resting on a baking dish, so the water can drip away as the ice melts.

This is the time you really need to rely on your local fishmonger (aka the guy working behind the fish counter). Tell him what you're doing and that you need a piece of fish he'd be comfortable serving raw. If he tells you "the tuna," it's carpaccio time. You'll want a white fish for ceviche; snapper is probably our favorite, mackerel is great too, and scallops are delicious—as long as they're super fresh. You have lots of options when it comes to curing fish, though fatty fish are best (that's why salmon is such a classic). People always seem to find these preparations daring and exciting; all the glory of hand-rolled sushi without covering your hands (and the kitchen) in sticky rice.

If you are making carpaccio or salt-cured fish (like our Tequila-Cured Salmon, page 307), it is incredibly important that you slice the fish as thin as possible. If your knife skills aren't quite Iron Chef Japan level, try the following method: Slice the fish as thin as you can, then lay a piece of plastic wrap flat on the countertop and rub it with a small amount of oil. Place the fish on the oiled plastic wrap and cover with a second sheet of plastic. Pound the fish lightly with the flat side of a meat tenderizer or the bottom of a small saucepan until the desired thickness (paper thin) is reached.

Here are some great ways to prepare raw or nearly raw fish:

Carpaccio/Tartare/Seared Rare—Tuna, scallops: Remember to slice thin and season well. Dress with bold flavors such as sesame oil, hot sauce, shallots, radishes, and herbs.

Ceviche—Snapper, mackerel, swordfish, marlin, shrimp, scallops: Lemon and lime juice do all the work here. Just remember to finish with freshly chopped herbs, such as cilantro, chives, or parsley. And don't forget to add a few fresh chiles to spice it up.

Cured—Trout, salmon, halibut, hamachi: Pack in a salt-sugar mix (page 307) or brine (page 208) to preserve.

Red Snapper Ceviche

Relaxing in Seaside, Florida, with our friends Lacy and Jeff Phillips, Jamie raided the fish cooler looking for lunch. Before the girls could even change out of their suits, Jamie had whipped up this snapper ceviche as a last-minute, light lunch. The great thing about his marinated fish is that it's just as good between a warm, corn tortilla, topped with shredded cabbage, tomatoes, and red onion marmalade (page 177), as it is served from a bowl with tortilla chips. Pop a Corona and enjoy.

serves 4

2 boneless, skinless fillets of mild white fish (about 1 pound), or about 1 pound scallops or shelled shrimp, cut into bite-size pieces

2 scallions, thinly sliced

1 jalapeño, minced

2 limes

1 lemon

good-quality extra virgin olive oil or lemon oil

1½ teaspoons kosher salt, plus more as needed

freshly ground pepper to taste

hot sauce

2 tablespoons chopped fresh cilantro leaves

Slice the fillets with a very sharp knife as thinly as possible. If your slices are long (over 1½ inches), cut them into shorter pieces. Place these in a stainless-steel or plastic bowl sitting inside another bowl of ice (you want to keep the fish as cold as possible throughout the entire process).

Add the scallions and jalapeño (for a milder ceviche, remove the seeds and ribs first—this is where most of the heat comes from) to the bowl. Squeeze in the lime and lemon juice; don't let any seeds get in there. Add 1 tablespoon olive oil and the salt. Mix well and refrigerate for 20 to 30 minutes.

Remove the ceviche from the fridge and taste. Adjust the seasoning, adding salt, pepper, hot sauce, lemon or lime juice, or olive oil as needed. The fish should be turning opaque by now. This curing action caused by the acid in the citrus juice will continue, so avoid mixing the ceviche too far in advance; an hour or two before serving is fine. Stir in the cilantro just before serving.

Spicy Red Onion Marmalade

Wrap your snapper ceviche (page 176) in soft corn tortillas and top with this sweet, sour, and spicy onion jam for a gourmet take on fish tacos. Or just serve this marmalade in a small dish, along with a bowl of ceviche and good-quality tortilla chips.

makes approximately 1 cup

1 tablespoon extra virgin olive oil

1 medium red onion, cut into thin julienne

1 whole dried red chile, or pinch of red pepper flakes

kosher salt and freshly ground pepper

2 tablespoons granulated sugar

¼ cup red wine vinegar

Heat the olive oil in a medium sauté pan over high heat. Add the onion and chile to the pan and stir well with a wooden spoon. Season with salt and pepper. Cook until very tender, about 10 minutes. Reduce the heat if there is any browning; you may also need to add a tablespoon or two of water if the pan gets dry. When the onion is fully cooked, turn the heat up and add the sugar. When the sugar begins to brown, carefully stir in the vinegar. Simmer until the vinegar has cooked away. Taste; there should be a balance of sweet and sour with a background of heat. Allow the mixture to cool to room temperature. Remove the chile before serving.

Keeps refrigerated up to 3 weeks. This recipe is easily doubled or tripled.

Carrot-Ginger Soup with Lime, Shrimp, and Avocado

This recipe can make a soup or a puree—depending on your mood and the occasion. For a girls' lunch in our new apartment, Jamie stuck around for longer than he was supposed to in order to show Brooke how he would serve it if he had been invited to the party. First, he'd opt for more of a puree than a soup—less potential spillage for the girls and their nice outfits. Next, he'd serve it up in appetizer-size portions in little white bowls and then create a colorful stack of shrimp and avocado. Jamie was right on all counts, and the puree was the hit of the party.

serves 6

LIME DRESSING

⅛ teaspoon ground coriander

1 teaspoon fresh lime juice

1 tablespoon extra virgin olive oil

pinch of kosher salt

a few grinds freshly ground pepper

18 fresh shrimp (21/25 count), shells on

2 cups chicken stock (more for a soup, less for a puree)

2 tablespoons extra virgin olive oil

2 teaspoons ground ginger

1 cup minced onion

6 cups grated carrots

salt and freshly ground pepper

½ cup cream (omit to make soup ultralight)

2 limes, juiced

1 avocado, cut into wedges

good-quality extra virgin olive oil for serving

Whisk together all the ingredients for the dressing and set aside.

Rinse the shrimp, with their shells on, under cold water. Bring the chicken stock to a boil in a small saucepot. Add all the shrimp at once and cover with a tight-fitting lid. Turn the heat off and let the pot stand for 5 minutes. Remove the shrimp with a slotted spoon and reserve the chicken stock. When the shrimp are cooled, peel and devein them and toss with the lime dressing.

In a medium saucepot, heat the olive oil over high heat. Add the ginger and cook until aromatic. Stir in the onion and sauté until translucent. Add the carrots and mix with a wooden spoon to coat with the oil, onion, and spice. Pour the stock into the pot through a strainer. Bring the mixture to a boil and season to taste with salt and pepper. Reduce the heat to a simmer and cook the carrots until tender, about 12 minutes.

When the carrots are tender, transfer the mixture to a blender and puree until smooth. Return the puree to the pot and stir in the cream. Bring the soup to a boil and stir in the lime juice as needed. Adjust the seasoning with salt and pepper. Transfer to a large bowl and chill in the refrigerator.

Divide the soup among 6 café-au-lait-size bowls. Garnish with 3 shrimp each, a wedge of avocado, and a drizzle of good-quality olive oil.

BIG EATS FOR THE BIG GAME

We're from the South, where certain sporting events are more celebrated than many national holidays. And the Big Game (it's always the Big Game no matter how inconsequential the match-up) is always a good excuse for a party!

Jamie's idea here is to cook up big, hearty, full-flavored food that'll either help you usher in a hangover or help you get over one. (No avant-garde cooking allowed and no precious little salads or bites of cheese!) He makes old favorites even better with a new ingredient or two—think smoked trout in your creamy chip dip and bourbon in your brownies—and whips up a Game Day cocktail to go with the washtub of beer. Chili and cornbread, shrimp and chorizo skewers, and a duo of dips cover all bases while boozy brownies split the uprights.

Beefy Southwestern Chili

Jamie's ideal Saturday: beer, football, and our baby daughter dressed in a tiny Florida Gators cheerleading uniform. All that and a really good bowl of chili. The key to this recipe is to slowly, slowly (did we say slowly?) brown the beef until it's super crispy and has great, dark color. It's all about starting off right, so also make sure to season your beef at the beginning, when it's raw, not after it's been simmering for an hour.

serves 6 to 8

canola oil

2 pounds ground beef, 85 to 90 percent lean

4 ounces bacon, chopped (optional)

2 teaspoons kosher salt

½ teaspoon freshly ground pepper

1 tablespoon chili powder

1 tablespoon ancho chile powder

1 teaspoon smoked paprika

1 medium yellow onion, diced

2 poblano or green bell peppers, diced

1 tablespoon minced garlic

2 cups canned plum tomatoes, with juice

1 pound dried black beans, soaked overnight

about 2 cups water or chicken stock

3 ears yellow corn, kernels cut from the cobs
    (about 1½ cups)

GARNISHES

cilantro

scallions

Cheddar cheese

sour cream

tortilla chips

In a large, heavy-bottomed pot, heat just enough canola oil to cover the bottom—about 2 tablespoons—over medium-high heat to the smoking point. Add the meat(s) and season well with the salt, pepper, chili and ancho powders, and paprika. Cook until well browned and all the moisture has evaporated. This process should take at least 15 minutes. Taste the meat and adjust the seasoning with salt and pepper if necessary.

Add the onion to the pan of sizzling meat and cook until softened. Next, add the peppers and continue cooking for about 5 minutes more. Stir in the garlic and cook until aromatic. Add the tomatoes. Bring the mixture to a boil and add the soaked beans.

Add water to cover the beans by about 1 inch. Bring the mixture to a simmer and add a good pinch of salt. Simmer until the beans are tender, about 1 hour. Add more water if the level of liquid drops below the beans.

Stir in the corn and continue simmering about 5 minutes more. Give a final seasoning and serve with garnishes.

In a pinch, substitute canned beans, but reduce the amount of water in the recipe. Add only enough to cover the contents of the pot by ½ inch.

CALL IN THE SUBS

Lighten Up—Substitute ground chicken or turkey in this recipe for an equally delicious but lighter meal. But since you're going to load it up with sour cream and Cheddar cheese anyway, why bother?

Jalapeño-Cheddar Cornbread

Sometimes cornbread made with 100 percent cornmeal can be like peanut butter sticking to the roof of your mouth—and we don't mean that in a good way. We love cornmeal, but we find that the best cornbread, one with a lighter crumb, is a combination of cornmeal and regular flour. You'll find that the proportions in this recipe are just right. The bread is light and fluffy (with little bits of jalapeño studded throughout!), while still managing to have a nice, coarser texture.

makes one 10-inch round pan

8 tablespoons (1 stick) unsalted butter, or ½ cup
    vegetable oil
1½ cups cornmeal
1 cup all-purpose flour
2 teaspoons kosher salt
2 teaspoons baking powder
1 teaspoon baking soda
¾ cup whole milk
1 cup buttermilk
3 large eggs
2 or 3 jalapeños, seeds and ribs removed, minced
    (about ¼ cup)
1 cup grated Cheddar cheese

Preheat the oven to 425 degrees.

Melt the butter or heat the vegetable oil in a 10-inch cast-iron skillet.

In a large bowl, combine the cornmeal, flour, salt, baking powder, and baking soda and blend well. In a separate bowl, whisk together the milk, buttermilk, and eggs. Stir the wet ingredients into the dry and gently mix together until just combined and smooth. Be very careful not to overmix. Stir in the melted butter, the jalapeños, and cheese. The batter will be thick but fluid. Pour the batter into the heated pan and bake until lightly browned and set in the center, 20 to 25 minutes.

Homemade Rosemary Potato Chips with Smoked Trout Dip

Party dips aren't typically innovative, but when we received our fifth dip tray as a wedding gift, Jamie vowed he would invent something interesting, and delicious, to fill our growing collection. You've got all your dip standards here—sour cream, chives, lemon, and mustard—but smoked trout, with its mild flavor and rich smokiness, makes it something that everyone will talk about even longer than that game-winning catch. Plus homemade potato chips? Your friends might never leave. . . .

serves 8 plus

DIP
2 medium red onions

2 cups sour cream

¼ cup whole-grain mustard

dash of Worcestershire sauce

dash of Tabasco sauce

juice of 1 lemon

5 ounces smoked trout

2 tablespoons thinly sliced fresh chives

CHIPS
6 Idaho or russet potatoes

Vegetable oil for frying

kosher salt

2 tablespoons chopped fresh rosemary

freshly ground pepper to taste

For the dip, cut the onions into slices, keeping the layers together in full rounds. Lightly oil a hot grill or cast-iron skillet and place the onions cut side down on the heated surface. Cook on one side until completely blackened and charred. Turn and char the other side. When all the onions are cooked, cool them completely and roughly chop. Combine the onions, sour cream, mustard, Worcestershire, Tabasco, lemon juice, and trout in a food processor. Puree until thoroughly mixed but not smooth. (To make the dip without a food processor, finely chop the onions and break the trout into small pieces by hand, then blend with the remaining ingredients.) Stir in the chives and adjust the seasoning to taste.

For the potato chips, slice the potatoes thin (less than ⅛ inch) on a mandoline. Place the sliced potatoes in a bowl and rinse under cool running water until the water in the bowl is clear. Drain and dry very well with paper towels or spin in a salad spinner. Heat a large pot of vegetable oil to 350 degrees. Add the potatoes in batches and fry until crisped. When they are brown, remove the potatoes from the oil and drain on paper towels. Season immediately with salt. When all the chips are cooked, toss in a bowl with the rosemary and freshly ground pepper.

CALL IN THE SUBS

Don't Force It—There's nothing like homemade potato chips, but the technique does require a little practice, so if you're running short on time, buy a good-quality, kettle-fried potato chip at the grocery store.

Shrimp and Chorizo Skewers with Roasted Garlic–White Bean Dip

This is a little more sophisticated than it has to be for the guys on game day, but they won't complain when they dip the plump, marinated shrimp and spicy chorizo into the smoky, almost whipped bean dip.

makes 24 skewers

MARINADE

2 cloves garlic, grated

1 lemon, zest grated and juiced

1 teaspoon ancho chile powder

1 tablespoon chopped fresh oregano

2 teaspoons kosher salt

¼ cup extra virgin olive oil

24 medium shrimp, peeled and deveined

4 to 6 links chorizo sausage

extra virgin olive oil

salt and freshly ground pepper

Combine all the ingredients for the marinade in a bowl and stir until the salt is dissolved. Add the shrimp and toss well to coat. Cover and refrigerate until ready to use.

Slice the chorizo into rounds, approximately the same thickness of the shrimp. Brush the excess marinade off the shrimp. Curl each shrimp around a chorizo slice and thread onto a skewer. Brush with olive oil and season lightly with salt and pepper. Cook on a hot grill or under the broiler, turning once, until the shrimp are firm and no longer opaque at the center.

Roasted Garlic–White Bean Dip

1 head garlic

2 tablespoons extra virgin olive oil, plus more
    for drizzling

kosher salt and freshly ground pepper

2 cups drained canned white beans

½ teaspoon smoked paprika

½ teaspoon sriracha hot sauce

Preheat the oven to 350 degrees.

To roast the garlic, cut the top off the whole head of garlic so the cloves are just exposed. Drizzle with a small amount of olive oil and season with salt and pepper. Wrap the garlic in a packet of aluminum foil and bake until the garlic is very aromatic and golden brown, 40 minutes.

Once the garlic is roasted and cool enough to handle, squeeze the whole head from the root to pop the roasted cloves out of the top and into a food processor. Add the beans, paprika, sriracha, and olive oil to the food processor and puree until smooth. Season to taste with salt and pepper and thin with water if needed.

CALL IN THE SUBS

No Beans? No Problem!—A quick dipping sauce is as easy as whipping up a batch of mayo (page 96), adding some paprika and cayenne, mashing one head of roasted garlic into a paste, and—like Bob Marley said—stir it up!

Mint Julep Brownies

Mint juleps are the classic Kentucky Derby cocktail made from bourbon, fresh mint, powdered sugar, and crushed ice . . . and Jamie just so happens to be obsessed with them. As an homage to his favorite drink, he created these bourbon-flavored brownies that get iced down with a mint glaze and are then garnished with a few sprigs of the green stuff. Warning: You must be a big fan of Kentucky's finest to enjoy this dessert. But if you are, it doesn't get much better than Jamie's sweet concoction of chocolate and booze!

makes 2 to 3 dozen brownies

¾ cup (1½ sticks) unsalted butter, plus more for the pan

4 ounces semisweet chocolate, bar or chips

1 cup granulated sugar

½ cup bourbon

2 large eggs, beaten

1 teaspoon vanilla extract

½ cup all-purpose flour

½ teaspoon kosher salt

ICING

4 tablespoons (½ stick) unsalted butter, at room temperature

4 ounces cream cheese

2 cups powdered sugar

1 teaspoon mint extract

1 tablespoon bourbon

GARNISH

fresh mint sprigs

Preheat the oven to 325 degrees.

Grease a 9-inch square baking pan with butter and set aside.

Combine the butter, chocolate, sugar, and bourbon in a small saucepot. Place the pot over medium heat and stir occasionally with a wooden spoon until the mixture comes to a simmer and the chocolate is melted. Remove the pan from the heat and stir in the eggs and vanilla. Fold in the flour and salt until fully incorporated. Pour the batter into the baking pan and spread evenly. Bake until a toothpick inserted into the center comes out clean, 40 to 45 minutes. Cool completely on a rack before cutting or icing.

For the icing, cream the butter and cream cheese with an electric mixer. Gradually beat in the sugar and mix until smooth. Beat in the mint extract and bourbon. Ice the cooled brownies. Cut into medium-size squares and garnish the brownie plate with sprigs of fresh mint.

THE NEXT LEVEL

While the brownies are cooling, brush them with an additional ¼ cup bourbon to boost that boozy Kentucky flavor.

TRADING ONION RINGS FOR WEDDING RINGS/BAR FOOD

Now that we're married, we feel we might have traded in our favorite fried, fatty, passable bar food—particularly those delicious onion rings—for a couple of wedding rings. Instead of hanging out in bars, we spend more time in our apartment or at our friends' homes. (We already landed the best guy/girl at the corner pub, so what's the point in milling around the tap?) No complaints about the social side of things.

However, we do miss the food—bar food—the down-and-dirty, eat-with-your-hands, indulgent bites that are usually fried, almost always include cheese, and pair perfectly with an ice-cold beer. Here, we've reinvented some classic, at-the-counter eats like chicken wings, spinach and artichoke dip, and Banana Pepper Poppers for the easygoing home cook. We've also thrown in some new favorites like Dixie Caviar and mini deep-dish pizzas (made with puff pastry). The idea here is to make food that people really want to eat. Someone's going to have to slap your hand away before you can resist another bagel chip slathered in our pimiento cheese. So while you won't find any elegance or refinement in these next pages, you will find irresistible food that makes you feel a little guilty—but it's so dang good, you just don't care. Oh, and these recipes are all set up to be made 100 percent ahead of time so there'll be no last-minute preparation or stress.

BAR FOOD MUSTS

- **FRIENDLY**—You want to make friendly food. Yep, food has a personality all its own. So you don't want anything that's too precious or gourmet. When you and a stranger pull up to a platter of Banana Pepper Poppers, we'll guarantee you that the oozing, gorgeous goodness will get a conversation started. See if that happens with salmon mousse.
- **MOBILE**—No, not that thing over the baby's bed. You need food that travels well—not across state lines, but from the kitchen bar over to the margarita station and then over to the television.
- **PACKS A FLAVOR PUNCH**—Big flavors should come in small packages when it comes to bar food. A small morsel should be loaded with just the right amount of spice, crunch, and cool.

Slice and Bake Mini Deep-Dish Pizzas

This is a really clever use of store-bought puff pastry—that ready-made, buttery dough that bakes into light, crisp layers. We cut the chilled dough into little rounds, put a slice of Roma tomato on top, sprinkle it with shredded Parmesan and basil, and pop it into a hot oven. Within minutes, you have a fabulous pizza. That's a great way to kick off your bar food feast.

makes approximately 20 pizzas

4 Roma or plum tomatoes

2 cloves garlic, thinly sliced

2 tablespoons chopped fresh basil

½ teaspoon kosher salt

freshly ground pepper to taste

1 package frozen puff pastry

4 tablespoons (½ stick) unsalted butter, melted

finely grated Parmesan cheese as needed

THE NEXT LEVEL

Make larger "pizzas" with heirloom tomatoes and fresh mozzarella. They're not as "poppable," but topped with a salad, they make a killer light lunch!

THE NEXT LEVEL

Add some favorite pizza toppings before they go into the oven—pepperoni or Italian sausage takes these pizza bites from fun to fought over.

Preheat the oven to 400 degrees.

Slice the tomatoes into rounds ¼ to ½ inch thick and gently toss in a bowl with the garlic, basil, salt, and pepper. Leave the tomatoes to marinate while you work with the dough.

It is best to work with puff pastry while it is partially frozen—as it warms, the dough softens and becomes greasy—so take one sheet out of the freezer at a time. Punch out rounds of the pastry dough with a round cookie or biscuit cutter or use a knife and trace around the rim of a glass or small bowl. The rounds of dough should be ¼ inch wider in diameter than the tomatoes (this makes your "pizza crust"). Arrange the rounds of dough on an aluminum-foil-lined baking sheet, leaving 1 inch between the pieces. Brush the tops of the rounds with the melted butter and sprinkle with Parmesan cheese.

Remove the tomatoes from their marinade and pat dry with paper towels, but leave any basil or garlic that clings to the tomato. Place a slice of tomato in the center of each round of dough and cover with more Parmesan cheese. Bake until the dough rises up around the tomatoes and browns slightly, about 12 minutes. Serve warm.

Buttermilk Fried Chicken Wings and Blue Cheese Dip

Instead of Buffalo-style, these are Southern-style wings coated in buttermilk, tossed in a flour mixture of garlic, cayenne, thyme, and marjoram, and fried up extra crispy. If you're not Southern—and your crib was not within crawling distance of a cast-iron Dutch oven or deep fryer—you might be intimidated by pots of hot oil. Don't be! We walk you through the process, step by step, and the end result is skin with such an amazing crunch that you won't want to dunk the wings in a butter and Tabasco bath.

serves 12 plus

10 pounds chicken wing pieces

1 tablespoon Tabasco or other vinegar-based hot sauce

1 to 2 quarts buttermilk

3 cups all-purpose flour

½ teaspoon dried thyme

½ teaspoon dried marjoram

1 teaspoon powdered onion

1 teaspoon powdered garlic

1 teaspoon cayenne

2 tablespoons kosher salt, plus more as needed

2 teaspoons freshly ground pepper

Vegetable oil for frying

Combine the chicken, hot sauce, and enough buttermilk to cover the chicken completely in a bowl and mix well. Leave on the countertop for 1 to 3 hours, or refrigerate for up to 24 hours. Just before frying, pour the chicken into a colander and let drain.

In a large bowl, mix the flour with the dried spices and seasonings. One by one add the chicken pieces and make sure to coat well with flour on all sides. Leave them in the bowl with the excess flour while you wait on the oil.

Fill a large pot with oil to a depth of 4 to 6 inches and heat to 350 degrees (you can check the temperature with your candy thermometer).

Grab each piece of chicken and slap it back and forth between your hands a few times to knock off the excess flour before slipping it into the oil. As the wings go into the oil in batches, try to maintain a temperature of 325 to 350 degrees. Cook until golden, 8 to 10 minutes. Remove to a rack to drain and season immediately with salt. Cool for a few minutes and serve with Blue Cheese Dip (page 188).

TECHNIQUE TIP

Cooking too many wings at once causes the oil temperature to drop, which will keep your wings from becoming golden and crispy. The number of wings you cook at a time will depend on the size of the pot you use, but it should never be more than one-third full of chicken.

Blue Cheese Dip

Did you ever know that blue cheese dip was this simple? The good stuff has a creamy base, some bite (from lemon juice), a delicate onion flavor, and a generous amount of cheese. Make ours and never again request extra from your delivery boy.

makes 2 cups

8 ounces sour cream
6 ounces blue cheese, crumbled
1 tablespoon minced fresh chives
2 teaspoons fresh lemon juice
kosher salt and freshly ground pepper to taste
a few dashes of hot sauce, such as sriracha

Combine all the ingredients in a bowl and mix well. Store in the refrigerator until ready to serve. The dip is best when prepared a few hours to a day before serving.

Panisse (Chickpea Fries)

Although these very addictive little snacks hail from the south of France—think of them as steak-fry-sized polenta cakes—we first enjoyed them at Nizza in Hell's Kitchen. (Our Manhattan rent ate up our south of France vacation money.) Making the panisse batter is as easy as stirring up a pot of polenta (or grits)—it's all about you and the whisk. While you can deep-fry these in vegetable oil, as Jamie's recipe suggests, it's not necessary. Brooke prefers to pour about ½ inch olive oil into her cast-iron skillet set over a high flame and fry them (just not DEEP-fry them) until golden brown. Instead of cleaning up a big vat of dirty oil, Brooke pours herself another glass of white and pretends they did book that flight to Nice.

serves 6

2 tablespoons unsalted butter
2 cups whole milk
2 cups water
1 teaspoon kosher salt, plus more as needed
2 branches fresh thyme
1 bay leaf
½ cup dry polenta or cornmeal
½ cup chickpea flour, plus more for dusting
3 to 6 cups vegetable oil for frying
1 recipe Aioli (page 96)

Combine the butter, milk, water, salt, thyme, and bay leaf in a large pot and bring the mixture to a boil. When the liquid reaches a boil, mix the polenta and chickpea flour and whisk it into the pot. Add the mixture very gradually to avoid lumps or use an immersion blender instead of the whisk. Cook, stirring occasionally to keep the bottom from burning, over low heat until well thickened and tender, about 30 minutes. Remove the thyme and bay leaf.

Adjust the seasoning as needed and spread in a thin layer on a baking sheet lined with plastic wrap. Chill for 2 hours, until firm.

Fill a medium pot with approximately 4 cups vegetable oil, or to a depth of 2 to 3 inches. Using your candy/deep-fry thermometer to measure the temperature, bring the oil to 350 degrees. Cut the panisse into strips the size of french fries and roll each one in chickpea flour. Pat off the excess flour and fry in batches until golden brown. Drain on paper towels and salt immediately. Serve with aioli.

TECHNIQUE TIP

If you don't have a candy thermometer and want to know when it's time to drop your panisse in the pan, carefully drop a small piece of bread or a pinch of flour in the oil. If it bubbles rapidly the moment it hits the oil, then the oil is ready to fry. If the bubbling is slow or delayed, allow the oil a few more minutes to heat.

ON THE LIGHTER (AND CLEANER!) SIDE

Cut the cooled polenta into steak-fry-size pieces and arrange ½ inch apart on a greased aluminum-foil-lined baking sheet. Bake at 500 degrees until golden and crispy on the edges, 4 to 6 minutes.

SOUTHERN ANTIPASTI PLATTER

Nothing says down-home and delicious like a well-worn cutting board crowded with slivers of meat, bits of cheese, and little bowls filled with pickles and spreads. The Italians, with their innate sense of style and culinary savvy, have mastered the casual first course of the meal (*antipasto,* literally meaning "before the pasta," since pasta is always served before the protein in their succession of courses) with a colorful sampling of local cured meats and cheeses and any other small nibble that can be eaten with one hand while the other is occupied with a drink. We're both kind of in love with this "sampler platter" notion, so we adapted it to include our favorite Southern starters. Instead of Parmigiano, we offer our pimiento cheese. Since prosciutto can be expensive, we opt for smoked ham. And instead of briny olives, we go for pickles with a real kick. Put this antipasti platter in the right spot, because the party will surround it.

Foodie Favors (aka Adult Party Favors)

Party favors aren't just for kids. If you want your friends to remember your latest get-together, send them home with something a little special.

1. Homemade Seasoned Salts—Follow Jamie's awesome seasoned salt recipes on pages 61 to 63. Pour into brushed steel or clear glass spice containers and wave good-bye to your guests with a cooking suggestion or two.
2. Mini Booze Bottles—Send them home with mini bottles of spirits and your signature house cocktail recipe on a 3 x 5 card that's tied around the neck of the bottle.
3. Chocolate—Homemade chocolates are a snap to assemble. Just melt chocolate discs (from your local baking supply store) and then pour them into shaped molds. Stick the molds in the freezer for an hour and voilà! Orange rinds and dried apricots can also take a dunk into the chocolate bath. With all your beautiful chocolate creations, your friends might start calling you Lady Godiva!
4. Cookie/Cake/Brownie Mix in a Jelly Jar—From the *Joy of Cooking* to Duncan Hines, all baked goods recipes begin with the sentence "Combine dry ingredients." Why not mix together the cocoa, flour, and seasonings, pour it all into a pretty jelly jar, and then provide your friends with your signature pound cake recipe on a 3 x 5 card? Tie a pretty bow or fasten a handsome piece of fabric around the top of the jar and call it a day. Oh, and you can also call yourself a mini Martha Stewart when you layer the ingredients like colored sand.

Dixie Caviar

Our city friends cock an eyebrow and ask in low, curious tones, "But, really, what IS it?" when we trot out our Dixie caviar. But this is no cover-up. Quite simply, Dixie caviar is a lesson in Southern chic—knowing how to dress up the little you've got and make it look and taste enviably delicious. A seventy-five-cent can of black-eyed peas and a cup of corn sub in for three-hundred-dollars-an-ounce fish eggs. Spot-on seasoning with garlic, red pepper flakes, and vinegar does the rest. We call it a little bit country, a little bit classy.

serves 6 to 8

1 shallot, minced

2 cloves garlic, minced

¼ teaspoon red pepper flakes

¼ cup white wine vinegar

1 tablespoon granulated sugar

2 tablespoons extra virgin olive oil

one 15- to 19-ounce can black-eyed peas, or 1½
    cups cooked fresh black-eyed peas, drained

1 cup corn kernels, cooked

1 red bell pepper, minced

2 tablespoons chopped fresh parsley

kosher salt and freshly ground pepper

Combine the shallot, garlic, red pepper flakes, vinegar, and sugar in a small sauté pan. Bring the mixture to a simmer, stir to dissolve the sugar, and remove from the heat immediately. Transfer the mixture to a large bowl and stir in the olive oil. Add the remaining ingredients, blend well, and season to taste with salt and pepper. Refrigerate the mixture for 1 hour, allowing the flavors to hang out and get to know one another.

Pimiento Cheese

Brooke landed in The New York Times *when she began selling every Southerner's favorite spread of roasted red peppers and Cheddar cheese. Murray's Cheese on Bleecker Street was her outpost, and after the article ran in the paper, demand quickly outstripped her supply. New Yorkers couldn't get enough! The secret's in the sriracha, so don't even think about calling in the subs.*

serves 1 if that one is Brooke or Jamie; otherwise, serves 8

1 pound red bell peppers

1 tablespoon extra virgin olive oil

1 teaspoon kosher salt, plus more as needed

freshly ground pepper to taste

1 pound Cheddar cheese (sharp or mild), grated

4 ounces cream cheese, at room temperature

½ cup mayonnaise

pinch of granulated sugar

sriracha hot sauce to taste

plain bagel chips or pita chips

VIETNAMESE SECRET SAUCE

Sriracha has gained a cult following over the past couple of years, heralded everywhere from *Saveur* to *Good Housekeeping.* The mixture of sun-ripened chiles and garlic can be found on almost every restaurant table in New York City's Chinatown because of its subtle, sweet heat. If you can't find the red squeeze bottle with the green cap at your local grocery or specialty food store, run to your computer and order a bottle online now! Huy Fong Foods, Inc.—www.huyfong.com.

Preheat the oven to 450 degrees.

Toss the peppers in a large bowl with the olive oil, salt, and pepper. Lay the peppers out on a baking sheet and roast in the oven until the skin is blistered and the flesh tender, about 20 minutes. Remove from the oven and set aside. Or place the peppers directly over a high flame on the stovetop or a grill. Turn occasionally until the skin is completely blackened on all sides.

When the peppers are cool enough to handle, peel them by pulling away the skin in large pieces; you may need to use the edge of a knife to scrape away the more stubborn bits of skin. Tear the peppers open and remove all the seeds. Do not rinse the peppers; it's better to leave a little skin on the peppers than to wash away some of the flavor.

Place the peppers in a food processor and pulse until well chopped but not smooth. Small chunks of pepper should remain. Remove the peppers to a large mixing bowl. Stir in the Cheddar and cream cheese. Beat vigorously with a wooden spoon until well combined. Stir in the mayo, some salt, pepper, a pinch of sugar, and the sriracha (start with just a teaspoon). We really like sriracha here because of its subtle sweetness and assertive heat. It adds a complexity to this dip that a regular hot sauce cannot bring. Serve with chips.

Pickles

For the down-home, homemade stuff, see Jamie's pickles on page 207.

Wickles Pickles

Alabama-made goodness. These are a must for any decent pantry. While it's always a blast to make things from scratch, we eat these faster than Jamie could make them, so we typically order by the case (www.wickles .com).

Sliced Ham

Since this won't be served with bread or mayo to cover it up, you need to search out a really good ham. Go to the deli counter and ask to taste a few different types. Boar's Head is a trustworthy brand that is fairly easy to find. Nicer grocery stores might carry hams made by natural producers such as Niman Ranch and Applegate Farms.

Banana Pepper Poppers

How many stuffed jalapeños can you really "pop"? They're too spicy and the pepper itself overwhelms the flavor of the cheese. Banana peppers, on the other hand, are much milder—with more of a sweet pickle flavor— and are infinitely more "poppable." We first came up with this recipe as a way to help Jamie's uncle Jay clear out his garden. It was midsummer and his well-tended plot was overflowing with banana peppers. What to do? Bundle together sharp Cheddar and cream cheese, stuff the peppers, coat them in well-seasoned breadcrumbs, and fry them. Even though we'd seen this on bar menus before, it never occurred to us how easy it would be to do at home. One bite of the banana poppers oozing with melted cheese, giving off their sweet heat and the gentle scent of coriander, and we were hooked.

makes 12 poppers

12 banana peppers

2 ounces cream cheese, at room temperature

1 cup grated Cheddar cheese

¼ teaspoon ground coriander

1 tablespoon chopped fresh cilantro

½ to 2 teaspoons sriracha hot sauce to taste

1 cup all-purpose flour

3 large eggs, beaten

2 cups plain dry breadcrumbs

canola or vegetable oil as needed

COOLING DOWN YOUR HOT POPPERS

Want to make sure that perfect golden crust sticks to your peppers? Giving the pepper time to rest in the fridge before frying will help the crust hang on.

Cut a slit down one side of each pepper. Gently open the peppers and scrape out the seeds with a small spoon. Blend together the cream cheese, Cheddar, coriander, cilantro, and hot sauce. Transfer the cheese mixture to a sturdy plastic bag and cut off the corner. Squeeze the cheese filling into the peppers through the slits. Press the peppers back together to close.

Set out 3 shallow bowls. Fill the first with flour, the second with beaten eggs, and the third with breadcrumbs. Working one at a time, roll the filled peppers in flour, dip into the eggs, then coat with breadcrumbs. Transfer the peppers to a pan and arrange in a single layer. Refrigerate for at least 30 minutes before cooking.

Fill a wide pot with oil to a depth of 2 to 3 inches. Heat the oil to 350 degrees or until a piece of bread sizzles when dropped into the oil. Fry 3 or 4 peppers at a time until golden brown on all sides. Remove the cooked peppers to a plate lined with paper towels to drain and cool slightly before serving.

TIP

On the Lighter Side—If you're not up for a frying adventure, you can skip the breading and bake the stuffed peppers "naked" in a preheated oven at 450 degrees until melted and gooey.

Spinach-Artichoke Dip

Brooke will go to a sports bar with Jamie and watch a lap or two of NASCAR, but there's one stipulation—the sports bar in question must have an amazing spinach and artichoke dip. Because only about two downtown bars are up to the task, we end up staying home and making our own. We'll say this: once you've enjoyed a bubbling pan of the good stuff, you'll never be able to eat the gummy mess again. The trick is the roux. The butter and flour mixture needs to be stirred with a wooden spoon until it's supersmooth and has taken on a nice tan color, then you can add all the delicious bits, which will be the base for all the spinach, artichoke, and cheesy goodness in the pot. The final touch is a generous sprinkling of provolone, Jack, and mozzarella.

serves 6

4 tablespoons (½ stick) unsalted butter

2 cloves garlic, grated

¼ cup grated onion

¼ cup all-purpose flour

one 6-ounce bag spinach leaves, cleaned and trimmed

1½ cups milk

kosher salt and freshly ground pepper

6 ounces marinated artichoke hearts, drained and sliced

1 cup grated cheese, provolone, Monterey Jack, mozzarella, or a mixture

¼ cup finely grated Parmesan cheese (optional for a final, salty flourish on the finished pan of dip)

Preheat the oven to broil.

Place a wide sauté pan or heavy pot over medium heat and add the butter, garlic, and onion. Cook gently until the mixture sizzles and no longer smells of raw onion. Stir in the flour. The mixture will thicken immediately, but continue stirring until it takes on a tan color. Add the spinach and cook until wilted, being sure to scrape the sides of the pan so the flour mixture doesn't burn. When the spinach is completely tender, add the milk and stir vigorously so there are no lumps of flour. The mixture should be very thick. Simmer a few moments while you adjust the seasoning with salt and pepper. Mix the sliced artichoke hearts into the mixture and transfer to an 8-inch square baking dish. Scatter the grated cheese over the top and broil until golden brown and bubbly. Finish with the Parmesan, if using.

THE NEXT LEVEL

Be sure to buy good-quality artichoke hearts. We typically skip the canned or jarred varieties and head for the prepared foods department at a grocery store like Whole Foods. There we scoop the best-looking artichokes from the salad bar and bring them home for the ultimate party starter.

Chocolate-Guinness and Butterscotch Pudding

This subtly boozy dessert makes a dramatic, professional-looking presentation but doesn't require quitting your day job and getting a "grande diplome" from Cordon Bleu. Preparing it in a clear dish or a juice glass lets everyone see the sweet, golden layer of butterscotch pudding as it rests on top of the deep, rich chocolate and Guinness. Then again, there's something to be said for surprises—serve these up in ceramic dishes and watch everyone's eyes light up as they discover the spoon-licking layers of this dessert. Either way, it's guaranteed that the bowls will leave the table clean.

serves 8

one 14.9-ounce can Guinness

½ cup whole milk

2 large egg yolks

2 tablespoons cornstarch

½ cup semisweet chocolate chips

BUTTERSCOTCH PUDDING

2 tablespoons cornstarch

1½ cups whole milk

1 large egg

1 large egg yolk

2 tablespoons unsalted butter

¾ cup light brown sugar

1 teaspoon kosher salt

1 tablespoon unsalted butter, cold

½ teaspoon vanilla extract

2 teaspoons bourbon (optional)

Pour the Guinness into a small saucepot and bring to a boil. Reduce the heat and cook at a simmer until 1 cup remains.

While the Guinness simmers, add the milk, egg yolks, and cornstarch to a medium bowl and whisk to combine. Slowly whisk the reduced Guinness into the bowl. Return the mixture to the saucepot and place on the stove over medium heat. Stir constantly with a wooden spoon or spatula until the mixture returns to a simmer, at which point it should be well thickened. Remove the pot from the heat, add the chocolate chips, and continue stirring until completely melted.

Divide the still-warm pudding among 8 custard cups, 8 small bowls, or about 14 shot glasses, filling each just halfway. Set aside to cool while you prepare the butterscotch pudding.

Place a fine-mesh strainer and clean bowl next to the stove.

In a separate bowl, combine the cornstarch with ¼ cup of the milk and whisk until smooth. Whisk in the egg and egg yolk.

Melt 2 tablespoons butter in a medium saucepot; add the brown sugar and salt and cook until bubbling and slightly darkened. Remove the sugar from the heat and carefully whisk in the remaining 1¼ cups milk. Switch to a wooden spoon and add the egg mixture; return the pot to medium heat and stir constantly until thickened.

When thickened and bubbling, immediately pour the pudding through the strainer into the waiting bowl. Stir in the cold butter, vanilla, and bourbon, if using, while the pudding is still hot. Press a piece of plastic wrap directly on the surface of the pudding to prevent a skin from forming. Chill thoroughly.

To assemble, fill each of the cups of Guinness pudding the remainder of the way with the butterscotch and place in the refrigerator to firm before serving, about 2 hours. If not serving immediately, cover with plastic wrap while storing in the refrigerator, up to 1 week.

WHEN YOUR BACKYARD IS THE BIGGEST ROOM IN THE HOUSE

We're young and kinda poor. To top it off, we live in New York City. This means that our bathroom is the size of a Porta-Potty and the rest of our apartment—kitchen, living room, bedroom, and nursery—is approximately the size of Fergie's shoe closet. Entertaining more than four people can get a little hairy.

While we want to believe that when we move to the 'burbs, we'll be able to entertain seventy-five at a clip in our living room, the truth is, our backyard will most likely be the biggest "room" in the house. The best place to entertain will be on the grass, beneath the shade of an oak tree with a bluebird or two as party crashers. That's why we think it's so important to have a great roster of outdoor eats and "grillables" in your cooking repertoire. You need a cold salad or two (make sure to refer back to our "Moveable Feast" chapter for a big list of these) and then a whole bunch of easy things to throw on the grill. As a new host/ess, you'll get even more points if you get your friends involved in the meal—have one grill the chicken while another assembles the s'mores.

Farmers' Market Slaw

There seem to be a lot of gimmicky slaws out there now-adays with crunchy noodles, nuts, and the like. Ours couldn't be simpler. Its success relies solely on great farmers' market vegetables that have been shredded (or sliced on the mandoline) and tossed with the lightest of dressings. Remember—you don't want your slaw to compete with your hot dog, barbecue chicken, or pork butt; you want it to be a light, fresh accompaniment.

serves 6

1 teaspoon caraway seeds, crushed

¼ teaspoon granulated garlic

pinch of cayenne

2 teaspoons celery seeds or celery salt

3 tablespoons cider vinegar

½ head red cabbage (about 12 ounces)

2 medium carrots (about 4 ounces), grated

1 zucchini

1 yellow squash

1 red bell pepper

kosher salt and freshly ground pepper to taste

granulated sugar

2 to 4 tablespoons mayonnaise

ESSENTIAL EQUIPMENT

Mandoline or Box Grater—A mandoline is a great tool for preparing slaw, for it slices vegetables precisely and extremely thin. If you don't have one (though you should have followed our Kitchen Registry and zapped one at the wedding store), a sharp knife and a standard box grater will still get the job done just fine.

In a small bowl, combine the caraway, garlic, cayenne, celery seeds, and vinegar. This will allow the flavors of the dressing to develop while you prepare the vegetables.

Cut the half head of cabbage into quarters and trim away any of the thick core. Then slice each piece as thin as possible. The cabbage can also be shredded using a mandoline or food processor. After finely shredding the cabbage and grating the carrots, cut the zucchini and squash into a thin julienne using a mandoline. Avoid cutting the seeds in the center; use only the skin and firm flesh. Peel the pepper with a vegetable peeler, remove the seeds and ribs, and cut into very thin strips.

Mix all the vegetables together in a colander and toss with salt, pepper, and a pinch of sugar. Set this in the sink with a weighted bowl on top and leave for 30 minutes to extract the excess water from the vegetables. After draining, squeeze to extract all the remaining water possible from the vegetables and place in a clean bowl. Add the dressing and mix well. Stir in just enough mayonnaise to bind and season with salt and pepper. The flavor will improve considerably over the first few hours. Keep covered in the refrigerator for up to 7 days. Remove from the fridge 1 hour before serving when possible.

PEPPER PEELING PET PEEVE

When peppers cook or take a long bath in a mixture with acid (vinegar), their skins toughen, leaving bits that are difficult to chew or wind up stuck in your teeth. Peeling peppers before cooking or marinating eliminates this problem and also gives you thinner, nicer-looking strips of pepper for your slaw.

Warm Tomato Salad with Bacon Vinaigrette and Goat Cheese

When you live with a chef, this is the kind of dish you end up with after cleaning out the fridge midsummer. After Jamie came across a hunk of leftover goat cheese and a few strips of raw bacon on the bottom shelf, he jetted a few blocks north to the farmers' market with a seasonal ingredient list and an idea. He thought it'd be fun to make a warm tomato salad for a change; Brooke and their sixth-floor neighbors couldn't have agreed more!

serves 6 to 8

2 pounds heirloom tomatoes, assorted shapes
    and colors
sea salt or kosher salt and freshly ground pepper
    to taste
4 ounces sliced bacon, chopped
1 shallot, minced
2 tablespoons red wine vinegar, plus more
    as needed
2 tablespoons extra virgin olive oil
4 ounces fresh goat cheese
fresh basil leaves as needed

Trim away the tough core around the stem of each tomato and cut the tomatoes into ½-inch-thick slices. Arrange the slices in a single layer in a tightly overlapping, concentric pattern in a large gratin or casserole dish. Season with salt and pepper.

Place the bacon in a medium sauté pan and cook over medium-high heat until lightly colored and sizzling. Add the shallot and cook until translucent, about 1 minute. Remove from the heat and deglaze the pan with the vinegar. Whisk in the olive oil. Season to taste with salt and pepper and add more vinegar if the dressing tastes too oily.

Preheat the oven to 500 degrees or heat the broiler.

Pour the bacon vinaigrette over the tomatoes in the baking dish. Crumble the goat cheese into bits and scatter over the tomatoes. Place the pan on the top shelf of the oven and bake until the cheese is just softened, only 2 minutes or so. Tear the basil into bits and distribute over the top. Serve warm.

THE SPICE OF LIFE

A variety of tomatoes in this salad is what makes it great. You'll know the time is right to make this salad when you go to your farmers' market or roadside stand and see tomatoes in all the colors of the rainbow. Some of our favorites: green Zebra, purple Cherokee, Brandy-wine (red and yellow), and Early Girl.

BBQ'd Chicken Halves

Anyone can douse drumsticks, breasts, and thighs with sugary bottled sauce and then throw everything onto a smoking grill. In fact, Brooke's dad did this for years while she and her sisters feigned excitement and secretly fed the family poodle charred, rubbery chicken beneath the table. Barbecue Night simply translated into Mom's-Night-Out-With-a-Glass-of-Pink-Zin, and it didn't matter how bad the food was for the members of the family left behind. For the sake of young husbands and dads everywhere, Jamie's written a barbecue chicken recipe that will turn out plump, juicy birds thanks to his bourbon brine. Basically the chicken absorbs the brine and then, when the meat is cooked, some of the liquid remains trapped inside the muscle fiber. All that osmosis business means one thing—the best, juiciest chicken you've ever eaten!

serves 6 plus

BRINE

3 quarts water

½ cup kosher salt

¾ cup brown sugar

1 whole head garlic, cut in half

½ cup bourbon (optional)

6 branches fresh thyme

1 bay leaf

1 teaspoon black peppercorns

4 cups ice

3 whole chickens, split in half (2 to 3 pounds each)

Creole Seasoning (page 63)

To make the brine, combine everything except the ice in a saucepot and heat on the stove until the salt and sugar are dissolved. Place the ice in a large bowl. Pour the heated solution over the ice and stir to cool rapidly.

Place the chickens in a large container and pour in the brine. Make sure the chicken is completely covered. You may add up to 3 more cups of water to cover completely if necessary. Leave the chicken to brine in the refrigerator or in a cool place with bags of ice added to keep the temperature below 40 degrees. Brine overnight but not more than 36 hours.

Remove the chicken from the brine, pat dry, and lay out in a single layer on a rack. Lightly season the chicken on both sides with the spice mix. Preheat a grill, smoker, or the oven to 250 degrees and cook the chicken, turning occasionally, until a thermometer registers 160 degrees at the thigh, approximately 80 to 90 minutes.

TECHNIQUE TIP

Slow and Low—That's the magic formula for tender, juicy barbecue. Long cooking and very low heat turns out the most succulent meat this side of Memphis. And if you're missing the sauce, brush on a good, thick layer of your favorite type in the last 15 minutes of cooking or serve the sauce on the side.

Grilled Swordfish Medallions in Lemon, Capers, and Olive Oil

This just kinda sings of the Mediterranean. The trick is marinating the swordfish after you grill it. That way, the fish warms the oil, drawing out all of the flavor from the herbs and spices. By the time you set the table and pop your first bottle of Vermentino, you have tender, beautifully perfumed slices of swordfish.

serves 4 to 6

1½ cups extra virgin olive oil, plus more as needed

2 tablespoons capers in brine, drained

3 cloves garlic, sliced

2 branches fresh marjoram

2 branches fresh thyme

1 teaspoon red pepper flakes

1 lemon, ½ thinly sliced, ½ juiced

1 tablespoon kosher salt

1 teaspoon coriander seeds, ground

1 teaspoon fennel seeds, ground

1 teaspoon black peppercorns, ground

1 pound swordfish loin, trimmed and sliced ¼ inch thick

Combine the olive oil, capers, garlic, marjoram, thyme, red pepper, and lemon slices and juice in a heatproof container—a large gratin dish is perfect.

In a separate bowl, combine the salt, coriander, fennel, and black pepper.

Preheat a grill or cast-iron grill pan to high. Brush the medallions of swordfish with olive oil (not the mixture that is sitting aside in the heatproof dish, just plain olive oil) and season lightly with the spice mixture. Place the pan of seasoned olive oil next to the grill. Quickly cook the fish on both sides so it is well marked but not quite cooked through. Carefully remove the fish from the grill and place in the seasoned olive oil bath. Allow the fish to marinate for at least 30 minutes before serving.

Serve the swordfish slightly warm.

THE SPICE OF LIFE

The marinating oil and fresh lemon juice makes an excellent dressing for lettuces and blanched or grilled vegetables (think green beans and asparagus).

Chicken-Apple Sausages with Celery and Apple Slaw

When Jamie took a turn on Food Network, the judges gave him a mystery basket of ingredients and crazy time constraints. In the time it takes most people to boil a pot of water, he transformed plain ground chicken and a couple of apples into a juicy entrée topped with a beautiful, bright, crunchy salad. There might not be a clock ticking in your kitchen, but this recipe will definitely be a hit at your judges' table (even if that's a picnic table in your backyard). This recipe does not double or triple exactly—the seasoning mixture can season up to 3 pounds ground chicken. So double the ingredients (onion through oregano) for 5 pounds of meat or simply increase each slightly for 3 to 4 pounds.

serves 4

SAUSAGE
about 4 tablespoons extra virgin olive oil
¾ cup finely minced or grated onion
5 cloves garlic, minced
kosher salt
1 large apple, grated (Braeburn, Honeycrisp, or Golden Delicious)
scant ½ teaspoon smoked paprika
scant ½ teaspoon fennel seeds, crushed
¼ teaspoon red pepper flakes
½ teaspoon plus a pinch dried oregano
¼ cup bourbon
2 pounds ground chicken

SLAW
1 apple, cut into thin julienne
2 ribs celery, thinly sliced
1 teaspoon Dijon mustard

1 tablespoon extra virgin olive oil
Fresh lemon juice
kosher salt and freshly ground pepper

toasted bread for serving

To prepare the sausage, add 2 tablespoons of the olive oil in a medium sauté pan over medium heat. Add the onion, garlic, and 1 teaspoon salt and sweat until very tender but not browned. Add the grated apple along with its juices and the spices and oregano. Cook this mixture until dry. Deglaze the pan with the bourbon and reduce until the pan is dry again. Cool the seasoning mixture.

Place the ground chicken in a large bowl, stir in the seasoning mixture, and stir with a wooden spoon to combine thoroughly.

Form the seasoned chicken mixture into the desired shapes (patties or links). Heat a nonstick or cast-iron skillet over medium heat. Add the remaining 2 tablespoons olive oil and brown the sausages in the pan. Transfer to a rack and bake in a 350-degree oven to finish cooking through. If you have a grill, cook the sausages over medium-high heat until cooked through.

For the slaw, combine the apple, celery, mustard, and olive oil in a small bowl. Mix well and season to taste with lemon juice, salt, and pepper.

Serve the cooked sausages on top of toasted bread (preferably sourdough) with the apple-celery slaw on top.

Corn Salad

We call it corn salad, but this is really the perfect dip for tortilla chips. Think of it as the more manageable version of your favorite Mexican corn on the cob smothered in queso fresco and sprinkled with ancho chile powder. But instead of having to pick corn kernels out of your teeth and hunt down queso fresco (it's even hard to find in our gourmet food stores in the West Village), you can enjoy this low-maintenance salad with staples from your fridge. No dental floss required!

serves 4

4 ears corn
1 tablespoon extra virgin olive oil
kosher salt and freshly ground pepper to taste
¼ teaspoon paprika
1 teaspoon mayonnaise
pinch of cayenne, plus more as needed
2 teaspoons fresh lemon juice, plus more as needed
3 tablespoons finely grated Pecorino Romano

Shuck the corn and rub with the oil, salt, and pepper. Cook on a hot grill or in a 450-degree oven until the kernels are browned or slightly charred. Set aside to cool.

Combine the paprika, mayonnaise, cayenne, and lemon juice in a medium bowl and mix well. With a very sharp knife, cut the corn kernels from the cobs. Stir the kernels and dressing together until the kernels are thoroughly coated. Stir in the cheese. Season to taste, adding more salt, pepper, cayenne, or lemon juice as desired. Serve with tortilla chips.

PICKLE BAR

Pickling vegetables was once more *have to* than *want to*. When summer's garden grew more than you and the neighbors could eat, two options remained:

1. Turn the hard-wrought veggies into compost, *or*
2. Break out the jars and put up for winter.

Then came airplanes and refrigerated trucks. Next, everyone had freezers in their homes. Innovation and technology coupled with the indomitable American spirit to deliver whatever we wanted, even when whatever we wanted meant "fresh" asparagus in January. Who cared if the green stalks on our dinner table were flown in from Peru?

Times have changed. Everything old is new again and farmers' markets and local produce have become all the rage. Guess what else is popular? Pickled veggies. But pickled cukes and cauliflower offer much more than a trendy way to prove to all your friends that you're a dedicated locavore. Pickling veggies means creating textures and flavors in everyday vegetables that would otherwise be impossible. Tart, sweet, spicy, and crunchy—cucumbers never had it so good.

There are two types of pickles—quick pickles and the ones just like Grandma used to make, those that sat on the shelf for weeks or months before you could think of cracking the seal. All of these recipes below can be ready to eat within twenty-four hours. But if you want the old-fashioned experience, everything here, plus Chow-Chow (page 209), can be put up in sterilized jars and stored in a cool, dark place for months. These jarred pickles make a great (and inexpensive!) hostess gift for when you attend summer dinners or barbecues.

Pickled Mushrooms

Best for fancy little mushrooms like chanterelles or Asian varieties like hon-shimeji.

makes 1 pound

½ cup white wine or cider vinegar
2 tablespoons kosher salt
2 tablespoons granulated sugar
1 small dried chile, or ¼ teaspoon red pepper flakes
1 teaspoon coriander seeds (optional)
1 pound mushrooms

In a small saucepot, bring all the ingredients except the mushrooms to a boil.

Cut any larger mushrooms in halves or quarters to make bite-size pieces. Quickly rinse the mushrooms if necessary and thoroughly pat dry. Place the cleaned mushrooms in a small plastic, ceramic, or stainless-steel container. Pour the boiling pickling mixture over the mushrooms and refrigerate for at least 12 hours. They will keep up to 2 weeks.

Bread and Butter Pickles

Bread and Butter are Jamie's favorite breed of pickle. Always made from sliced cucumbers and heated in their brine, they're also the fastest to make. Brooke loves them because they're sweet and crunchy—plus, you can make them as spicy as you want (a little jalapeño mixed in the brine does the trick for us).

serves 12 plus, or serves 2 for a few weeks

3 pounds Kirby cucumbers, sliced

1 yellow onion, diced

1 green bell pepper, diced

1 red jalapeño, diced

½ cup kosher salt

4 cups granulated sugar

2 teaspoons ground turmeric

2 tablespoons mustard seeds

1 teaspoon celery seeds

3 cups cider vinegar

2 cups white wine vinegar

Toss the cucumbers, onion, peppers, and salt in a colander. Place the colander in a bowl and place another bowl on top of the vegetables. Fill the top bowl with heavy cans and refrigerate for 3 hours.

Mix the sugar, turmeric, mustard seeds, celery seeds, and vinegars in a stainless-steel pot and bring to a boil. Press the vegetables in the colander to extract any liquid and add to the simmering pot. Wait for the mixture to return to a boil.

Pour the boiling-hot mixture into sterilized jars and fill to within ¼ to ½ inch of the tops. Wipe the rims and seal. Cool, check the seals, label, and store in a cool, dark, dry place. Let stand a minimum of 24 hours before serving.

Instead of jarring, these pickles can be cooled and stored in the refrigerator in a plastic or glass container with a tight-fitting lid and kept for 6 weeks, if they last that long!

HOT! HOT! HOT!

Sterilizing jars before filling with pickles ensures your veggies will be safe to eat 6 months from the day that you make them. Improper canning can result in the growth of bacteria inside the jar, specifically botulism, which if ingested is sure to put a damper on your day. Sterilize jars and lids by bringing a large pot of water to a boil and placing the jars and lids in the water. Make sure that both are completely covered by the water and leave them to boil for 6 minutes. Any tongs or other tools used to handle the jars should be boiled as well. Remove the jars and lids from the water and place on a clean surface to fill. When filling, make certain your hands never touch the rims or interior of the jars or lids. Hands on the outside only. Everything else should be handled with sterilized tongs.

Pickled Carrots, Cucumbers, and Radishes (Bánh Mì Style)

The simple crisp pickles that you find on Vietnamese sandwiches. This mixture is also the perfect topping for our Spicy Beef Salad (page 80).

serves 4 to 6

1 cup thinly julienned or coarsely grated carrots
1 hothouse or English cucumber or 2 medium Kirby
     cucumbers, cut in half, seeded, and cut into
     half-moons ¼ inch thick (2 cups)
1 cup thinly sliced radishes (optional)
1 tablespoon kosher salt
2 tablespoons granulated sugar

BRINE
5 tablespoons granulated sugar
1 cup distilled white vinegar
1 cup water

Combine the carrots, cucumber, and radishes, if using, with the salt and sugar in a large bowl. Stir the vegetables for 3 minutes with a wooden spoon to season them and release their water. Rinse well under cold water, then squeeze completely dry in a clean kitchen towel. Set aside in a clean bowl.

Bring the sugar, vinegar, and water for the brine to a boil in a small saucepot. Pour the boiling liquid over the vegetables and leave to marinate for at least 1 hour before serving. Keeps for 3 weeks refrigerated.

Chow-Chow

Chow-chow is a pickled relish that, in our opinion, is one of the South's great contributions to the condiment table. In the hopes that you'd give the processed green relish a rest, we wanted to share with you this sweet and spicy mixture of pickled peppers, jalapeños, and cabbage. It's the perfect topping for any sort of grilled meat sandwich.

serves 6 to 8

1 head green cabbage, chopped

1 yellow onion, diced

1 green bell pepper, diced

1 red jalapeño, minced

¼ cup kosher salt

1 cup granulated sugar

2 teaspoons ground turmeric

2 tablespoons mustard seeds

1 teaspoon celery seeds

1½ cups cider vinegar

1 cup distilled white vinegar

Toss the cabbage, onion, peppers, and salt in a colander. Place the colander in a bowl and place another bowl on top of the vegetables. Fill the top bowl with heavy cans and refrigerate for 3 hours. This will press any moisture out of the vegetables.

Combine the remaining ingredients in a stainless-steel pot. Bring the mixture to a bare simmer over low heat and stir well to make sure everything is dissolved. Press the vegetables in the colander to extract as much water as possible. Add the vegetables to the hot liquid and bring to a boil for 30 seconds. Remove from the heat and cool completely before storing in the refrigerator for up to 1 month.

CHOW WHAT?

Some say that the Chinese workers who boxed and shipped spices and pickles to the States and to England coined the term "chow chow." Because of the different mixture of foods and goods packed together, the immigrant merchants called it "chow chow," a word that later was used to describe a mixture of vegetables and other ingredients packed together as a sweet pickled dish.

Grilled Fingerling Potatoes with Wilted Arugula

There's something special about small fingerlings instead of big, foil-wrapped baked potatoes. The smaller tubers happen to grill up nicely, and they make a downright elegant side dish when tossed with fresh arugula and Parmesan. We spoon these onto one of the half-dozen trays we received as wedding gifts and let the heady aroma of garlic, rosemary, and thyme do the talkin'.

serves 4 to 6

2 pounds fingerling potatoes, cut lengthwise in half

1 tablespoon plus 2 teaspoons kosher salt

4 cloves garlic, crushed

1 branch fresh rosemary

2 branches fresh thyme

¼ cup plus 3 tablespoons extra virgin olive oil

½ teaspoon freshly ground pepper

1 red onion, sliced into ½-inch rings

6 ounces fresh arugula

¼ cup shaved Parmesan cheese

Place the cut potatoes in a medium pot and cover with cold water. Add 1 tablespoon salt and place on the stove over high heat. As soon as the potatoes reach a boil, drain through a colander.

Combine the garlic, rosemary, thyme, the ¼ cup olive oil, 2 teaspoons salt, and the pepper in a bowl. Add the drained warm potatoes and mix well. Leave to marinate for at least 30 minutes. Drain any liquid that has come from the potatoes and place the potatoes on a grill preheated to high. Cook the potatoes until tender and moderately charred. At the same time, grill the sliced onion until fully charred and blackened on both sides.

Remove the potatoes from the grill, discarding the herbs (which have probably caught on fire by now anyway), and place in a large bowl. Chop the charred onion and add it to the bowl along with the arugula, the 3 tablespoons olive oil, and the Parmesan. Mix well, allowing the heat from the potatoes and onion to wilt the arugula.

ESSENTIAL EQUIPMENT

Shaved Parmesan—Break out your vegetable peeler to cut thin, delicate slices of cheese that are just right for this salad and so many others.

Grilled Peach Sundaes with Salted Caramel Sauce

Everyone remembers a gorgeous dessert—especially one that's hot off the grill. When peaches are at their juicy, sweet best in July and August, we halve and pit the locally grown beauties (Jersey peaches when we're in New York; Alabama or Georgia peaches when we're at the beach), toss them onto the grill, and then stir together a homemade salted caramel sauce. After the vanilla bean ice cream has rested on the counter until it's just soft enough, we begin constructing our very Southern sundaes. Each spoonful is at once warm and cool, savory and sweet, from the fruit, ice cream, and ooey-gooey goodness of the caramel.

serves 4

2 ripe peaches
vanilla ice cream
Salted Caramel Sauce (recipe follows)
optional garnishes: chopped nuts (peanuts, pecans, walnuts), chocolate chips, fresh berries

Cut the peaches in half and remove the pits. Preheat a grill to high. Place the 4 peach halves cut side down on the grill. Cook for 2 minutes and remove the peaches to 4 separate bowls so the grilled sides are facing up. Top each with a large scoop of vanilla ice cream and spoon over a generous amount of the caramel sauce. Add garnish, if using.

Salted Caramel Sauce

makes 2 cups

¼ cup water
2 cups granulated sugar
8 tablespoons (1 stick) unsalted butter, cut into pieces and chilled
1 cup cream
1 tablespoon kosher salt

Combine the water and sugar in a medium saucepot. Turn the heat to medium and stir often until the sugar is dissolved. Continue cooking until the sugar is caramelized; it will develop a rich brown color and read 260 degrees on a candy thermometer, though taking its temperature is not necessary. The sugar will take about 12 minutes to caramelize, but it will take about 7 minutes before the sugar begins to brown. Once the sugar starts to color, stir often and watch carefully (the sugar will go from caramel to burned in just about 2 minutes).

Remove the pan from the heat, add all of the butter at once, and stir until melted. Carefully add the cream—the mixture may bubble rapidly—and whisk until smooth. Stir in the salt. Serve hot or set aside to cool and store tightly covered in the refrigerator, up to 3 weeks. Reheat in the microwave; or on top of the stove, bring ¼ cup water to a boil in a small pan, add the cold sauce, and bring to a simmer.

S'mores

We have a special thing for s'mores. It all started around the bonfire at summer camp when we were ten years old. Jamie tried to woo Brooke with a graham cracker, marshmallow, and chocolate bar sandwich—it just seemed like the quickest way to her heart. Even though Brooke opted to go to the end-of-session dance with another boy, Jamie would finally have his chance, eighteen years later, when we honeymooned at Palmetto Bluff. Every night we left our warm cottage along the banks of the May River and followed the flickering lights to the main lawn. A blazing bonfire and buffet tables laden with long, elegant skewers, chocolate bars, and platters of graham crackers awaited us. S'mores Hour had become the new Happy Hour. Suddenly we felt like kids again. We were at summer camp. Jamie—and the s'more—had gotten the girl! For one final touch, we add the other childhood pairing—peanut butter and jelly— into the mix. This makes for an unforgettable, rich finish to your backyard bash.

serves 8

2 packages graham crackers, broken in half
   to form squares
16 large marshmallows
metal skewers or 12-inch bamboo skewers
1 cup grape jelly
1 cup strawberry preserves
1 cup peanut butter
2 to 3 chocolate bars, broken into pieces
   (2 squares chocolate per s'more)

Stack the graham crackers on an attractive platter. Place 1 marshmallow at the end of each skewer and arrange them on the platter next to the graham crackers. Put the grape jelly, strawberry preserves, and peanut butter in 3 separate bowls, each with its own spreader or small knife, and place on the platter as well. Find a spot for the chocolate pieces on the platter, put it down somewhere near the grill or fire pit, and stand back.

The Girl Scouts of America aren't just do-gooders— they're great little chefs. The first recorded s'mores recipe appeared in their 1927 publication, *Tramping and Trailing with the Girl Scouts.* Really, who better to come up with a warm chocolate bar and roasted marshmallow sandwich than a troop of sweets-loving six-year-old girls who huddle around a campfire every Saturday night?

EVERYDAY COCKTAILS

Cocktail hour is adult recess time. One good drink makes life warm and easy (or maybe just a little easier to handle). That's why you need to pick a cocktail and make it yours. Do like Brooke's grandparents did and every day, at 6 P.M., pull out the shaker and rocks glasses and make a memory. We both love the notion that they had a special drink—a special concoction that they considered uniquely their own—set aside for that particular time of day. For them, it was as simple as vodka on the rocks with a twist of lemon; for us, it can get as fancy as Blackberry Tequila Sunrise. Whatever it is, two sips will probably coerce you to move over to his side of the swing (or couch) and forget the fact that he left your dry cleaning on top of the car. One drink apiece, never any more, and, finally, you're able to let your shoulders down and enjoy each other again. The conversation is leisurely, the air is light, and dinner becomes a pleasant continuation of your sunset ritual.

Thrifty Bartender: Serve House Cocktails, Save Some Cash

As a host, it's easy to fall back on wine (and to fall over when you've had too much of it). Uncork, pour, and serve. But the truth is that wine can really push up your bar bill. So while you'll still serve vino with the meal, consider mixing up house cocktails during the apéritif or cocktail hour. By investing in several top-shelf bottles of booze, serving cocktails before dinner will be less expensive in the long run than serving many bottles of inexpensive wine.

How We Stock Our Bar
Vodka—Grey Goose, Ketel One
Bourbon—Maker's Mark, Bulleit
Gin—Hendrick's, Tanqueray
Tequila—Cuervo Silver
Rum—Sailor Jerry's
Grand Marnier
Triple Sec
Bitters
Club soda and ginger ale (buy small bottles to minimize waste)

Jamie's Genius Margarita

The Margarita Secret: homemade, lime-flavored simple syrup. That and the freshest, juiciest limes you can get your hands on. Nope—it's not about the tequila! There. We said it. And by following the steps below, you'll know how to make your own special syrup. All right, now we're not as indispensable at all those football/Cinco de Mayo/pool parties, but we thought we should finally reveal the secret behind Jamie's Genius Margarita.

serves 4

6 ounces fresh lime juice
6 ounces Lime Simple Syrup (recipe follows)
4 ounces Triple Sec
8 ounces tequila
ice cubes
salt for glasses
lime wedges for garnish

In a cocktail shaker, combine the lime juice, lime syrup, Triple Sec, and tequila with 3 or 4 ice cubes. Shake vigorously until well chilled. Strain through the top of the cocktail shaker into salt-rimmed martini glasses or short rocks glasses filled with ice. Garnish each with a wedge of lime.

Lime Simple Syrup

makes approximately 2 cups,
enough for 3 batches margaritas

zest of 2 limes removed in strips with a vegetable peeler
1 teaspoon kosher salt
1 cup granulated sugar
2 cups water

Combine the lime zest, salt, sugar, and water in a medium saucepot and bring to a boil. Stir well so all the sugar dissolves. Strain through a fine-mesh strainer and cool. Store in the refrigerator for up to 2 weeks.

To Patrón or Not to Patrón

Save your money for good limes and do not buy top-shelf tequila. There is absolutely no reason to use the expensive stuff to make margaritas. By mixing the tequila with Triple Sec and lime juice, the flavor of Mexico's finest just gets lost. We like midrange tequila like Jose Cuervo Silver or Gold. (Brooke likes the smoothness of Silver; Jamie thinks Gold is more "interesting.") Same goes for the Triple Sec. Save your orange-flavored Cointreau for more refined cocktails that don't involve salt and strong citrus. Better yet, use the Cointreau in a gourmet chocolate dessert (chocolate mousse, page 265, anyone?). A midrange bottle of Triple Sec works perfectly well for our irresistible margs.

Watermelon Margarita

The midsummer, so-good-it's-dangerous watermelon margarita came about as a bargaining chip. The bartenders at Highlands Bar & Grill needed Jamie and his sous chef, Brian, to help juice and sieve the forty-pound watermelons whose juice would infuse a half dozen of their seasonal cocktails. The chefs agreed to help on one condition: the bartenders would have to guarantee them an icy tumbler of the magenta-hued juice—spiked with tequila—at the end of dinner service. The bartenders complied and summer weekends were never the same. In fact, Jamie's pretty sure that these margaritas were the only reason that Brooke stuck around that long, hot Alabama July.

serves 6 to 8

12 ounces watermelon juice
2 ounces lime juice
4 ounces Triple Sec
8 ounces silver tequila
1 lime, cut into wedges
salt for glasses (optional)

To make watermelon juice, cut fresh watermelon into chunks, place in a blender or food processor, and puree until smooth. Pour the puree through a fine-mesh strainer. One medium watermelon will make 6 to 8 cups juice.

Fill a large pitcher halfway with ice. Add the watermelon juice, lime juice, Triple Sec, and tequila and stir to chill thoroughly. Rub a lime wedge around the rim of a martini glass and dip the glass into a plate of salt to coat the rim. Fill with the mixed margarita and garnish with the lime wedge.

BOURBON FOR EVERY SEASON

By now, you've noticed Jamie's obsessed with bourbon. While it's not an everyday libation in our house, bourbon, the famed American whiskey made primarily from corn, is the first thing he reaches for on special occasions, whether that means a dinner party with friends or a Sunday afternoon off work (a rarity when you're a chef). So it's only natural that he's figured out a way to drink it, just right, every season. Take a look at Jamie's year-round repertoire of cocktails made from Kentucky's most famous export. A little cucumber juice here and a splash of peach and soda water there make Jamie's bourbon indulgences far more social than just sipping it straight over ice. After all, Brooke needs him to tend bar and do the dishes—not crawl into bed at seven o'clock.

Spring Kirby Birby

2 to 3 ounces cucumber juice, or to taste
ice cubes
3 ounces bourbon
juice of 1 lemon, strips of zest reserved for garnish
splash of ginger ale
cucumber slices for garnish

To make cucumber juice, set a box grater over a large bowl and grate fresh cucumber into the bowl. Set a fine-mesh strainer over a separate bowl. Pour the grated cucumber into the strainer, then press on the gratings to extract as much juice as possible.

Fill a large cocktail shaker with ice. Pour in the bourbon, cucumber juice, and lemon juice. Shake vigorously to chill. Strain into 2 rocks glasses filled with ice. Top with a splash of ginger ale and garnish with lemon zest and cucumber slices.

Summer Peach Press

Some drinks are better made in pitchers. Big batches are easy to mix up, and you're able to see all the gorgeous elements—such as peaches, lemon slices, and fresh mint—floating inside the fat, round, or tall glass pitcher. Best of all, it's easy to bartend for a crowd, and a drink like our Peach Press is definitely best enjoyed with friends.

serves 6 to 8

2 branches fresh mint
2 ripe peaches, pits removed, cut into quarters
3 slices lemon
ice cubes
2 cups bourbon
1 cup club soda
1 cup ginger ale
mint leaves for garnish
peach slices for garnish

Combine the mint, peaches, and lemon in the bottom of a glass pitcher. Press with a wooden spoon or long muddling stick until the mint is bruised and the peaches are crushed. Fill the pitcher halfway with ice and pour in the bourbon. Stir until thoroughly chilled; there will be a layer of condensation on the outside of the pitcher. Just before serving, add the club soda and ginger ale. Serve in highball glasses, garnished with mint leaves and peach slices.

Fall Apple Cart

In New York, when the weather turns cold, the Union Square Greenmarket has little to offer except for crisp, delicious apples from upstate. Well, those and locally made apple cider, apple butter, and baked goods made with apples. As a tribute to our adopted hometown and its most famous fruit, Jamie matched fresh apple cider with bourbon, adding a slice of ginger to the mix for its unmistakable flavor pick-me-up.

serves 2

1 slice fresh ginger, about the size of a quarter and
    ¼ inch thick
2 lime wedges
ice cubes
2 ounces apple cider
2 ounces bourbon
2 ounces orange-flavored liqueur
1 ounce fresh lime juice
½ ounce simple syrup (recipe below; omit the ginger
    and mint)
apple slices for garnish

Muddle the ginger and lime wedges in a cocktail shaker, fill with ice, and add the remaining ingredients. Shake vigorously to chill. Strain into cocktail glasses filled with ice and garnish with apple slices.

Winter Blood Orange Old-Fashioned

See page 268 of New Traditions.

Ginger Moscow Mule

Ginger beer is like root beer, not Budweiser. And here it lends a little sweetness and a lot of kick.

serves 4

6 mint leaves
2 ounces Ginger Syrup (recipe follows)
2 ounces fresh lime juice
6 ounces vodka
ice cubes
4 ounces ginger beer

In the bottom of a cocktail shaker, muddle the mint leaves with the ginger syrup and lime juice. Add the vodka and fill with ice. Shake to chill. Strain into rocks glasses filled with 3 or 4 large ice cubes. Top each glass with approximately 1 ounce ginger beer.

Ginger Syrup

makes 2 cups

1 cup granulated sugar
1 cup water
¼ cup thinly sliced peeled fresh ginger
2 branches fresh mint

Combine all the ingredients in a saucepot. Bring to a boil and cook until the sugar is dissolved. Cool completely. Store in the refrigerator for up to 1 month. Strain before using.

Blackberry Tequila Sunrise

The trick to the "sunrise" effect is making each drink in its own glass. When made properly, the color of this drink goes from deep purple at the base, fades through shades of red, and finally lightens to become a soft orange at the top of the glass. We put a tip jar on the kitchen counter when we (successfully) pour these!

serves 2

8 blackberries, plus more for garnish
2 strips orange zest
2 teaspoons granulated sugar
4 ounces tequila
ice cubes
1 cup fresh orange juice
club soda as needed (2 to 4 ounces)

Place 4 blackberries, 1 strip orange zest, and 1 teaspoon sugar in the bottom of each of 2 collins (or other tall) glasses. Muddle to release the berry juice and dissolve the sugar. Add 2 ounces tequila to each glass and stir to combine. Fill each glass with ice and add ½ cup orange juice. Finish each glass with a splash, 1 to 2 ounces, of soda water. Garnish with blackberries.

Planter's Punch

Though the ingredient list reads more tiki bar than Charleston single, Planter's Punch was created at the very swank hotel Planter's Inn in Charleston. This is a classy cocktail whose roots, like the city itself, are steeped in British West Indies culture. Fresh pineapple, orange, and lime juices (all those happy flavors we love from trips to the Bahamas) mixed with rum make it almost too easy to enjoy.

serves 4

6 ounces spiced rum, such as Sailor Jerry's
3 ounces light rum
3 ounces fresh lime juice
3 ounces simple syrup (page 43) or Ginger Syrup (page 218)
6 ounces pineapple juice
6 ounces fresh orange juice
grenadine (optional)
crushed ice
orange bitters

In a pitcher, combine the spiced rum, light rum, lime juice, simple syrup, pineapple juice, and orange juice and stir well to combine. If using grenadine, place ½ tablespoon at the bottom of each of 4 tall rocks glasses. Fill the glasses with crushed ice and pour in the rum mixture. Add 2 dashes of bitters per glass and stir.

Basil Gimlet

The vodka gimlet is a classic cocktail . . . that can be a bit of a country club snoozer. To jazz up the mainstay ingredients (vodka, soda water, lime juice), we muddle the lime and sugar with fresh basil leaves to give the drink a bright, fresh flavor that tastes like summer in a glass.

serves 2

1 lime
3 fresh basil leaves
1 teaspoon granulated sugar
3 ounces vodka
ice cubes
club soda

Cut the lime in half, then cut each half into 4 wedges. Reserve 2 wedges for garnish. Place the remaining 6 pieces of lime in a cocktail shaker; add the basil leaves and sugar. Muddle until the sugar is dissolved. Pour in the vodka, fill the shaker with ice, and shake to chill thoroughly. Fill 2 rocks glasses with ice cubes. Strain the vodka into the glasses, garnish each with a lime wedge, and top with a splash of soda.

Grapefruit Cocktail

Refreshing and just tart enough to tease your taste buds before a big meal, our grapefruit cocktail is a fabulous way to make your apéritif hour lively.

serves 2

1 lemon
1 tablespoon granulated sugar
4 ounces gin
6 ounces fresh grapefruit juice
ice cubes

Cut the lemon in half, then cut each half into 4 wedges. Reserve 2 wedges for garnish. Place the remaining 6 pieces of lemon in a cocktail shaker; add the sugar and muddle to dissolve. Add the gin and grapefruit juice, fill the shaker with ice, and shake to chill thoroughly. Fill 2 rocks glasses with ice and strain the gin into each glass. Garnish each drink with a lemon wedge.

PART 2

New Traditions

We have to eat. It might as well be a celebration. Right?

As we set out on our first year together as a married couple, we made a pact with each other to enjoy the little moments, the "off" nights, the small meals in between feasts. But more than anything, we vowed to create our own traditions. Sure, we'd still do a big bird for Thanksgiving. But we'd do it our way and start cooking it at brunch time with Bloody Marys, Irish coffee, a basket of oysters, and a platter of beignets. (When the turkey goes in the deep fryer, the Apalachicola oysters and the New Orleans breakfast treats get their own hot-oil bath!)

Other times, a girl just needs an excuse to slip into a pair of heels and a little knit dress and sip a champagne cocktail. Brooke uses Thursday nights with *Real Housewives* as an excuse to have a "New Housewives" mini cocktail party for her newly married girlfriends. Everyone sips The Smackdown, Brooke's ginger, grapefruit, and tequila cocktail, and nibbles on homemade Blue Cheese Crackers with Fig Chutney and Sugar Snap Peas with Orange and Mint. Or, in the case of Jamie and the Kentucky Derby, a two-minute race in Louisville becomes a reason to have an all-day party in New York. He stirs up frosted goblets brimming with bourbon and mint and turns out tray after tray of Cornmeal Gougères filled with Country Ham Cream. (He also looks forward to any opportunity to wear his seersucker blazer and not be made fun of.) As a hostess, Brooke considers these "No-Pressure Parties" (check out her page in this section dedicated to these relaxed get-togethers) a lot more fun than the days filled with expectation, anxiety, and too many of other people's traditions.

In this section, we're inventing reasons to be with friends, get a little fancy, and eat and drink really well. While "Life As We Know It" reads like a greatest hits of our cooking repertoire—the recipes meant to be mixed and matched—the food in "New Traditions" is meant to be prepared as entire menus for all the new, special occasions in your life. Is there something wrong with that? We say, if there's not a celebration on the calendar, make one up!

VALENTINE'S DINNER: PLAYING CUPID IN THE KITCHEN

Jamie (claims that he) thinks Valentine's Day is for fools and for new loves. But, year after year, on February 14, he acts like a 4-star cupid and surprises Brooke with blueberry pancakes in bed (page 26), actually putting away his laundry, and cooking up a wonderful dinner to end the day. The truth is, these somewhat clichéd holidays really do take on special importance when you're newly married. They're just an excuse to be sweet—and eat decadent food. What's so wrong with that?

A few Valentine's dinner do's and don'ts:

DO

- While you might be staying in, do dress up like you're going out to dinner. A little blush and a close shave go a long way.
- Do write a short-but-sweet love note and slip it beneath the plate. Anything that you write is infinitely more meaningful than a purchased thought.
- Get out the nice dinnerware and cloth napkins. Yes, tonight is worth it.

DON'T

- "Romantic holiday" shouldn't mean "hangover." While it's always tempting to drink too much on the big night, don't. Open a "split" (a "split" is a half bottle) of champagne while you both put the finishing touches on dinner. Share a nice bottle of Pinot Noir with your meal. Any more joy juice than that and you won't be able to remember whether you supped on peanut butter and jelly or pistachio-crusted lamb.
- While you want to impress, don't opt for a list of recipes that's so involved—and beyond your current skill level—that you'll still be busy in the kitchen (and not in the bedroom) at midnight. Really new to the cooking world? Make half of our Valentine's recipes this year and half next year. Our point is romance—not raggedy fingernails and bloodshot eyes.
- Don't put off all shopping, prepping, and table setting until February 14. Make a big effort to follow our Prep Ahead for Nooky sidebars and spread out the duties. The more organized and prepared you feel, the more you'll enjoy the big night.

Smoked Salmon Pizza

This thin-crust pizza is perfect for a home kitchen because the crust can crisp up at a lower temperature. And there's no slow-simmering tomato sauce. All you do is spread the warm pizza dough with thick sour cream, sprinkle with salted capers, and finish off with ribbons of smoked salmon. These pizzas are light and elegant and prove to be a really fun way to start your romantic evening together. Brooke recommends buying Eastern Nova salmon—it's the mildest variety of the smoked stuff that you can find.

makes two 8- to 10-inch round pizzas or
one 18- x 13-inch pan pizza (full-size baking sheet)

CRUST

1¼ cups water, lukewarm (about 100 degrees)

1 packet (2¼ teaspoons) active dry yeast

1 teaspoon salt

1 cup whole-wheat flour

2½ cups all-purpose flour, plus more as needed

2 tablespoons olive oil, plus more for greasing
the bowl and baking sheets

TOPPING

8 ounces sour cream

1 tablespoon fresh lemon juice

pinch of kosher salt, plus more as needed

freshly ground pepper to taste

2 tablespoons olive oil

2 shallots, thinly sliced

4 ounces smoked salmon, sliced paper thin

2 teaspoons capers, chopped

Combine the water and yeast in a small bowl and whisk to dissolve. In a separate bowl, stir together the salt, flours, and olive oil to mix well. When the yeast mixture begins to foam, after 7 to 10 minutes, stir it into the flour. Mix with a wooden spoon until just combined. The mixture should pull into a smooth ball. Transfer the dough to a clean bowl that has been lightly greased with olive oil. Cover with plastic wrap or a clean kitchen towel and set aside on the countertop for 45 minutes.

Remove the dough from the bowl to a floured work surface. Punch the dough down by pressing the air out of it with floured hands. Gently knead the dough and divide it into 2 pieces if making 2 pan pizzas; leave it whole if making a single large one. Roll each piece of dough into a ball under the palm of your hand. Then, on a lightly floured work surface, roll into a flat disc with a lightly floured rolling pin. Finish stretching the dough by hand. The pizzas are now ready to top.

PREP AHEAD FOR NOOKY

This pizza dough is best when made the night before and left to proof in the refrigerator overnight. Follow the directions above but rest the covered dough in the refrigerator rather than on the countertop. When you're ready to make pizza, remove the dough from the fridge, punch it down, and roll out as needed.

The pizza crust can be baked up to 1 hour before topping and serving. Rewarm the baked crust slightly before topping.

Place the sour cream in a small fine-mesh strainer lined with a coffee filter set over a bowl. Drain for 20 minutes. (By extracting the excess water or moisture, you'll be left with a super-rich and flavorful sour cream.) Remove the sour cream from the strainer, stir in the lemon juice, a pinch of salt, and pepper.

Preheat the oven to 500 degrees.

Line 2 baking sheets with aluminum foil. Rub each with olive oil or spray with a nonstick spray. Place a stretched pizza dough in the center of each pan. Drizzle each dough with 1 tablespoon of the olive oil and spread evenly over the surface with your fingers. Scatter the sliced shallots on the pizza and season with salt and pepper. Bake in the heated oven until the edges are golden brown, about 7 minutes.

Remove the baked dough from the oven and cool slightly before spreading each with a generous layer of sour cream. Arrange the slices of salmon on top and scatter with the capers. Slice and serve slightly warm or at room temperature.

No Substitutions, Please

Follow the recipe and use the good stuff.

1. Fresh lemon juice (not bottled)
2. Fresh garlic (not jarred or preminced cloves)
3. Good wine that you can sip AND use for the recipe (not bottled "cooking" wine)
4. Fruity (Italian) or mellow (French) extra virgin olive oil
5. Kosher salt (not iodized)

Sicilian Lobster Salad

The idea here is luxury. Buttery lobster, both sweet and meaty, is tossed in a blood-orange citrus dressing along with hearts of palm, slivered almonds, and radicchio. (How often do you eat like that?!) If you decide to buy your lobster precooked (a move Brooke highly recommends), this exotic showstopper is just about as easy to whip up as a bowl of chicken salad.

serves 2

LOBSTER

1 live 1½-pound lobster, or 1 lobster tail plus
    2 claws, cooked
8 cups water, plus more as needed
1 tablespoon distilled white vinegar
2 teaspoons kosher salt

DRESSING

2 tablespoons blood orange juice, reserved from
    segmenting the orange for the salad
2 teaspoons fresh lemon juice
pinch of granulated sugar
1 tablespoon minced shallot
¼ cup good-quality extra virgin olive oil
kosher salt and freshly ground pepper

BUTTER SAUCE

¼ cup water
2 teaspoons kosher salt
1 teaspoon cayenne
1 lemon, zest grated and juiced
8 tablespoons (1 stick) unsalted butter, cut into
    small chunks

SALAD

1 small head radicchio, cored and thinly sliced
2 cups baby spinach, loosely packed
⅔ cup sliced hearts of palm
kosher salt and freshly ground pepper
2 tablespoons sliced almonds, toasted
1 blood orange, cut into supremes (page 14),
    juice reserved

Preheat the oven to warm or just below 200 degrees.

To prepare the live lobster, bring the water, vinegar, and salt to a rapid boil in a pot large enough to hold the lobster. Prepare a large bowl of ice water. Carefully place the lobster in the boiling water headfirst; this will reduce the chances of the tail flipping and splashing boiling water on you. Cook for 3 minutes and remove immediately to the ice water. Rest the lobster in the ice water for 5 minutes to allow it to cool completely. Remove the tail and claws from the body. Then, with your kitchen scissors, cut down the edge of the shell to remove the tail meat in one piece. Whack the claws with the back of a chef's knife to extract that meat in one piece.

While the lobster is cooling, prepare the salad dressing. Combine the juices, sugar, and shallot in a small bowl. Set aside for 15 minutes for the flavors to come together. Whisk in the olive oil and season to taste with salt and pepper.

Slice the lobster tail into rings ½ to 1 inch thick. Place in an ovenproof dish along with the claws.

For the butter sauce, in a small saucepan, combine the water, salt, cayenne, and lemon zest and juice; bring the mixture to a boil. Remove from the heat and add all of the butter at once. Whisk rapidly until the butter is melted into the sauce.

Pour the butter sauce over the lobster meat, cover tightly with aluminum foil, and place in the 200-degree oven to keep warm.

To assemble the salad, combine the radicchio, spinach, and hearts of palm in a medium bowl. Season with salt and pepper and toss with the dressing (you won't need it all). Drain the warm lobster on paper towels and pat off the excess butter. Divide the greens between 2 plates and arrange half of the lobster on top of each. Scatter with the toasted almonds and tuck the blood orange supremes into the greens.

PREP AHEAD FOR NOOKY

All parts of the salad can be prepped ahead and stored covered in the refrigerator until ready to serve. The lobster can be cooked up to 24 hours in advance and stored, tightly wrapped, in the refrigerator. Thirty minutes before serving, complete the lobster preparation as described above, reheating the meat in the butter sauce.

TECHNIQUE TIP

When possible, buy canned hearts of palm in whole pieces. Slice the pieces into rounds ¼ to ½ inch thick.

Pistachio-and-Mint-Crusted Lamb Rack

At Jamie's first 4-star cooking gig in Manhattan, this lamb rack was the "go-to" luxury entrée for A-list private dinner parties. The foodies at the table always prodded the waiter for the recipe. How was the lamb perfectly seared and yet the crust remained so incredibly moist and flavorful? Of course, Jamie never revealed his secret . . . until now.

serves 2 to 4

one 8-rib rack of lamb, frenched (cut from the top
    of the bones and the exposed bones are
    scraped clean)
1 teaspoon kosher salt, plus more for the lamb
¼ teaspoon freshly ground pepper, plus more
    for the lamb
2 tablespoons olive oil or canola oil
5 tablespoons unsalted butter, at room temperature
½ cup dry or fresh breadcrumbs
¼ cup pistachio nuts, finely ground
1 tablespoon chopped fresh mint leaves
1 tablespoon Dijon mustard

Season the lamb generously with salt and pepper. Place a heavy skillet over high heat and add the olive oil. When the oil begins to smoke, place the lamb fat side down in the skillet and sear until deeply colored. Stand the rack up to brown its top, then roll over to brown the bone side. Remove from the pan and cool on a rack.

Place the butter, salt, and pepper in a bowl; beat with an electric mixer until light and fluffy. Add the breadcrumbs, pistachios, and mint. Stir the mixture with a wooden spoon to combine well and form a ball. Transfer to a sheet of wax or parchment paper; place another piece of wax paper on top. Press the ball flat between the sheets of paper. Roll out the mixture ⅛ inch thick with a rolling pin. Keeping the rolled mixture flat, freeze at least 10 minutes, or up to 2 weeks if tightly covered.

Preheat the oven to 450 degrees. Put a rack on the top shelf in the oven.

Twenty-five minutes before serving, remove the butter mixture from the freezer and cut a rectangular shape from it the same size as the fat side of the rack. Brush the fat side of the rack with the Dijon mustard. Remove the paper from one side of the cut piece of frozen butter crust. Press the crust onto the rack over the mustard, allowing your hands to warm it and shape it to the rack. The mustard will act like a delicious glue, helping to hold the buttery crust in place. Remove the remaining piece of paper.

Place the lamb crust side up on an aluminum-foil-lined baking sheet. Roast until a thermometer inserted into the center (NOT through the crust!) reads 130 degrees, 12 to 14 minutes. Remove and rest on a rack for 8 minutes before carving to serve.

Unused pieces of the crust can be put together and rerolled to be used again. Store unused portions tightly covered in the refrigerator.

PREP AHEAD FOR NOOKY

Once you've placed the crust on the lamb rack, the whole thing can be refrigerated and held up to 24 hours before its final roasting. Just don't forget to leave enough time for the lamb to rest after it's cooked! Slice too soon and you'll risk leaving that gorgeous crust behind on your cutting board.

Restaurant Daniel

The ultimate 4-star French dining experience (outside of France) is at Restaurant Daniel, the crown jewel of Daniel Boulud's dining empire. Make a trip to the Upper East Side for a once-in-a-lifetime meal in the casually elegant lounge or the refined and fancy main dining room. **Restaurant Daniel**—60 East 65th Street, New York City 10065; Tel-212.288.0033; www.danielnyc.com.

Parsnip Puree

A nice, skinny-jeans-friendly alternative to mashed pota-toes. While the parsnips blend up to be just as creamy as the tubers, they're lighter and altogether better for you. Plus they pack a ton more flavor—parsnips have the earthy bite of turnips crossed with the sweetness of carrots.

serves 2 to 4

4 tablespoons (½ stick) unsalted butter

1½ pounds parsnips, peeled and sliced

1 tablespoon minced garlic

1 Idaho or russet potato, peeled and chopped

2 teaspoons kosher salt, plus more as needed

½ cup cream

freshly ground pepper to taste

Melt 2 tablespoons of the butter in a large saucepot. Add the parsnips and sauté for 3 to 4 minutes until just softened. Add the garlic and cook until aromatic, 30 to 60 seconds. Stir in the potato and cook for 1 minute more. Cover the vegetables completely with water, add the salt, and bring the mixture to a simmer. Cook until completely tender, about 10 minutes. Pour through a colander and let drain for 2 to 3 minutes to remove as much moisture as possible, or your puree might turn into parsnip soup. Transfer to a blender, add the cream and the remaining 2 tablespoons butter, and process until smooth. Return to the pot and hold over a low flame to keep warm, or gently simmer to thicken if the puree is too thin. Season to taste with salt and pepper.

PREP AHEAD FOR NOOKY

This puree can be made, then held, covered with alumi-num foil, in a warm (200 to 250 degrees) oven for up to 2 hours before serving.

TECHNIQUE TIP

Parsnips are very low in starch, so they can run through the blender to become silky smooth without getting gummy or tacky. Never try to make mashed potatoes with a food processor or blender.

Roasted Brussels Sprouts

Well-seasoned, roasted Brussels sprouts are almost as addictive as french fries. The outer layers get crisp and a little bit brown, while one bite yields tender yet toothsome flesh. When we teach our winter classes at the Institute of Culinary Education, we always include this recipe. We think Brussels are a much maligned veggie that deserve their place in the sun—especially when gilded with warm brown butter, Parmesan, almonds, and lemon zest. Make these midwinter when Brussels are at their seasonal peak.

1 pound Brussels sprouts, cut in half

1 cup minced yellow onion

3 cloves garlic, crushed

2 tablespoons extra virgin olive oil

kosher salt and freshly ground pepper to taste

2 tablespoons unsalted butter

¼ cup sliced almonds

grated zest of 1 lemon

2 tablespoons finely grated Parmesan cheese

Preheat the oven to 425 degrees.

Combine the Brussels sprouts, onion, garlic, and olive oil in a large bowl. Toss well and season with salt and pepper. Spread in a single layer on a baking sheet and roast until tender and lightly browned on the edges, about 15 minutes. Transfer to a large bowl.

Melt the butter in a small sauté pan over high heat until it begins to brown. Remove from the heat and stir in the almonds to toast lightly. Pour the butter and almonds into the bowl with the Brussels sprouts. Add the lemon zest and Parmesan and toss to coat. Adjust the seasoning with salt and pepper. Cover to keep warm until ready to serve.

SO YOU THINK YOU CAN COOK?

Dreaming of leaving behind the cubicle for a day job behind the stove? Before telling your boss to stuff her memos where the sun don't shine, test out the culinary world after hours (and after you've punched your time card). The Institute of Culinary Education offers both recreational and professional programs—after 6 P.M.—that teach you everything about the culinary arts. So right when you'd normally enjoy happy hour, you'll be whisking a pot of béchamel and boning a chicken. Now doesn't that sound like fun? Or if you're in the mood for a different date night, sign up for our couples' cooking classes. We chop, we sear, we julienne—and we serve amazing house cocktails after all the knives have been put away!

The Institute of Culinary Education—50 West 23rd Street, New York City 10010; Tel-800.522.4610; www.iceculinary.com.

Cinnamon-Spiced Chocolate Cake

This reminds us a little bit of Mexican hot chocolate. The cocoa, the cinnamon, and the vanilla really work their magic together to create a chocolate dessert that's just different enough to be memorable.

makes 12 individual cakes

1½ cups all-purpose flour, plus more for the molds

1 teaspoon baking soda

1 teaspoon kosher salt

1 teaspoon ground cinnamon

¼ teaspoon ground allspice

¼ teaspoon ground cloves

4 ounces semisweet or bittersweet dark chocolate

8 tablespoons (1 stick) unsalted butter, plus more
  for the molds

1 cup granulated sugar

1 teaspoon vanilla extract

2 large eggs

1 cup whole milk

1 cup cream, whipped

TECHNIQUE TIP

Whipped Cream—Pour 1 cup cold cream into a chilled bowl. Add 1 tablespoon sugar and 1 teaspoon vanilla extract. With a handheld electric mixer or a whisk, beat vigorously until well thickened and the cream holds firm peaks. Just make sure not to overwhip the cream. You'll know this has happened when it's become grainy and watery.

Preheat the oven to 350 degrees.

Combine the flour, baking soda, salt, cinnamon, allspice, and cloves in a large bowl and set aside. Melt the chocolate and the butter in a double boiler or the microwave and whisk until smooth. Add the sugar, vanilla, eggs, and milk to the melted chocolate mixture and whisk until smooth.

Add half of the dry ingredients and fold together with a spoon or spatula. Repeat with the remaining dry ingredients.

Butter and flour twelve 8-ounce ramekins, custard cups, or disposable aluminum cups. Invert and tap on the counter to expel the excess flour. Fill each cup three-quarters of the way with batter and tap gently or use a spatula to smooth. Space the cups 1 to 2 inches apart on a baking pan. Bake until the edges look firm and dry and the centers are slightly soft, approximately 14 minutes. Cool briefly and remove the cakes from the baking cups. Garnish each with a dollop of whipped cream.

This recipe makes enough batter for 12 cakes, but if it's just the two of you for a special evening, the excess batter can be refrigerated for up to 5 days, so you can have fresh baked cakes the next morning with coffee . . . and again for lunch. The batter can also be frozen for up to 3 months. To use, pull the batter out of the freezer the day before baking and allow it to thaw completely in the fridge.

PREP AHEAD FOR NOOKY

It's no problem to serve these cakes fresh from the oven (they're amazing that way!). As soon as the lamb comes out of the oven, scoop the refrigerated cake batter you made the day before into prepared cups and pop into the oven to bake. By the time the lamb has rested, been carved, and is on the plate, the cakes will be ready to come out of the oven. They can cool while you eat your lamb.

Thrifty Table

Hurricane Lamps Without a Storm in Sight: Growing up down South, on the water, every self-respecting Junior Leaguer and hostess owned a set of antique, cut-glass hurricane lamps. (I'm betting the lamps were worth more than their owners' station wagons.) Thankfully, now you can find these fabulous, simple candle covers at almost any craft store for about $10. I love to place a tall pillar candle inside the lamp and fill it with seasonal decorations. Some of my favorites include summertime shells and starfish; chocolate Easter eggs and Peeps; seasonal berries and small Christmas tree balls; little, brightly colored candies for Valentine's (Red Hots, peppermints); or bright fall leaves and twigs. People always comment on them and vow to make some for themselves.

Thrifty Table: Basics

Brooke admits she'd spend our baby daughter's college fund on pretty plates, glasses, and table do-dads if Jamie would let her. There's just something about table accessories that makes her heart skip a beat.

But, the truth is, you don't need a lot to set a nice table. It's the gorgeous food you've lovingly prepared that should be the focus. So here's a list of basics—with a few tricks thrown in—that will make your brunch, lunch, or evening spread a simple, elegant, THRIFTY affair.

Most of these "extras" and do-dads can be found at your local craft store, Target, Walmart, or Bed Bath & Beyond.

- White cloth napkins ($10/set of 8)
- Clear glass vases: 2 short and square, 1 regular ($5 each)
- Bud vases: 6 to line the center of the table ($2.50 each)
- Clear hurricane lamps: 2 ($10 each)
- Pillar candles ($3 to $20 each)
- Votive candles ($10, bag of 100)
- Large, plain wooden cutting board ($45)—For rustic, elegant presentations of cheese, fruit, charcuterie, mixed antipasti, and general h.o.d.'s.
- Tablevogue ($49/$39)—This ingeniously designed natural-colored tablecloth transforms drab, all-purpose tables into elegant dining, buffet, or bar tables. The handsome box pleats dress things up for an overall vibe of casual chic, while the stain- and wrinkle-resistant fabric keeps things practical. This is one table accessory that won't budge—or bruise your wallet. It's absolutely perfect for year-round entertaining.

SPRING LUNCH

The first beautiful, mild day of the year is a reason to celebrate. When we were both living in Brooke's studio in SoHo, we'd use the first warm breeze as an excuse to lug her kitchen table and chairs outside onto the patio and pop a bottle of rosé. We'd sort through the gorgeous spring loot we had picked up at the farmers' market—fiddlehead ferns, asparagus, sweet peas, mushrooms, butter lettuces, and young, creamy goat cheese. By the time we made our way through a crotin (a "crotin" is a round of young, French goat cheese) and a loaf of bread, a vegetable ragout was simmering on the stove and a juicy cut of lamb was roasting in the oven. Friends and upstairs neighbors would be over in an hour to join us at the table outside.

Whether you decide to cook up our spring meal as part of a religious celebration or because your favorite lily of the valley is finally on display outside of Walmart, personalize this menu. Or as our West Coast friends say, "Own it!" Buy produce that is local to your area and try out that funky vegetable that's always piqued your curiosity. Above all else, order a case of well-priced rosé—pink wine is a chance to celebrate the return of warm weather!

Easter Ham, Asparagus, and Morel Gratin

When we were growing up down South, Easter Sunday was a big deal. Our dads wore ties (and didn't complain for once), and our moms and aunts cooked up one of the biggest lunches of the year. But because church lasted past noon, a lot of the food had to be made in advance and then heated at the last minute. This gratin—in some form or another—was the ladies' best friend and always made an appearance on the buffet. Granted, they might have used button mushrooms instead of morels, but the idea is still the same. This is just a simple layered casserole made with the best seasonal ingredients. Tying this dish all together is a very good homemade version of cream of mushroom soup.

serves 6 to 8

1 bunch large asparagus (12 to 14 spears)
4 tablespoons (½ stick) unsalted butter
2 leeks, diced and rinsed (about 2 cups)
kosher salt and freshly ground pepper
8 ounces boiled ham, cut into cubes
1 tablespoon minced garlic
2 cups morel mushrooms, trimmed and washed
2 tablespoons all-purpose flour
2 cups chicken broth
½ cup cream
½ cup finely grated Parmesan cheese
6 soft-boiled eggs, cut into quarters
1½ cups fresh breadcrumbs

Bring a large pot of salted water to a boil and prepare a large bowl of ice water. Trim the woody ends from the asparagus and drop the spears into the boiling water. Cook until just tender, 2 to 3 minutes; then remove immediately to the ice water. When cool, set aside on paper towels to drain.

Melt 2 tablespoons of the butter in a large pot over high heat and add the leeks. Season lightly with salt and pepper, stir in the ham, and cook until the leeks are softened. Add the garlic and mushrooms and cook until the pot is dry, about 5 minutes.

Stir in the remaining 2 tablespoons butter. When completely melted, add the flour and cook until a thick paste forms. Slowly add the chicken broth to the pot, stirring constantly so the mixture will be smooth. Bring the mixture to a boil and season to taste with salt and pepper. Reduce the heat and simmer until well thickened, about 5 minutes. Stir in the cream and remove from the heat.

Preheat the oven to 425 degrees.

Cut the cooled asparagus into 1- to 2-inch pieces. Stir the asparagus and Parmesan cheese into the pot and mix thoroughly. Transfer the mixture to a 1- to 2-quart oval baking dish, then press the quartered eggs into the cream mixture. The gratin can be held for up to 12 hours.

Scatter the breadcrumbs over the gratin and place in the hot oven on the top rack. Bake until golden brown on top and bubbling around the edges, 10 to 15 minutes. Serve hot.

TECHNIQUE TIP

For perfect soft-boiled eggs every time, bring a pot of salted water to a boil. Carefully add the eggs to the boiling water with a spoon. Simmer the eggs for 7 minutes and transfer to a bowl of ice water. Remove the eggs from the water when completely cooled, about 5 minutes. Store refrigerated in the shell and peel just before eating.

Morel Mushrooms

These little beauties are a specialty of spring. If you can't get your hands on them or they're out of your price range (both equally likely), you can substitute chanterelles, porcini, or even crimini mushrooms. But a more accessible and economical option would be to look for dried morels or a mix of mushrooms that contains dried morels. To cook with dried mushrooms, first soak them for 15 minutes in room-temperature water, then lift them from the soaking water to leave any sand or grit in the bottom of the bowl. Transfer them to a pot of chicken stock and simmer until tender. This will prepare the mushrooms for eating and give the stock a phenomenal flavor!

Roasted Lamb with Persillade and New Potatoes

Our moms always made lamb in the springtime—just not like this. (Sorry, Mom . . . I hope you still set out my stocking at Christmas.) Theirs tended to be a little tough and a bit "gamey." Really, that's how most people think of lamb; it's the "other dark meat" (and not in a good way). But if cooked properly—and coated with a wonderful herb crust—lamb can be mellow and delicious. Our roast doesn't require a lot of tending to. We just rub it down with a whole lot of minced garlic, thyme, parsley, and rosemary (also known as persillade), stick it in a pan, and throw a few potatoes in the bottom of the pan to absorb the cooking juices. Then we set the timer for one hour and head to the patio to enjoy the springtime sun.

serves 8 to 10

PERSILLADE

2 tablespoons chopped fresh parsley

2 tablespoons chopped garlic

1 tablespoon fresh thyme leaves

1 tablespoon chopped fresh rosemary leaves

3 tablespoons extra virgin olive oil

2 teaspoons kosher salt

½ teaspoon freshly ground pepper

LAMB

one 2- to 4-pound boneless lamb roast from the
    shoulder or leg (ask the butcher to butterfly it)

kosher salt and freshly ground pepper

extra virgin olive oil

3 pounds small new red or Yukon Gold potatoes,
    cut in half

For the persillade, combine the parsley, garlic, thyme, and rosemary in the center of a cutting board and chop together until well blended. Transfer the mixture to a bowl and stir in the olive oil, salt, and pepper.

The day before cooking the roast, lightly season all the surfaces with salt and pepper and place in the refrigerator, uncovered, resting in a pan to catch the juices. Remove the roast from the fridge 2 hours before cooking. Lay the meat flat on a cutting board, pat dry with paper towels or a clean kitchen towel, and rub the persillade mixture over all the surfaces. Roll the meat tightly back to its original shape and tie with 3 pieces of butcher's twine—once around the center and again 2 inches from the ends.

Preheat the oven to 325 degrees.

Place the lamb in a roasting pan, drizzle with about 2 ounces of olive oil, and transfer to the oven to cook on the center rack. After 1 hour of cooking, add the cut potatoes to the pan around the lamb. Return to the oven to cook. For a leg, cook to a temperature of 140 degrees in the thickest part of the roast, 1½ to 2 hours. For a shoulder, cook to an internal temperature of 150 degrees, approximately 2 hours. Remove the pan from the oven and transfer the cooked potatoes to a separate dish so they don't soak up excess fat. Leave the roast to rest on the stovetop for a minimum of 30 minutes before slicing.

Persillade (pur-SEE-yad) is a mixture of chopped parsley combined with other seasonings such as garlic and a variety of other herbs. It can be added at the beginning of the cooking process for roasts or other large items or at the end, with small meats and vegetables.

Brooke on the Bottle—Rosé Wines: Thrifty Spring Fling

After a winter of overpriced reds, rosé wines are as welcome as a light spring tan. But first, you've got to banish visions (and flavors) of your mom's sweet, pink Zinfandel from the '70s and '80s.

A good rosé is dry, crisp, and floral. She's an actress to boot. While she can play like a red wine, with her fruit and body, she can also display the freshness and acidity of a white. This versatility means that she pairs with a wide array of foods—everything from take-out Chinese to the first spring lamb roast.

And here's the fun part—she's cheap! Okay, "affordable" would be the nicer word, but if you compare her to her French sisters, she's a steal at $15 (or less) a bottle. This has to do with a number of factors, but a biggie is AGE. Don't believe in the "vintage rosé" hullabaloo—rosé wines are meant to be enjoyed young, about a year or two after they're bottled.

Kind of like that mental checklist that helped you find Mr./Mrs. Right, take this checklist with you next time you visit the wine store. You'll walk away happy . . . and a little pink.

Best Regions for Rosé Wine
Southern France
Southern Italy
Northern Spain

Desirable Characteristics
Nice Fruit
Good Acidity
Light in Texture, Full in Flavor

Notes (the wine will taste like several of the below—though not ALL of the below)
Fresh Strawberry
Raspberries

Watermelon
Cherry
Herbs (depending on the region, the herby flavors could include thyme, rosemary, sage)

Grapes (my completely biased list of the grapes that make the best bone-dry rosé)
Grenache
Syrah
Cinsaut (or a combination of the latter three grapes)
Tempranillo

Sautéed Radishes

Unsalted butter, fresh radishes, and sea salt are a classic French nibble. The clean, bright flavors have a way of prepping a palate for deliciousness to come. We took this same principle and heated it through—turning a cool radish starter into a warm side dish. This is the perfect partner for the heavier lamb roast.

serves 4

1 tablespoon extra virgin olive oil

1 clove garlic, thinly sliced

3 cups quartered radishes

½ teaspoon kosher salt, plus more to taste

1 teaspoon finely grated lemon zest

1 tablespoon chopped fresh dill

1 tablespoon unsalted butter

freshly ground pepper

Place the olive oil and garlic in a large sauté pan over medium heat. When the garlic begins to sizzle, add the radishes and salt. Turn the heat to high and cook until the radishes are just tender, about 5 minutes. Add the lemon zest, dill, and butter and toss until the butter melts and the radishes are well coated. Remove from the heat and season to taste with salt and pepper.

MAKE AHEAD

The radishes can be sautéed up to a day in advance. Cook them as directed up to the point of adding the lemon zest, dill, and butter to the pan. Then, when you're ready to serve, finish the preparation with those last items, which should only take a couple of minutes.

Lemon Icebox Pie

Pull a bar of cream cheese from the fridge, a can of condensed milk from the pantry, a few lemons from the fruit basket, and you've got lemon icebox pie. Puckery and easy.

serves 8 to 10

CRUST

2 packages graham crackers, ground

½ cup granulated sugar

½ teaspoon kosher salt

¾ cup (1½ sticks) unsalted butter, melted

FILLING

finely grated zest of 1 lemon

one 8-ounce package cream cheese, at room
      temperature

1 cup sweetened condensed milk

½ cup fresh lemon juice (2 to 3 lemons)

Preheat the oven to 325 degrees.

For the crust, combine the graham cracker crumbs, sugar, and salt in a medium bowl. Mix well and stir in the melted butter to moisten. Press the crumbs over the bottom and up the sides of a 10-inch springform pan. Bake for 10 minutes and cool completely.

For the filling, combine the lemon zest and cream cheese in a bowl and beat with an electric mixer until light and fluffy. Add the sweetened condensed milk and continue mixing until smooth. Stir in the lemon juice and pour into the prepared crust. Freeze until set, about 2 hours. Serve chilled.

THE NEXT LEVEL

Dress Her Up—Try any of these garnishes to make your pie even more impressive: whipped cream, chopped hazelnuts, mint, or candied lemon zest.

DERBY DAY

The Kentucky Derby isn't a very big deal in New York City, but it certainly is in our apartment. Jamie dons his seersucker suit, watches all the pre-race coverage, makes sure that the bar is stocked with powdered sugar and crushed ice for his mint juleps, and then begins to turn out tray after tray of the most delectable cheese puffs stuffed with Country Ham Cream. Meanwhile, Brooke's hidden in a corner of the kitchen, elbow deep in chocolate ganache, rolling out dozens of bourbon truffles for post-race party favors. Even if you don't give a hoot about horse racing, Jamie's gougères and Brooke's truffles are reason enough to host your own Kentucky-themed, bourbon-heavy shindig!

Sweet Pea or Asparagus Soup Shots

Everyone gets a little excited when you hand them a shot glass—even if it's filled with soup. Here, we begin with a base of vichyssoise—a classic onion and potato soup—and add in sweet peas and parsley. You can turn it into the soup of your choice by pureeing in any cooked vegetable. The vibrant green of the sweet peas and asparagus make this beautiful. It's just as good cold as it is hot, which makes it a great do-ahead appetizer.

serves 12 plus as a "shot,"
or 4 to 6 as a first course

2 tablespoons unsalted butter

2 cups thinly sliced Vidalia or yellow onion

3 cloves garlic, sliced

2 teaspoons kosher salt, plus more to taste

2 cups peeled and diced Idaho potato (1 large)

3 cups water

4 cups sweet peas (two 10-ounce packages, frozen)

1 cup packed fresh mint or parsley leaves

or

2 bunches standard asparagus, thinly sliced with woody ends removed (3 to 4 cups)

1 cup packed fresh parsley or chervil, or ⅓ cup minced chives

1 cup sour cream or crème fraîche

freshly ground pepper

Place a medium saucepot over high heat, add the butter, and cook until lightly browned. Stir in the onion, garlic, and salt and sauté until translucent. When the onion is well softened, add the potato and water and bring the mixture to a simmer. Simmer until the potato can be easily crushed with the back of a spoon, about 15 minutes.

While the soup base is simmering, bring a pot of salted water to a boil. Add the peas or asparagus and herbs to the boiling water. Cook the vegetables until tender, 3 to 4 minutes. Pour into a colander and cool completely under cold running water. Leave the colander in the sink to drain while the potato soup base cooks.

Transfer the soup base to a blender in batches and process until smooth, or puree in the pot with an immersion blender. Add the sour cream and blanched vegetables; process again until smooth. Season to taste with salt and pepper. Serve hot immediately; the green color will fade as the soup remains hot. For a chilled soup, cool quickly by whisking the soup in a metal bowl set over another bowl of ice and refrigerate until ready to serve.

TECHNIQUE TIP

To keep your soup the brightest green, completely cool the soup base before pureeing your green veggies into it. This soup makes a perfect lunch with one of our sandwiches (pages 130 to 135). Garnish your bowl with a spoonful of sour cream and crumbled bacon!

HOW TO TRIM ASPARAGUS

How much is too much and when is it not enough? Trimming asparagus might seem tricky, but it's really not. Just hold the asparagus spear by its tip and by the base. Apply pressure until it snaps into 2 pieces. Wherever it naturally snaps is the dividing point between the tender flesh of the asparagus and its woody end. Use that spear as a reference point for where you will cut the rest of the asparagus.

LIKE A BUNCH OF FLOWERS

Think of asparagus like fresh-cut flowers—they need to be stored in water. It's best to loosely wrap a rubber band around the bunch of asparagus and arrange the spears in a standing position in a shallow pan of room-temperature water. If you do store asparagus this way, you can keep them on the countertop and out of the fridge.

Cornmeal Gougères

The addition of cornmeal and Country Ham Cream to the gougère is Jamie's Southern twist on a French classic. Supposedly the French word gougère *refers to a centuries-old baking technique and means "a bread roll baked under ashes." However, we think there's an alternate translation. Roughly, it's "impress the pants off your guests with these light-as-air cheese puffs." The classic French accompaniment to the gougère is bubbly. There's something about the savory, cheese-flecked dough and champagne that primes your taste buds for an evening of delicious eats.*

makes 2 to 3 dozen gougères

1½ cups whole milk

1½ cups water

¾ cup (1½ sticks) unsalted butter

1½ cups cornmeal, plus a bit more for topping

1½ cups all-purpose flour

2 teaspoons kosher salt

½ cup grated Gruyère cheese

7 large eggs

finely grated Parmesan cheese for topping

Preheat the oven to 425 degrees.

In a wide, heavy-bottomed saucepan, bring the milk, water, and butter to a boil over high heat. In a separate bowl, mix the cornmeal, flour, and salt. When the liquid reaches a boil, add the dry ingredients and beat vigorously with a wooden spoon. Continue to cook, stirring often, over very low heat for 5 minutes. The dough should be a smooth, shiny ball that has pulled cleanly from the sides of the pan.

Remove the dough to a bowl and beat with an electric mixer to release some of the steam. With the mixer still running, add all the Gruyère cheese and beat until incorporated. Next begin adding the eggs one at a time—waiting for each to be fully incorporated before adding the next. When all of the eggs have been added, place the dough in a pastry bag fitted with a large round tip, or put it in a heavy ziplock bag and snip off the corner to create an opening no larger than ½ inch.

Using baking sheets lined with parchment paper or silicone liners, pipe the dough into small, mounded domes, no more than 1 inch in diameter. When all of the dough is piped, wet the tip of your finger and smooth the top of each gougère. Go back over the sheets and sprinkle a small amount of cornmeal and Parmesan over each mound of dough.

Bake in the preheated oven for 6 minutes. Turn the pans 180 degrees and drop the temperature to 350 degrees. Bake until golden brown and cooked through (the inside should not be "doughy"), about 10 minutes more.

WORTH THE TROUBLE

We're not going to try to pull the whip-these-up-in-a-jiffy wool over your eyes. But what we will do is make you a promise—if you go to the effort to make these (with or without the country ham cream), your friends WILL talk about them, and your chef skills, for days. And then they'll reciprocate, and you'll likely see your party invites increase by 400 percent.

Country Ham Cream

So good, it's probably illegal in Alabama. . . . Our gougère filling is sinfully rich thanks to a healthy dose of cream. Bourbon brightens the flavor, then pureeing ham and onions into the liquid sends it into the meaty, slightly salty stratosphere.

makes 3 cups

4 ounces country ham or prosciutto ends
(don't spend the money on expensive
slices of good ham here)

¼ cup water

1 yellow onion, finely diced

1 cup bourbon

3 cups cream

Trim all of the fat from the ham and place the fat and water in a small saucepan over medium heat. Heat until the fat is rendered. Add the onion and continue cooking until very tender—being careful not to let it brown. Dice the ham meat, add it to the pan, and cook for 2 minutes more. Deglaze the pan with the bourbon and reduce until the pan is dry. Add the cream and simmer gently until well thickened. Carefully put the entire mixture in a blender and puree until smooth. Transfer the pureed cream to a piping bag fitted with a small metal tip and fill the gougère (see below).

THE NEXT LEVEL

The baked gougères can be filled with Country Ham Cream (above). Fill a pastry bag fitted with a fine piping tip with the cream. Use the piping tip to pierce the side of the gougère and squeeze the cream in, like filling a jelly doughnut. Alternatively cut the gougère in half, add a small spoonful of the cream to the hollow center, and replace the top. Or serve the cream on the side as dipping sauce.

Bourbon-Cured Trout

We say bourbon "cured" trout, but our "cure" is more of a boozy marinade than a lengthy curing process. First, the trout bathes in the brine, which gives it that salty, slightly sweet cured flavor. Then it's on to the grill to be cooked through and pick up a gentle smokiness. Super tender, savory fish is your reward for organizing, planning—and marinating!—ahead.

serves 6 to 8

4 pan-dressed trout, or 8 boneless fillets

3 cups water

1 cup bourbon

1 cup kosher salt

1 cup brown sugar

1 tablespoon black peppercorns

3 cloves garlic, crushed

1 bay leaf

4 cups ice cubes

THE NEXT LEVEL

Make your grilled trout into a killer crostini. To build this perfect bite, start with a toasted round of baguette, add a dollop of sour cream and then a cucumber slice. Rest a small piece of grilled trout on the cucumber and finish with a sprig of dill or a single parsley leaf.

Quickly rinse the trout under cold water and pat dry. Place in the refrigerator, uncovered, while preparing the brine.

Combine the water, bourbon, salt, sugar, peppercorns, garlic, and bay leaf in a medium saucepot. Bring the mixture to a boil so that the salt and sugar dissolve. Remove from the heat and stir in the ice. Cool the mixture completely and pour over the trout. Leave the trout to brine in the refrigerator for 4 to 6 hours.

Remove the trout from the brine and pat dry. Grill or broil skin side down for 3 to 5 minutes, until just cooked through. If cooking whole fish, turn once halfway through the cooking process.

TECHNIQUE TIP

Pan-dressed trout have been cleaned so that all of the bones of the spine, ribs, and belly are removed without separating the fillets or removing the head. It looks like a whole fish, head and all, but is actually 2 cleverly presented boneless fillets. If you'd rather not meet your dinner face-to-face, go for the boneless fillets, but leave the skin on—it will protect the meat while it cooks.

Bourbon Bacon and Oyster Brochettes

You say skewer, we say brochette (bro-SHETT). But any way you pronounce it, Jamie's come up with his own pretty darn amazing surf-and-turf hors d'oeuvre. He sees it as the "perfect bite": oyster, bacon, and pickle. In one mouthful, you get briny, smoky, and tart. These light pickles pair perfectly with oysters and bacon but may be substituted with Bread and Butter Pickles (page 207) or any jarred variety as long as they're not too sweet.

makes 12 brochettes

PICKLES
2 Kirby cucumbers, cut lengthwise in half and sliced
2 tablespoons salt
1 cup ice, crushed if possible
1 cup distilled white vinegar
2 cloves garlic, crushed
1 teaspoon red pepper flakes
½ cup granulated sugar
2 sprigs fresh dill, or ½ teaspoon dried dill

6 slices thick-cut bacon
½ cup bourbon
12 oysters, shucked

To make the pickles, toss the sliced cucumbers with 1 tablespoon of the salt and place in a colander. Cover with the crushed ice and leave in the sink to drain for 2 to 3 hours.

Remove any remaining ice and give the cucumbers a quick rinse. Squeeze dry in a clean kitchen towel and place in a heatproof container. (This little step makes the pickles extra crisp but can be skipped if time or space doesn't allow.)

Bring the remaining ingredients along with the remaining 1 tablespoon salt to a rapid boil and pour over the cucumbers. Cover tightly and refrigerate overnight. The cucumbers will be ready in 12 hours.

Cut the bacon slices in half and arrange in a single layer in a baking dish. Bring the bourbon to a simmer in a small pot and pour over the bacon. Wrap tightly with aluminum foil and set aside to allow the bourbon to infuse the bacon, 15 minutes.

Wrap each of the half slices of bacon around an oyster and secure with a small skewer. Place these back in the baking dish with the bourbon until ready to cook.

Quickly cook the brochettes on a hot grill or under the broiler until the bacon is browned and the oysters are plumped. While the oysters are cooking, the bourbon bath should be brought to a boil before the cooked brochettes are returned to the dish. Just before serving, place a pickle at the end of each skewer.

TECHNIQUE TIPS

Any good seafood market sells shucked oysters. They typically come in pint-size containers packed in some of their own liquid. Keep the container stored on ice in the coldest part of the refrigerator until ready to use.

Thick-cut bacon from the deli case works great, but if you can get slab bacon from the butcher's counter, you'll be doing even better. Cut the bacon into chunks slightly smaller than the oyster; give it a bourbon bath.

Chocolate Bourbon Truffles

Chocolate truffles take their name and shape from their earthier counterpart—those wild, and wildly expensive, subterranean mushrooms. Lucky for us, the sweet, make-at-home variety are really economical. These bite-size delicacies are nothing more than chocolate ganache—quite simply, melted chocolate with some sort of natural additive (like cream or butter) that keeps them soft. A classic finishing touch is to roll the chocolate balls in cocoa powder. The cocoa resembles the loose dirt that clings to the real mushrooms once they're dug up from the root systems of oak and elm trees.

makes 3 to 4 dozen truffles

1 cup cream

2 tablespoons (¼ stick) unsalted butter

16 ounces bittersweet chocolate, broken into small
      pieces

2 tablespoons bourbon

OPTIONAL TRUFFLE COATINGS:
semisweet cocoa powder, finely ground almonds
        or hazelnuts, shredded sweetened coconut,
        or powdered sugar

Bring the cream to a boil in a saucepot over medium heat. Add the butter and chocolate to the boiling cream, remove from the heat, and stir until smooth. Pour the chocolate mixture into a bowl and stir in the bourbon. Refrigerate until firm.

Set up a workstation: Fill a coffee mug with hot water from the tap. Place a teaspoon or melon baller in the water. Place a baking sheet that will fit in the refrigerator on the countertop and line with wax paper. Scoop small "balls" of chocolate onto the wax paper, dipping the spoon back into the water between scoops. Continue until the tray is full, then refrigerate until firm, at least 1 hour. Make small plates of whatever coating you choose: cocoa powder, ground nuts, coconut, or powdered sugar.

Remove the chocolates from the fridge and roll each ball between the palms of your hands to make them round. (Be prepared—this is a messy job!) Roll in the plates of coating and refrigerate to firm. Remove from the refrigerator 1 hour before serving.

ALL CHOCOLATE IS NOT CREATED EQUAL

You walk down the baking aisle and you're bombarded with dozens of different chocolate brands, each one touting its superiority and "cocoa-ness." How to choose? We've tried them all, so just trust us. Brooke's favorite, easy-to-find, top-shelf brands are Scharffen Berger and Ghirardelli. Check out their labels and choose the bars that have between 63 and 72 percent cocoa—the percentage reflecting the cacao content (aka how much of what you're buying is actually derived from the cocoa bean). The remaining percentage is filler—the sugar, vanilla, and myriad "extras" that make the chocolate bar more appealing to the masses. But you're not just everybody . . . you're a discerning chef-in-the-making! Go for the good stuff!

The Perfect Mint Julep

Jamie has enjoyed a lot of bourbon in his day—often garnished with mint, and sometimes finished with a splash of soda. But he never knew how to make a "proper" mint julep until he became buddies with Adam Harris, New York City's king of all things bourbon. Sadly, Adam is now plying the residents of Austin with his delicious creations and expertise, but Jamie and Brooke still toast him every May.

serves 1

1 teaspoon superfine or granulated sugar

4 mint leaves

crushed ice

2 ounces Maker's Mark bourbon

mint sprigs

powdered sugar (optional)

Place the superfine sugar and mint leaves in a silver julep cup, and muddle to release the aroma of the mint. Add enough crushed ice to fill the cup halfway. Pour in the bourbon and stir until frost forms on the outside of the glass. Add more crushed ice until it is mounded just over the top of the cup. Stick 3 or 4 mint sprigs into the center of the ice and insert a straw through the mint all the way to the bottom of the cup. Cut the straw off about 2 inches above the mint and dust the top with powdered sugar. Sipping a julep should be a dual sensory experience—the short straw makes the nose fill with the scent of mint while you taste the sweet bourbon.

ESSENTIAL EQUIPMENT

Mint Julep Cup—If your family hasn't passed down to you a set of century-old julep cups, chances are you don't have any. No worries. Even without a proper julep cup, you can still make a great mint julep in a rocks glass. Just promise us, no red plastic cups. Ever.

No-Pressure Parties

Inviting friends over comes with a certain set of pressures. You feel like you have to spring clean, even if it's December ("Dust bunnies and last year's catalogs be gone!"), fill every platter in the house with savory goodies, and churn out nightclub-worthy cocktails. Combine that with the pressure of a big holiday like New Year's Eve and you're bound to combust. Why not take it easy and entertain on the "off" nights? You can have just as much fun on December 30th as on December 31st. Check out Brooke's list of No-Pressure Parties and host one of your own.

Instead of: Baby Shower
Try: Sprinkle (the low-key equivalent of a shower that is given for your sister/cousin/girlfriend's second or third child)
Instead of: New Year's Eve
Try: December 30
Instead of: Oscar Night
Try: The finale of your favorite reality TV show
More fun excuses to throw low-key parties: Housewarming, Wine Tasting, Chocolate Party, Show Off Your Goodies (display your new wedding loot), or Game Night

GIRLS' NIGHT IN

Brooke invites the girls over under a premise—playing Scrabble, watching *Real Housewives,* checking out Baby Parker's chubby thighs. But, really, all anyone cares about is good food, a relaxing drink, and catching up on life.

The game plan for Girls' Night In is to treat your girlfriends to restaurant-quality nibbles and drinks and to maybe show off a little bit in the process. Pull out your wedding loot! Climb to the top of your pantry and dust off all those platters and serving pieces! Open that package of cute cocktail napkins!

Everything on this menu, except for the shrimp, is meant to be made in advance. So the day of the party, all you need to do is fill little bowls with our sugar snap peas, unmold the torta onto a big platter, pop the blue cheese rounds into the oven, and whisk together the coconut sauce for the shrimp. The food is easy on the hostess (you!) and easy on the eyes. One important menu-planning trick for a cocktail party: always feature foods that can easily be eaten with one hand. Your right hand holds a cracker, while the left balances a glass of wine. You don't want to do the cocktail plate, fork, and knife juggle! Dessert, however, is a two-handed affair. Pass around a big glass bowl of orange and cinnamon-spiced chocolate mousse and let everyone serve themselves as little or as much as their hearts desire.

Blue Cheese Crackers

Brooke loves doing the cheese platter and cracker thing. But, finally, feeling like she needed to step up her game as a hostess, she sat down in earnest with Jamie to devise a new h.o.d. to please the girls. He asked her what they all love. "Well . . . cheese and crackers." In the end, we decided to make our own blue cheese crackers by whipping up a big batch of cheesy, buttery dough and freezing it into a log. Once it firms up, you have the equivalent of slice-and-bake cookies. With your new chef's knife, slice the dough into rounds, place them on a cookie sheet, and then pop them in the oven. While they bake, prepare one of our toppings or our fresh fig chutney (page 257). We love Maytag for a domestic blue and Bleu d'Auvergne for a little bit fancier, more subtle French cheese.

makes 2 to 3 dozen crackers

8 tablespoons (1 stick) unsalted butter, at room
  temperature
½ teaspoon kosher salt
1 teaspoon freshly ground pepper
8 ounces blue cheese, crumbled or roughly
  chopped
1 large egg
1½ cups all-purpose flour

Place the butter, salt, and pepper in a bowl and beat with an electric mixer until light and fluffy. Add the blue cheese and continue mixing until thoroughly incorporated. Scrape down the sides of the bowl and beat in the egg to loosen the mixture. Fold in the flour with a spatula.

Lay a piece of plastic wrap flat on a clean countertop. Turn the mixture out of the bowl onto the plastic wrap and form it into a long cylinder along the bottom third of the wrap. Pull the wrap up over the dough and continue rolling toward the top of the plastic wrap. Twist the ends of the wrap tightly to help form a compact cylinder about 2 inches wide and 6 to 8 inches long. Place the dough in the freezer to firm. Dough can be kept frozen, up to 3 months.

Preheat the oven to 375 degrees.

Remove the dough from the freezer and cut into ¼-inch slices. Arrange the slices at least ½ inch apart on an aluminum-foil-lined baking sheet. Bake until lightly browned, about 7 minutes. The surface of the crackers will look slightly oily and foamy from the butter; pat off the excess with paper towels. Remove to a rack to cool. Store at room temperature in an airtight container or a ziplock bag, up to 1 week.

Mushroom Topping

Pungent blue cheese and earthy mushrooms are natural complements. Just make sure to sauté the mushrooms until all the moisture has been cooked out. No matter how cute of a hostess you are, no one likes soggy crackers.

makes 1½ cups or topping
for about 24 crackers

1 tablespoon butter
8 ounces sliced mushrooms, any variety
kosher salt and freshly ground pepper to taste
1 tablespoon thinly sliced chives
1 to 2 tablespoons sour cream (optional)

Place the butter in a small sauté pan over high heat. When the butter begins to sizzle, add the mushrooms, season with salt and pepper, and sauté until completely tender and lightly browned, about 4 minutes. Remove the cooked mushrooms to a plate lined with paper towels to drain and cool. Roughly chop the mushrooms, then transfer to a small bowl. Stir in the chives and sour cream.

Tomato Topping

Tomatoes add a bite of freshness and acidity to our app. Their eye-popping color coupled with the fresh basil brings a lovely brightness to the platter.

makes 1½ cups or topping
for about 24 crackers

2 cups grape tomatoes, quartered, or 4 Roma or
    plum tomatoes, seeded, cored, and roughly
    chopped
1 clove garlic, minced
finely grated Parmesan cheese
extra virgin olive oil
1 tablespoon finely chopped sliced almonds
kosher salt and freshly ground pepper
4 to 6 fresh basil leaves, torn, for garnish

Combine the tomatoes, garlic, Parmesan, olive oil, and almonds in a food processor and pulse to a chunky but spoonable consistency. Season to taste with salt and pepper. Garnish with the basil.

BETTER THAN A SECRET SAUCE— CHUTNEYS AND RELISHES REVEALED

Relishes and chutneys are a great alternative to traditional sauces, those that require multiple steps and lots of "reduction" time (that's the time the sauce bubbles away on the stove, its flavors deepening and its consistency thickening). Relishes and chutneys also tend to get better as they sit, so we recommend that you make them in advance and store them at the back of your fridge. Check out these easy ideas on how to get some extra flavor on your plate—fast.

Fig Chutney

How impressed will your girlfriends be with homemade fig chutney on their crackers? The interplay of savory blue cheese and sweet figs is absolutely unforgettable. The next night, use the leftover chutney as a topper for a log of creamy goat cheese. Keeps for 10 days.

makes about 2 cups

⅓ cup red wine vinegar
pinch of ground cloves
½ teaspoon ground cinnamon
½ teaspoon freshly ground pepper
3 tablespoons brown sugar
1 teaspoon kosher salt
2 cups Black Mission figs, diced
1 lemon, zest grated and juiced

Combine all the ingredients except the figs and lemon in a small saucepot. Bring the mixture to a boil and reduce to a simmer. Stir in the figs and cook until softened and the mixture is well thickened, about 12 minutes. Remove from the heat and stir in the lemon zest and 1 tablespoon of the juice. Transfer to a ceramic or glass bowl and cool to room temperature.

Tomato Chutney

Our tomato chutney is a spiced—not spicy—tomato sauce with lots of texture. You'll be thankful to have it accompany your roasted pork tenderloin leftovers. This one's also delicious on any grilled or roasted fish, especially salmon. Keeps for 1 week.

makes about 2 cups

¼ cup canola or vegetable oil
1 tablespoon cumin seeds
½ teaspoon red pepper flakes
1 cup minced yellow onion
1 tablespoon minced garlic
one 14.5-ounce can chopped tomatoes
kosher salt and freshly ground pepper to taste

Heat the oil in a small pot over medium heat. Add the cumin and red pepper flakes and toast in the oil. When the spices are very aromatic, stir in the onion and garlic. Cook until translucent. Add the tomatoes and bring the mixture to a simmer. Cook at a simmer, stirring occasionally, until well thickened, about 15 minutes. Cool and season with salt and pepper.

Grapefruit and Avocado Relish

Sweet, sour, and rich, this relish has a lot to offer. Try it on grilled snapper instead of Pecan Sauce (page 94) or any other grilled or roasted fish. Keeps for 2 to 3 days.

serves 4 to 6

1 grapefruit

1 teaspoon red wine vinegar

pinch of granulated sugar

½ teaspoon kosher salt, plus more as needed

3 tablespoons extra virgin olive oil

1 avocado, pitted and diced

1 tablespoon chopped chives

freshly ground pepper to taste

Cut the grapefruit into supremes (page 14) and reserve 1 tablespoon of the juice. In a separate bowl, whisk together the reserved grapefruit juice, the vinegar, sugar, and salt until dissolved. Stir in the olive oil. Add the grapefruit, avocado, and chives. Stir together gently to avoid breaking the fruit or avocado and season to taste with salt and pepper.

Mango Chutney

Mango chutney is classic Indian fare. And, luckily, very easy to prepare. We think you'll love this as a sandwich spread—especially when wrapped around roasted and sliced pork or chicken. When you make a platter of grilled shrimp at your next cookout, offer a bowl of this sweet and spicy chutney on the side. Keeps for 10 days.

makes 3 cups

2 tablespoons extra virgin olive oil

1 teaspoon mustard seeds or ground mustard

1 teaspoon ground ginger

1 small red onion, minced

1 jalapeño, seeded and minced

¼ cup granulated sugar

¼ cup distilled white or white wine vinegar

2 ripe mangoes, peeled and diced

kosher salt and freshly ground pepper to taste

Heat the olive oil in a small saucepot over medium heat. Add the mustard and ginger and toast until aromatic. Stir in the onion and jalapeño and sauté until softened, about 5 minutes. Stir in the sugar and vinegar and bring the mixture to a simmer. Add the mangoes and simmer until tender, stirring occasionally to make sure nothing sticks to the bottom of the pot. Remove from the heat to cool and season with salt and pepper.

Grilled Corn and Roasted Red Pepper Relish

We think corn calls for more corn. Pour this smoky, sweet relish into a serving dish and set it next to a big bowl of corn tortilla chips. It's also great spooned on top of grilled or roasted chicken and served with a small salad of spinach or arugula. Keeps for 2 to 3 days.

serves 4 to 6

3 ears yellow corn, shucked
2 tablespoons extra virgin olive oil, plus more to
    brush the corn
kosher salt and freshly ground pepper to taste
1 red bell pepper, roasted, peeled, and diced (see
    page 86 for roasting instructions)
1 tablespoon chopped fresh cilantro
1 tablespoon fresh lime juice

Brush the corn with olive oil and season with salt and pepper. Char on all sides on a hot grill or under the broiler. Cut the kernels from the cobs. In a medium bowl, combine the corn, roasted pepper, and cilantro. Mix well and add the lime juice and the 2 tablespoons olive oil. Season with salt and pepper.

Green Peach Relish

Tart, firm peaches scream for something a little fatty and succulent—think roasted or grilled duck breast or sliced flank steak. Keeps for 1 week.

serves 6 to 8

1 red onion, sliced into rings
extra virgin olive oil
2 firm peaches
1 tablespoon chopped fresh chives
1 lime, juiced
kosher salt and freshly ground pepper to taste

Brush the onion slices with olive oil and grill until well charred (completely black) on both sides. Remove the pits from the peaches and dice. Chop the charred onion and mix with the peaches and chives. Add olive oil and lime juice to taste. Season with salt and pepper.

Goat Cheese, Pesto, and Sun-Dried Tomato Strata

This savory cheese spread will become the Homecoming Queen of your girls' night buffet. (And around the holidays, the guys go crazy for this as well; Brooke's cousins fight for the rights to the butter knife when she sets this out on the Christmas sideboard.) The alternating layers—"strata" means "layers"—of goat cheese, tomatoes, and pesto make it a beauty inside and out. So that the lively flavors can have a chance to mingle, make sure to prepare this one day in advance.

serves 12

1 cup loosely packed, coarsely chopped spinach
    leaves
1 cup loosely packed fresh basil leaves
1 teaspoon minced garlic
¼ cup good-quality extra virgin olive oil
1 cup grated Parmesan cheese
kosher salt and freshly ground pepper to taste
8 ounces cream cheese, at room temperature
4 ounces goat cheese, at room temperature
¼ cup oil-packed sun-dried tomatoes, finely
    chopped
2 teaspoons fresh thyme leaves, finely chopped
¼ cup chopped toasted walnuts or pecans
Toasted baguette rounds or bagel chips for serving

In a food processor or blender, combine the spinach, basil, and garlic. While the machine is running, stream in the olive oil through the opening. Add the Parmesan and process until almost smooth. Season with salt and pepper.

In a medium bowl, whip the cream cheese and goat cheese together with an electric mixer until lightened and smooth.

In a small bowl, stir together the sun-dried tomatoes and fresh thyme.

Line a 3-cup bowl with plastic wrap, leaving a 4-inch overhang.

With a medium-size spoon, spread one-third of the cream cheese mixture in the bottom of the prepared bowl. Spread half of the pesto over the cheese. Sprinkle half of the walnuts over the pesto and then arrange half of the tomatoes over the walnuts. Repeat the layering with the remaining cream cheese mixture, pesto, walnuts, and tomatoes. Fold the plastic overhang over the top of the spread. Press gently to compact the mixture. Refrigerate for at least 2 hours but preferably up to 1 day.

To serve, unfold the plastic from the top and invert the strata onto a plate. Carefully remove the bowl and plastic wrap. Arrange baguette rounds and/or chips around the strata and serve.

TIME-STRAPPED HOSTESS

When Brooke is short on time (and it's winter and basil costs an arm and a leg), she'll buy premade pesto. To brighten it a bit, she adds a handful of spinach leaves, a branch or two of basil, and a little olive oil to smooth things out.

TECHNIQUE TIP

Spreads Like Icing—Just like when icing a cake, dip your spoon in a cup of lukewarm water when spreading the cream cheese and goat cheese mixture. This prevents the cheese from sticking to the spoon and the touch of moisture keeps the cheese smooth. Your layers will be intact and the final product will be gorgeous.

Brooke on the Bottle—Sip and Sup Like a "Real Housewife"

My favorite housewives are always playing in the sun, maxing out their credit cards . . . and drinking. It's a toss-up as to what they like to drink the most—white wine or margaritas. Things *really* get crazy when they drink both!

Thursday night is my standing *Real Housewives*/New Housewives cocktail party at the apartment. All my newly married girlfriends (and bachelorette besties) gather to watch the latest episode, sip, sup, and gossip like the ladies of leisure we're destined to be in our next lives.

I serve a combo of light fare and cheesy decadence, from skinny-jeans-friendly shrimp skewers to diet-be-damned goat cheese torta. But, most importantly, I take the time to tend bar like a pro.

With a little mixology help from Jamie, I pay homage to my favorite Housewives with two cocktails. For the white wine margaritas, I stir up a pitcher full of crisp Sauvignon Blanc, Cointreau, and fresh lime juice. Two of those make me feel warm and social, but thanks to the substitution of wine for tequila, I leave the lampshades alone and don't sing along to the theme music. The Smackdown (something that occurs on every episode) is an occasional indulgence—a crazy, delicious combination of fresh grapefruit juice and the aforementioned Crazy Water, tequila. I stick to just one of these because I don't want to be cast as the newest Housewife.

GIRLS' NIGHT COCKTAILS

Watch out! While these cocktails go down smooth, they might make you act a little rough-around-the-edges—just like my favorite prime-time ladies.

White Wine Margarita

serves 6 to 8

4 ounces fresh lime juice (4 to 5 limes)
2 ounces fresh lemon juice
2 ounces fresh orange juice
¼ cup granulated sugar
4 ounces Cointreau or Triple Sec
1 bottle Sauvignon Blanc (preferably from New
     Zealand), chilled
ice cubes
lime wedges for garnish

Combine the fruit juices and sugar in a pitcher and stir until the sugar is dissolved. Stir in the Cointreau, wine, and a few ice cubes. Pour into wineglasses over a few ice cubes and garnish each with a lime wedge; salt optional.

The Smackdown

serves 4

6 fresh mint leaves
1 teaspoon granulated sugar
6 ounces tequila
4 ounces grapefruit juice
ice cubes
4 ounces ginger ale or club soda

Combine the mint leaves and sugar in the bottom of a cocktail shaker. Crush with a muddle stick until the sugar is dissolved. Add the tequila, grapefruit juice, and 4 ice cubes. Shake until well chilled. Stir in the ginger ale or club soda and strain into chilled martini glasses.

Shrimp and Pineapple Skewers

You've gotta embrace turning the big three-o. For Brooke that meant flying down to the Gulf, renting a beach house for the weekend, and throwing a Salty & Sweet–themed birthday party. (Because by age thirty, she thinks that you need to be a little of both to survive.) While our New York houseguests enjoyed several bottles of Chablis and waited for everyone else to arrive for the dinner party, Jamie, on a whim, whipped up several plates of these skewers to tide us over. A beautiful pineapple at the grocery store had caught his eye and so had a can of coconut milk from the ethnic food aisle. (Brooke thinks he was planning ahead—thinking he'd be tipsy at 4 A.M. and in need of a bowl of homemade coconut curry.) With about two pounds of sweet Pensacola Bay shrimp at his disposal, he knew that he had the makings for a memorable birthday h.o.d.—one that's a little salty and a little sweet.

serves 8

24 medium shrimp, peeled and deveined

1 pineapple, peeled and cut into 1- x ½-inch pieces

Ultimate Grill Salt or Creole Seasoning (page 61
    or 63)

2 tablespoons thinly sliced scallions

1 tablespoon minced garlic

1 tablespoon finely grated fresh ginger

2 jalapeños, seeded and chopped

one 13.5-ounce can coconut milk

extra virgin olive oil

Arrange the shrimp and pineapple chunks on 6-inch skewers. Sprinkle with grill salt.

Combine the scallions, garlic, ginger, jalapeños, and coconut milk in a small pot. Bring the mixture to a simmer over low heat and reduce by half. Transfer to a blender and process until smooth. Keep the coconut mixture warm while you cook the shrimp.

Brush the shrimp skewers with olive oil and cook on a preheated grill or on a baking sheet beneath the broiler approximately 2 minutes per side. Drizzle the coconut milk mixture over the shrimp and serve warm with the remaining coconut sauce as a dip.

Sugar Snap Peas with Orange and Mint

These peas are fun finger food that are actually healthy. The citrus and the mint kind of act like palate cleansers so you can move back and forth between the blue cheese crackers and the shrimp skewers no problem!

serves 6

6 cups sugar snap peas

1 tablespoon coarse sea salt

2 teaspoons finely grated orange zest

1 teaspoon extra virgin olive oil

one dozen torn mint leaves

Trim the stem ends from the peas and rinse them in a colander under cold water. Bring a large pot of well-salted water to a rapid boil. Prepare a bowl of ice water. Drop the peas into the boiling water; cook until tender-crisp, about 2 minutes. Remove immediately to the ice water. Cool completely and drain well.

While the peas are draining, combine the salt, orange zest, and olive oil in a bowl. Mixing the salt with oil only (no liquid), keeps it from dissolving into the dressing. This gives the peas a delicious salty crunch. When the peas are well dried, toss with the oil mixture and mint. Serve slightly chilled.

Chocolate Mousse au Chez Janou

Our first "vrai" chocolate mousse experience was in Paris at Chez Janou, a little Provençal restaurant on the Right Bank. One of Jamie's former culinary students lived a few doors down and suggested that she and her husband meet us at Janou for a late dinner. After several stunning courses of bright vegetable terrines, simply prepared seafood, and house-made pasta, we declared that we couldn't eat another bite. Then we looked one table over. The most luscious-looking glass bowl of chocolate mousse rested between the couple, a smaller bowl of whipped cream to the side. After they finished cleaning their plates, they served themselves a spoonful more. We had to have it—and we knew we had to do the communal bowl of chocolate mousse thing at our next party stateside. Our orange- and cinnamon-scented chocolate mousse is the best you'll ever eat (unless you're at Chez Janou, of course).

serves 6

8 ounces semisweet chocolate

1 tablespoon unsalted butter

¾ cup cream

grated zest of 1 orange

pinch of ground cinnamon

6 large egg whites

2 tablespoons granulated sugar

Combine the chocolate and butter in a heatproof bowl. This will be your serving bowl so choose a clear glass or colored ceramic bowl at least 1 quart in size. Bring the cream, orange zest, and cinnamon to a boil, pour it over the chocolate, and let sit for 3 minutes. Stir to combine and continue whisking until smooth.

Whip the egg whites to soft peaks. Gradually add the sugar and continue whisking until stiff peaks form. Gently fold the whipped egg whites one-third at a time into the chocolate mixture. Refrigerate, covered with plastic wrap, for at least 1 hour.

Chez Janou

For a taste of Provence, visit this Right Bank gem. Not only can you graze on the perfect h.o.d. sampler platter of little fried fish, cold ratatouille, and olive tapenade while you sample their selection of eighty different pastis, but you can also indulge your inner chocaholic with the best ever communal bowl of chocolate mousse. **Chez Janou**—2 rue Roger Verlomme, 75003 Paris; Tel-33 01 42 72 2841; www.chezjanou.com.

Garlic: Five Favorites

1. **Sweet Roasted Garlic Spread:** Cut the top off of a whole head of garlic, just enough to expose the tops of the cloves, leaving everything attached at the root. Place the garlic on a square of aluminum foil, drizzle with olive oil, sprinkle with salt, and seal the foil to make a pouch. Roast at 425 to 450 degrees for 35 to 40 minutes. Serve with a crusty baguette.
2. **Garlic-Infused Olive Oil:** Lightly crush (smash with the side of your knife) whole cloves of garlic (you can leave the skins on). Place the crushed cloves in a small saucepot and add enough olive oil to cover completely. Turn the heat to medium and let the oil and cloves lightly bubble for 10 minutes. Strain the oil and discard the cloves. Keep the oil refrigerated for up to 3 months. The oil is perfect to drizzle on salads, popcorn, and pasta dishes.
3. **Garlic Crust:** On a Microplane or the fine side of a box grater, finely grate garlic cloves. Mix the gratings with olive oil, salt, and pepper. This mixture makes the perfect rub for roasts and chicken and is great to incorporate into Jamie's homemade seasoned salts (pages 61 to 63). Keeps for 1 week.
4. **Fresh Garlic Finish:** For a burst of flavor, finish off sautéed veggies with a shower of finely sliced or minced fresh garlic.
5. **Ghost Garlic:** That is, sneak it in there. Prepare your favorite dishes with lightly crushed whole cloves rather than chopped, minced, or sliced. When you have finished cooking, remove the large pieces before serving. The flavor will remain, though it will be a touch lighter than if you had prepared the dish using chopped.

BACHELOR FEAST

Our wedding came about so fast, Jamie never had a final blowout with his guys. But if he could have, it would have gone something like this: a group of his best buddies sitting on the back porch with a fire pit and glasses of bourbon to keep warm, thick steaks on the grill, and a great football game on TV.

If you're planning your own night with the guys, this menu's got it all. The mac-n-cheese is easy to make in advance and only gets better if you let it sit around. Let the blue cheese butter hang out in the freezer while you wait for the steaks to finish cooking. That just leaves the men and the meat. Since nearly every guy is a self-proclaimed expert, why not let them all cook their own over a bed of hot coals? And the only way to top a big fire is more fire, so finish off that bottle of bourbon by sending your apples up in a blaze and then pile them on top of vanilla ice cream. This food is so good, the ladies might try to sneak in for a bite. . . . Jamie will leave that up to you.

Blood Orange Old-Fashioned

When in season, blood oranges lend the perfect mix of sweetness and acidity to make a great glass of bourbon even better. But when blood oranges are not available, any good fresh orange will do. Just don't go for the OJ concentrate or the stuff that's been sitting on the grocery store shelf for a week!

serves 1

1 slice orange, rind on, cut in half
½ teaspoon granulated sugar
ice cubes
3 ounces bourbon
splash of club soda (optional)

Place the halved orange slice in the bottom of a rocks glass. Add the sugar and grind with a muddle stick or a spoon until the sugar is dissolved. Add enough ice to nearly fill the glass, pour in the bourbon, and stir until chilled. Top with a splash of club soda if desired.

Grilled Caesar Salad

A Caesar dressing that gets it just right is hard to find. There are so many things that can go wrong. It can be too eggy, too fishy, too puckery—just too "strong" (as Brooke's grandmother, Ms. Theda Ball, would say). But when it's made right, it's bold, tangy, and oh-so-good that you almost want to lick your salad bowl. Yes . . . go ahead . . . no one's looking! The only touch that makes Jamie's creamy dressing better is a salad of grilled romaine. Grilling the romaine over a high flame just warms the lettuces, giving them a great smoky flavor, without wilting or making them mushy.

serves 6

Caesar Dressing

makes 2 cups

2 large egg yolks (if you prefer, substitute
    2 tablespoons mayonnaise)
3 flat anchovy fillets, or more to taste, rinsed
    and drained
4 cloves garlic
¼ cup grated Parmesan cheese
1 tablespoon fresh lemon juice
1 tablespoon red wine vinegar
1 teaspoon Worcestershire sauce
1 tablespoon Dijon mustard
½ cup extra virgin olive oil
1 cup canola oil
¼ teaspoon freshly ground pepper

In a blender, puree together the egg yolks, anchovies, garlic, cheese, lemon juice, vinegar, Worcestershire, and mustard. With the blender still running, drizzle in the oils and process until the mixture becomes thick. Stir in the pepper and season to taste.

Worcestershire sauce is one of the most famous mistakes in the world of food. In 1835, Misters Lea and Perrins, two chemists in Worcestershire, England, were commissioned by the former governor of Bengal, India, to create a sauce to feed his hankering for curry. History remembers their original effort kindly as "unpalatable"; it was stored in the basement in a barrel and forgotten. Rediscovering the sauce two years later, they found their concoction had mellowed to become wonderfully flavorful. They began bottling and selling the sauce immediately and haven't stopped since.

Grilled Romaine

Yep, we want you to grill your lettuce. Not individual leaves of lettuce, mind you (that would prove very time-consuming and a little weird), but large wedges of romaine with their hefty, fragrant hearts. Just remember that a screaming-hot grill is the only way to impart the heads of romaine with a gentle, smoky flavor without cooking them into a mushy mess. If you don't feel like firing up a grill, our dressing is just as delicious on regular romaine.

serves 6

1 cup crusty bread cut into ½- to 1-inch cubes
1 teaspoon Creole Seasoning (page 63)
3 tablespoons unsalted butter, melted
3 heads romaine lettuce

Preheat the oven to 350 degrees.

Combine the bread, seasoning, and butter in a bowl and mix well. Spread in a single layer on a baking sheet and bake until lightly browned, about 10 minutes. Cut the heads of romaine in half lengthwise. Place cut side down on paper towels to drain.

Heat a grill or a cast-iron grill pan on high. Rub the grates of the grill with oil and place the romaine, cut side down, over direct heat. Grill just until marks appear, about 1 minute. Place half a romaine head on each plate. Drizzle with the dressing and scatter the croutons.

TECHNIQUE TIP

We can't stress this enough—a super-hot grill is a must for grilling your lettuce!

Ultimate Tomato-Bacon Mac-n-Cheese

Jamie won't settle for just shells and Cheddar when he's making mac-n-cheese, especially when the guys are coming over. He insists on cooking an over-the-top version of the old standby, incorporating every man's favorite ingredients—bacon and hot sauce—into the dish. Three cheeses with different tastes and textures— sharp Cheddar, fresh mozzarella, and aged Parmesan— make this the ultimate mac-n-cheese.

serves 4

1 pound penne pasta

8 ounces lean bacon or pancetta

about 2 tablespoons fat (unsalted butter or olive oil)

1 cup canned chopped tomatoes

¼ cup all-purpose flour

3 cups milk

2 cups grated Cheddar cheese

1 tablespoon sriracha hot sauce

kosher salt and freshly ground pepper

8 ounces mozzarella cheese, diced

1 cup grated Parmesan cheese

Preheat the oven to 400 degrees.

Bring a large pot of salted water to a rapid boil. Add the pasta and cook until just tender but not completely soft, about 10 minutes. Drain the pasta immediately and rinse with warm water to keep it from sticking. Set aside to drain.

Cut the bacon into a small dice or lardons and place in a large, heavy-bottomed pot over low heat. Slowly render the fat from the meat; you may have to add a little oil to help the browning if the bacon is extremely lean. When the meat is brown and crisped, remove it from the pot with a slotted spoon to drain on paper towels.

Measure the fat left in the pot and add enough butter to make 4 tablespoons (or discard any excess). Stir the flour into the hot fat and cook until a paste forms, about 3 minutes. Add the canned tomatoes and stir vigorously, cooking 3 minutes more, until the paste is dry and extremely thick.

Stir in 1 cup of the milk and mix thoroughly with a wooden spoon. Scrape any bits from the bottom of the pot and stir vigorously until a smooth, very thick paste forms. Whisk in the remaining 2 cups milk. Mix until smooth and bring to a simmer. Cook for 7 to 10 minutes at a simmer until thickened. Add the Cheddar and whisk until smooth. Stir in the hot sauce and season to taste with salt and pepper.

Mix the cooked pasta into the sauce and return to a simmer. Add the crisped bacon to the pot along with the diced mozzarella and turn off the heat. Stir the mixture together and transfer to a large gratin dish.

Cover the top of the pasta with grated Parmesan and bake until bubbling and golden brown on top.

THE NEXT LEVEL

In the summer, when tomatoes are at their juiciest and bursting with flavor, chop one or two (making sure to remove the seeds) and mix them into the pasta with the bacon and mozzarella.

How to Select the Perfect Steak

You only need two things for a great steak: quality meat and a hot grill. (While you're at it, throw in some kosher salt and freshly ground black pepper for enhanced flavor.) That means the onus of turning out a great steak rests squarely on the shoulders of the hunk of meat that you select. Here's what to look for:

Color—The color of the meat is a great indicator of how much it's been aged. Good or bad. Proper aging of steak yields a slightly darker, more brown color. It might not be the prettiest steak in the butcher's case, but it's the tastiest, with the richest, deepest flavor. Improper aging—aka steaks that have been sitting in the butcher's case too long—will look dull, slightly grayish. To recap: good aging—color deepens; bad aging—color fades.

Marbling—Those white flecks in the meat are fat, and fat is flavor! Look for a good quantity and an even distribution of the white stuff to ensure that every bite will be a flavorful one.

Size—When it comes to steak, size definitely matters. If the cut is too thin, it will be difficult to develop a good char on the outside without overcooking the interior. If it's too thick, you might burn the exterior before the interior reaches a level beyond that of steak tartare. Go for a steak that's at least ½ inch thick and up to 2 inches thick.

New York Strip Steak with Blue Cheese Butter

serves 4

4 New York strip steaks, 10 to 12 ounces each
kosher salt and freshly ground pepper

One hour before cooking, remove the steaks from the refrigerator, season lightly with salt on both sides, and leave at room temperature.

Preheat a grill. Turn one side of the grill to its highest setting and the other to medium.

Immediately before cooking, pat the surface of the meat dry with a paper towel and season generously again with salt and pepper. Place the steaks over the hottest part of the grill and cook until well colored on one side; turn and cook for a similar coloring on the second side. For medium-rare steak, cook 4 to 6 minutes per side; 6 to 7 minutes per side for medium. If the steak looks burned on one side before the time has passed, move it to the cooler side of the grill so it will continue to cook but color more slowly. Rest 6 minutes on a rack before serving.

Blue Cheese Butter

8 tablespoons (1 stick) unsalted butter
½ teaspoon kosher salt
1 teaspoon coarsely ground pepper
dash of Tabasco sauce
2 ounces blue cheese, crumbled
1 tablespoon minced fresh chives

Soften the butter completely at room temperature. With a wooden spoon, blend the salt, pepper, and Tabasco into the butter. Add the blue cheese and chives and mix gently. Leave the mixture at room temperature to spoon onto the cooked steaks. Or transfer to parchment paper or plastic wrap, form into a log, and chill; slice the butter as needed to top steaks as they come off the grill.

TECHNIQUE TIP

If your grill has a lid, only use it for preheating. Putting a lid on while cooking transforms it into an oven and changes cooking times greatly.

Compound Butters Revealed

Ordering the "bar steak," be it in Paris, Des Moines, or Denver, means a pile of skinny fries and a slab of grilled meat topped with a melting spoonful of butter infused with herbs and lemon zest. Why the addition of butter? Bar steaks are typically inexpensive cuts of meat that aren't quite flavorful or tender enough to star on their own; they need a vibrant supporting actor to give them a boost. Who better to rescue them than compound butter—the Betty White of the bar steak world? It lends just enough character, richness, and seasoning to the overall production without requiring a ton of effort from the director, the chef. Fancy red wine sauces—those high-maintenance starlets—need not apply!

But compound butters aren't only for steaks and fries. They can dress up all types of grilled meats or roasts and are great stuffed underneath the skin of chicken before roasting. Mixing in a spoonful of compound butter is a great way to finish off veggie side dishes and sauces too. Compound butters are also the brilliant way to extend the life of expensive seasonal mushrooms. Chanterelles, morels, and porcini can break the bank when bought in large quantities during their short peak seasons. But buying a small amount, a quarter pound or so, and blending them into a butter is an inexpensive and convenient way to keep their unique flavor in your kitchen year-round.

Everything You Ever Needed or Wanted to Know About Compound Butters

- Allow the butter to naturally soften to room temperature—don't even think about melting or microwaving it.
- Precook tougher ingredients that will be incorporated into the butter as needed—roasting vegetables like corn or peppers.
- Use an electric mixer to cream butter as you would for making cookies (the paddle attachment for a KitchenAid mixer is excellent).
- Beat the main ingredients into the butter until thoroughly mixed.
- Don't forget the salt and pepper—keep some bread or crackers nearby to taste for seasoning.
- Mix in the herbs by hand. Beating them with a mixer will deliver green butter.
- Place the butter on wax paper and roll into a log shape. Wrap the log in aluminum foil and store it in the freezer.

A few ideas:

Lemon and herb—for chicken or fish
Blue cheese and black pepper—for steaks (page 272)
Corn and chive—great for veggies and meats
Thyme and citrus zest—meaty cuts of fish or poultry
Roasted red pepper with chorizo and cilantro—shrimp, chicken, or veggies; adds a Southwestern flair
Parmesan, smoked paprika, and chiles—perfect on grilled corn on the cob or grilled or roasted pork

New York State Apples, Southern Style

Any night that starts with glasses full of bourbon is best ended with . . . more bourbon. But don't think this recipe will leave you breathing fire. We've included just enough of the good stuff to lightly perfume the apples. Get out the ice cream to soften because these babies are in and out of the sauté pan in five minutes.

serves 4

2 tablespoons unsalted butter
½ teaspoon kosher salt
3 tablespoons brown sugar
4 Golden Delicious apples, peeled, cored, and cut
    into wedges
½ cup bourbon
lots of vanilla ice cream

Melt the butter in a large sauté pan over medium heat. Add the salt and brown sugar and stir over medium heat until bubbling and thickened. Add the apples to the pan and cook, stirring often, until tender to the tip of a knife, about 5 minutes. Remove the pan from the heat and add the bourbon. Carefully place the pan back over the heat and allow the mixture to come to a boil. The alcohol will likely ignite so be careful with this step. If there are no flames, do not worry, for the alcohol can be cooked off by boiling the sauce for 30 seconds. When the sauce is nice and thick, remove the pan from the heat and set aside to cool for 5 minutes.

In the meantime, get your bowls out of the freezer and start scooping ice cream. Spoon the apples and their juices over the ice cream and serve immediately.

THANKSGIVING

When Thanksgiving, the first mega-holiday that might have tested our respective ideas of "tradition" rolled around, we were busy eloping. This was all fine and good; a bullet dodged. We were having a lovely time feeding each other french fries in Palmetto Bluff's heated pool overlooking the May River and the sea grass islands that lie beyond. And, really, how would we go about combining Jamie's family's tradition of doing a very casual backyard turkey fry with Brooke's family's belief that it's not a proper holiday meal unless everyone is seated with their own collection of crystal goblets and monogrammed flatware? Brooke floated in the saltwater pool, tried not to hyperventilate, and wondered if the favorite foodie holiday was going to be our downfall.

Three hundred and sixty-five days later, while writing this cookbook, we figured it all out. After acknowledging that Thanksgiving is our absolute favorite holiday because it's a day dedicated to eating—there's no awkward gift exchange or hoping that you both fall under the same religious umbrella—we set out to create a harmonious menu, one that reflects our past but mainly focuses on the new traditions of our present life together, now and in the future.

We have a *new* green bean casserole that demonstrates our everything-from-scratch kitchen dedication. We have a cheesy, curry-scented gratin reminiscent of our trips to Manhattan's "Indian Row" that urges you to give cauliflower a chance (who says broccoli is the only veggie worth baking?). And we serve a boozy, pear-scented sangria that makes us smile because it recalls our first Macy's Thanksgiving Day Parade. Follow the theme here? All of these dishes mean something to us and say something about our time together. We want you to use our recipes as a guideline and then create a menu that is wholly your own. Sit down with a bottle of wine and reminisce about the best dishes you've enjoyed together. Jot down ingredients; list flavors. And then, when Thanksgiving Thursday rolls around, create a New Traditions feast that no one in the family will ever forget.

Thrifty Table

Forget About Flowers: Decorating with fresh flowers (unless you have a garden) will cost more than your bar bill. Instead, create centerpieces from seasonal fruits and vegetables (apples, pears, quince, oranges, lemons, limes, pomegranates, artichokes, asparagus), fresh greenery, and berries. After the party's over, make a meal from your centerpieces!

TURKEY FRY

The perfect Thanksgiving turkey isn't about flawless technique—it's about vodka and oysters, back porches, and power tools (well, in our parents' neighborhoods down South at least).

Early morning, as the Macy's balloons gather on Central Park West in New York City, we like to slip out with our neighbors and fire up huge pots of oil, drop in turkeys, and watch expectantly as the big white birds turn golden brown.

Meanwhile, we're ready to warm up too, filling a cooler with ice, some unnecessarily expensive vodka, fresh orange juice, extra-spicy Bloody Mary mix, and a sack of bivalves from local bays. Inevitably, some of the oysters wind up rolled in cornmeal and joining the turkeys in the fryer. On the other side of the porch, a separate little fryer churns out beignets, those powdered New Orleans breakfast pillows of sin.

So, let's recap. While your "traditional" Thanksgiving morning has been spent pacing the kitchen and checking the oven, we're sipping cocktails, eating delicious fried things, and watching our turkeys bubble away to a golden, crispy goodness.

No need for jealousy! Follow our cooking plan—one that requires minimal coordination—and pull off a turkey party of your own. One caveat: you'll need special equipment . . . and a yard.

Fried Turkey

COOKING WITH POWER TOOLS

You'll need:

- propane tank and burner
- 32-quart stainless-steel pot with poultry rack or basket
- grab hook for lifting the turkey into and out of the hot oil
- 4 to 6 gallons frying oil (peanut-corn blend); you can buy big jugs of oil at any wholesale store
- deep-fry thermometer
- heavy-duty gloves (like welder's gloves or fire mitts)

Fellas, here's your excuse to head to the hardware store. Ladies, trick him into using his "power tools" so you get the morning off.

Here's a little taste of how the day should go:

7:00 Fire up the pots.
Coffee and beignets (page 279).
7:45 Oil hits 400 degrees—first turkey in the pot.
Start mixing up the hushpuppy batter (page 280)
8:30 First turkey comes out of the pot.
Doctor up the Bloody Mary mix (extra spicy), put orange and grapefruit juice into pitchers, open the vodka, and pop the prosecco (Champagne Buffet, page 42)!
8:45 Next turkeys are ready for the pot.
Rinse the oysters and start shucking. Mmmm . . . Bloody Marys and oysters—that's a good morning!
9:00 Vodka starts to set in.
Start frying hushpuppies to soak up the booze—you need to make it to your 3 P.M. naptime.

A 12- to 15-pound turkey is the ideal size for frying.

serves 8 plus leftovers

1 whole turkey, completely thawed if previously frozen
Creole Seasoning (page 63)
4 to 6 gallons oil for frying (see above for special equipment)

Twenty-four hours before cooking the turkey, remove it from its packaging and pat dry with a clean kitchen towel or paper towels. Remove any pieces from inside the bird. Rub the entire surface of the bird with a generous amount of seasoning. Put a handful of seasoning inside the bird and rub it into the inner cavity as well. Place the whole turkey in a roasting pan and refrigerate until ready to cook.

When ready to cook, remove the turkey from the refrigerator and leave out to warm at room temperature while you set up the fryer. Place the turkey frying pot in a grassless area at least 10 feet away from any trees or other plants. Never fry indoors or in a garage. Make sure the burner stand is level and extremely stable. Attach the propane tank and make sure the burner is firing properly. Fill the frying pot halfway with cold oil (allowing for displacement by the turkey) and place on top of the burner. Fire the burner to begin heating the oil. Monitor the temperature closely with a deep-fry thermometer while you prep the bird. Stand the turkey up to drain moisture from the cavity and pat the surface dry. Loop a piece of string around the end of the drumsticks and tie tightly to pull the legs together.

If using a poultry rack or stand, insert the long metal loop through the opening at the neck and feed it through so the end comes out near the legs you just tied together. Stand the turkey up so the breast side is facing down. Grab the end of the metal loop and lift to ensure the turkey is on the stand securely.

If using a basket, dry and tie the legs as above. Place the basket in the pot with the oil, but leave the turkey in the roasting pan until the oil reaches temperature.

When the oil reaches 400 degrees, pick up the turkey on its stand with the grab hook and carefully lower it into the hot oil. Wear gloves when doing this. If using the basket, grab the basket handle with the hook and slowly lift the basket out of the oil. Carefully place the turkey, breast side down, in the basket and slowly lower it into the hot oil. Add more oil if the bird is not completely covered.

The oil temperature will drop quickly; turn the burner to high to keep the oil from cooling too much. Monitor the oil temperature throughout the cooking and maintain a consistent temperature of 325 to 350 degrees. Cook for 3 minutes per pound. We typically cook a 12- to 15-pound turkey in 45 minutes or less. When the time is up, carefully and slowly lift the turkey stand or basket from the oil using gloves and the grab hook. Set the turkey down next to the pot and check the temperature at the thigh. The thermometer should read a minimum of 150 degrees. If the turkey is not fully cooked, return it to the oil. Place the cooked turkey in a clean roasting pan and loosely cover with foil. Let the turkey stand for at least 1 hour before carving.

Three or four turkeys can be cooked in a single batch of oil. More oil may need to be added between birds. When finished cooking, put your gloves on and remove the pot from the stand and set somewhere to cool safely. Disconnect the gas from the burner and make certain the valve is closed. When the oil has cooled completely (4 to 6 hours), pour the used oil back into the container it came in to transport it to a recycling facility or to discard.

Beignets

A pyramid of deep-fried dough pockets showered with powdered sugar is the only way to start your day in New Orleans (be it at 3 A.M. or 8 A.M.). But you can enjoy these beauties from your back porch just as you would from Café du Monde. All you really need is a good little fryer (we recommend the Fry Daddy and Fry Baby) and a jumbo-size bag of confectioners' sugar.

makes about 20 beignets

1 packet (2¼ teaspoons) active dry yeast

½ cup warm water

1 cup whole milk

3 tablespoons unsalted butter

1 large egg

1 large egg yolk

5 cups all-purpose flour, plus more for dusting

¼ cup granulated sugar

1 teaspoon kosher salt

oil for deep-frying

½ cup powdered sugar

1 tablespoon espresso powder

½ teaspoon ground cinnamon

Stir together the yeast and warm water and leave it to activate, about 5 minutes. Put the milk and butter in a small saucepot and warm over medium heat until the butter is just melted—don't let it get too hot! Crack the egg and egg yolk into a bowl and whisk in the milk mixture. Finally stir in the yeast mixture.

In the bowl of a food processor, combine the flour, granulated sugar, and salt and pulse to mix. With the processor running, add the yeast mixture in a steady stream. As soon as a dough forms, stop the processor and turn out onto a lightly floured work surface. Gently knead to form a smooth dough.

Divide the dough into 4 pieces. Working with one piece at a time and keeping the others well covered, with a rolling pin, roll the dough into a rectangle about ¼ inch thick and cut into 2-inch squares. Place the cut squares on a lightly floured tray while you roll out the remaining dough.

Preheat oil in a deep fryer to 375 degrees. Carefully drop the cut squares of dough into the hot oil in batches and fry until puffed and brown, about 2 minutes. While the beignets are frying, mix the powdered sugar, espresso powder, and cinnamon and put it in a flour sifter. Remove the cooked beignets from the oil and drain on paper towels. Dust with the sugar mixture and serve hot.

MAKE AHEAD

If you want fresh, hot beignets without your alarm going off at daybreak, make the dough the night before. Roll it out, cut it into squares, and keep refrigerated. In the morning, fry the beignets straight from the fridge.

Hushpuppies

Deep-fried cornbread balls—studded with corn kernels and bits of onion, if you're feeling fancy—could make anyone hush up, they're so delectable. But once upon a time, they were only meant for the lucky Southern pups that crowded the buffet at fish fries, barking and yelping for scraps of mullet and triggerfish. (Oh, come on now, don't think we Southerners are rednecks—Queen Elizabeth dines alfresco with her hunting dogs.) Ours is a good, classic hushpuppy recipe that can't be beat.

makes 3 dozen hushpuppies

1½ cups yellow cornmeal

½ cup all-purpose flour

1 teaspoon baking powder

½ teaspoon baking soda

1 teaspoon Creole Seasoning (page 63) or Cajun
    seasoned salt

1 cup whole milk or buttermilk

1 large egg

1 cup corn kernels, cut from the cob or frozen

2 tablespoons unsalted butter, melted

1 tablespoon honey

about 6 cups oil for frying

kosher salt

Combine the cornmeal, flour, baking powder, baking soda, and seasoning in a bowl and mix well. Combine the milk, egg, corn, butter, and honey in a blender and process to mix thoroughly, but stop before it forms a smooth puree. Pour the wet ingredients into the dry and stir to just combine. Let the batter rest for 15 minutes.

Bring a pot of vegetable oil, about 6 cups, to 350 degrees in a heavy pot or countertop fryer. Using a small ice cream scoop or 2 large spoons, drop the batter in large tablespoon-size scoops into the oil in batches. Cook until golden brown on all sides. Drain on paper towels and season lightly with salt immediately after removing from the oil.

TECHNIQUE TIP

An All-Day Affair—When you finish frying the beignets, pour the hot oil through a strainer lined with a coffee filter or thin, clean kitchen towel and return it to the fryer to be reused for frying your hushpuppies.

Curried Cauliflower Casserole

We don't know why cauliflower always seems to get passed over in favor of broccoli, especially around the holidays. If cooked properly (roasting—high and fast; poaching—slow and low), it can have a mild, really elegant flavor. This is a great "2nd & 6th"–inspired recipe (2nd Avenue and 6th Street is our favorite little stretch of Indian restaurants in New York's East Village). It incorporates one of Jamie's favorite seasonings—curry—and Brooke's all-time favorite cheese—Parmesan. The end result is a creamy, rich Indian casserole that bows enough to make our Thanksgiving buffet.

serves 6 to 8

4 tablespoons (½ stick) unsalted butter

1 medium yellow onion, diced

2 tablespoons curry powder

3 tablespoons all-purpose flour

2 cups whole milk, warmed

kosher salt and freshly ground pepper to taste

2 heads cauliflower, trimmed into bite-size florets

1 cup grated Parmesan cheese

Preheat the oven to 400 degrees.

Melt the butter in a large, heavy-bottomed pot. Add the onion and sweat until tender. Add the curry powder and cook until fragrant.

Stir in the flour and cook, stirring constantly, until the paste cooks and bubbles a bit (but don't let it brown), about 2 minutes.

Add the warmed milk and stir as the sauce thickens. Bring it to a boil. Add salt and pepper to taste, lower the heat, and cook, stirring, for 2 to 3 minutes. Simmer the sauce for 15 minutes.

Stir in the cauliflower and ½ cup of the Parmesan cheese. Season the mixture to taste.

Transfer to a gratin dish and cover the top with the remaining ½ cup Parmesan cheese. Bake for approximately 20 minutes. The gratin should be golden brown on top and bubbling on the sides.

TECHNIQUE TIP

Parmesan cheese helps this dish get its golden brown, crispy top—you know, the part that everyone will be fighting over at the table. Don't be shy with the cheese!

The *New* Green Bean Casserole

Green bean casserole is a stalwart of the Thanksgiving buffet. And guess what? It's usually not very good. How much can you really expect from a collection of cans (canned beans, canned mushroom soup, canned fried onion rings)? As one of our New Traditions, we decided to revamp the classic dish and make every component from scratch. This signals that we're going to do things our way, even if it takes a little more time. The payoff is a casserole loaded with flavor that we'd just as soon serve to Brooke's grandmother as we would to Brooke's gourmet girlfriend in town from Napa.

serves 6 to 8

1 ounce dried porcini mushrooms
3 branches fresh thyme
4 cups chicken broth
4 tablespoons (½ stick) unsalted butter
1 cup finely diced onion
2 cups cleaned and sliced crimini mushrooms
4 cloves garlic, minced
¼ cup all-purpose flour
1 pound green beans, trimmed
½ cup grated Parmesan cheese
1½ cups fresh breadcrumbs
1 recipe Crispy Shallot Topping (recipe follows; optional)

Combine the dried porcini, thyme, and chicken broth in a saucepot and simmer over medium-high heat until reduced by 1 cup.

In a separate pot over medium-high heat, melt the butter, add the onion, and sweat until tender. Add the crimini mushrooms and cook for 2 to 3 minutes more.

Stir in the garlic and flour and cook until the flour is thickened and a dark tan color.

Strain the chicken broth and whisk it into the mushroom mixture, adding the liquid gradually and allowing the mixture to become extremely thick when the first liquid is added, then thinning as the rest is whisked in.

Preheat the oven to 425 degrees.

Simmer the sauce, stirring occasionally, for about 15 minutes. The mixture (now called a "velouté") should be well thickened. Add the green beans and simmer for 5 minutes more.

Transfer the mixture to a 1- to 2-quart gratin dish and cover with the Parmesan and breadcrumbs. Place on the top shelf of the oven and bake until browned on top and bubbling on the sides, about 12 minutes. Remove from the oven and scatter Crispy Shallot Topping over the casserole.

Crispy Shallot Topping

If only every dish could be topped with fried mini onion rings. These are so outrageously delicious that Brooke isn't sure why we listed them as "optional." Come on, go the extra mile and start your own New Tradition!

4 shallots, very thinly sliced (preferably on a mandoline)
3 cups canola oil

Set up a strainer over a metal container and a pan lined with paper towels next to the stove.

Combine the sliced shallots and cold oil in a medium saucepot. Place the pot over medium heat and stir occasionally with a metal spoon as the oil begins to heat. The shallots will first bubble very gradually. When the bubbling becomes more rapid, the stirring should become constant, being careful not to splash the hot oil. The moment the shallots turn a deep golden brown, pour them through the strainer to separate them from the hot oil. Then spread the shallots in a single layer on the towel-lined pan to drain and cool quickly.

MAKE AHEAD

Prepare the mushroom velouté and green beans, transfer to the gratin dish, and cool. Store covered in the refrigerator. When space in the oven opens up, add the breadcrumbs and Parmesan at the very last minute and then bake. Storing the gratin with breadcrumbs and Parmesan on top before it is baked will keep the top from getting crispy.

Cranberry-Pecan Chutney

Traditional cranberry sauce can be a little one-note—it's all about overly sweetened, mushy berries. Our cranberry chutney, on the other hand, has crunch and layers of flavor.

serves 6 to 8

two 12-ounce bags fresh cranberries
2 tablespoons finely grated peeled fresh ginger
1 orange, zest grated and juiced
1 cinnamon stick
2 Granny Smith apples, peeled and grated
¼ teaspoon ground cloves
½ cup granulated sugar
kosher salt and freshly ground pepper to taste
1 cup chopped pecans, toasted

Combine all the ingredients except the pecans in a saucepot and bring to a simmer over low heat. Cook until thickened. Cool slightly before stirring in the pecans. Taste and adjust the seasoning.

MAKE AHEAD

This is one of those better-as-it-sits recipes, so don't be afraid to make this a day or two in advance.

Sweet Potato and Turnip Gratin

Jamie learned this super-simple, no-measurement beauty while working with Frank Stitt at Highlands Bar & Grill. The ingredient list couldn't be shorter and you can make it as big or as small as you like—that's where you fill in the measurements. Just alternate layers of sweet potatoes and turnips with a bit of cheese in between until the dish is filled to the brim.

> sweet potatoes
> large white turnips
> garlic
> kosher salt and freshly ground pepper to taste
> grated Gruyère cheese
> about 2 cups cream

Preheat the oven to 350 degrees.

Peel the sweet potatoes and turnips, then slice them into even rounds ⅛ to ¼ inch thick. Smash a clove of garlic and rub it around the inside of a gratin dish. Arrange an overlapping layer of sweet potatoes on the bottom of the gratin dish. Season the sweet potatoes with salt and pepper and sprinkle with some of the cheese. Top with a layer of turnips, overlapping them in the opposite direction (this will keep the gratin from falling over on your plate after it's cut). Again season and add some of the cheese.

Continue alternating layers until the gratin is full or you run out of vegetables. Pour in the cream until it is just visible around the edges and cover the top with a generous amount of cheese.

Bake until bubbly and well browned; a knife tip should easily pierce the center. Allow the gratin to sit for 15 to 20 minutes before serving.

TECHNIQUE TIP

Layering the vegetables in alternating directions (sweet potatoes clockwise, turnips counterclockwise) will make a sturdier gratin that is easier to cut and serve.

Arugula and Pomegranate Salad

For our first Thanksgiving together, just the two of us, Jamie created this salad. It's light and easy—kind of like a holiday without three dozen different opinions on how to cook the "perfect" turkey.

serves 4

8 ounces arugula

3 breakfast radishes

¼ head cauliflower

1 pomegranate, seeds removed, juice reserved

pinch of granulated sugar

½ lemon, juiced

2 to 3 tablespoons extra virgin olive oil

kosher salt and freshly ground pepper to taste

4 ounces ricotta salata

CALL IN THE SUBS

Breakfast radishes are shaped differently (they're more oblong) and have a different color (think more pink and white) than regular radishes. If you can't find this special variety at your grocery store or farmers' market, regular radishes will do just fine.

Ricotta salata is a semifirm sheep's milk cheese from southern Italy that has a salty, slightly tangy flavor. If you can't find it, substitute Parmesan, Pecorino, or mild feta.

Wash the arugula (preferably in your Kitchen Registry salad spinner) and dry thoroughly.

Thinly slice the radishes and florets of cauliflower on a mandoline or with a vegetable peeler. Cover with a damp paper towel and reserve.

In a small bowl, combine 3 tablespoons of the pomegranate seeds and any juice you collected when seeding them. Whisk in the sugar, lemon juice, and olive oil.

Combine the arugula and shaved vegetables in a large bowl. Gently toss with the dressing (you may not need it all, so add gradually) and season well with salt and pepper. Divide the salad among 4 plates, scatter about some extra pomegranate seeds, and finish by shaving a few slices of the cheese over the top with a vegetable peeler.

Thanks-gria

Living in New York City comes with a ton of hassle (astronomical rent, zero privacy, $30,000 preschool)— and a few perks. We consider the Thanksgiving Day Parade to be one of those perks; while the rest of the country has to turn on the television to watch Snoopy and the boy bands float down Broadway, all we do is hop the B train to the Upper West Side. (Jamie wants to clear the air—Brooke is the only one who enjoys the boy bands.) But when you decide to brave the crowds and the freezing weather to hit Central Park South, you need a libation—something to keep you warm and happy for five hours. Thanks-gria, our cold-weather, seasonal take on our favorite sangria, turned out to be so good packed in a thermos, sipped on a blustery morning, that we now serve it in an elegant glass pitcher at all of our holiday parties. First, quince and pears soak in Poire William, a pear brandy from Alsace. Then they're added to a pitcher of Beaujolais. It's easy and beautiful—the perfect mix-ahead drink for big get-togethers.

serves 8 to 12

1 piece star anise

1 cinnamon stick

1 tablespoon black peppercorns

2 lemons

½ cup granulated sugar

1 quince, cored and diced

2 pears, cored and sliced

2 cups Poire William pear brandy (also known as
     eau-de-vie)

2 bottles Beaujolais Nouveau, chilled

Tie the star anise, cinnamon, and peppercorns together in a piece of cheesecloth. Zest the lemon into strips and set aside. Squeeze the lemon juice into a bowl, add the sugar, and stir until the sugar is mostly dissolved. Add the quince, pears, and lemon zest; toss to coat the fruit with the lemon and sugar. Transfer the fruit to a large glass container, pour in the Poire William, and stir to completely dissolve the sugar. Add the sack of spices and refrigerate for a few hours or up to 2 days. An hour or two before serving, add both bottles of Beaujolais to the fruit and mix well. Remove the cheesecloth sack of spices. Serve chilled with some of the fruit in each glass.

Irish Stout and Pumpkin Mousse Tiramisu

Our winter "pick-me-up" (the literal Italian translation of "tiramisu") whips together mascarpone cheese and pumpkin puree. Next, to keep things unique, we dip the ladyfingers in Irish stout instead of coffee. The tartness of the beer really mimics the flavor profile of coffee while also giving it some zip. We bet everyone at your table will be stumped by the secret ingredient.

serves 12

CANDIED PECANS
1 large egg white
½ teaspoon kosher salt
½ cup granulated sugar
2 cups pecans

PUMPKIN MOUSSE
¾ cup mascarpone cheese
¼ cup light brown sugar
¾ cup granulated sugar
½ teaspoon ground ginger
½ teaspoon ground cinnamon
pinch of ground nutmeg
1½ cups unsweetened canned pumpkin puree
2 cups cream, chilled

BEER
2 cups Irish stout
1 cup granulated sugar
1 tablespoon cocoa powder
1 teaspoon ground cinnamon

one 15- to 17-ounce package ladyfingers

CALL IN THE SUBS

Mascarpone is the light Italian version of cream cheese. If you cannot find mascarpone at your local grocery or specialty food store, cream cheese is a fine substitution. Just expect your tiramisu to be a bit heavier and more dense.

Preheat the oven to 325 degrees.

For the pecans, whisk the egg white in a medium bowl until frothy. Add the salt and sugar and whisk a moment more; the mixture should be white and foamy. Stir in the pecans and turn out onto a baking sheet lined with parchment paper. Toast until golden brown and crisp, about 30 minutes. Cool on the baking sheet.

For the pumpkin mousse, combine the mascarpone, the brown sugar, ¼ cup of the granulated sugar, and the spices; beat with an electric mixer until light and fluffy. Mix in the pumpkin until smooth.

In a chilled bowl, whisk the cream to soft peaks. Add the remaining ½ cup sugar in a steady stream and continue whisking until stiff peaks form. Fold the cream one-third at a time into the pumpkin mixture, fully incorporating each addition before adding the next. Refrigerate to chill the mousse while you prepare the remaining ingredients.

Combine the stout, sugar, cocoa, and cinnamon and whisk until dissolved.

Coarsely chop the pecans.

Assemble in a trifle bowl, gratin dish, or individual glasses. Begin by dipping the ladyfingers into the beer one at a time and removing them immediately. Arrange them in a single layer on the bottom of the dish or glass. Add some of the pumpkin mousse and spread into an even layer about ½ inch thick. Scatter the chopped pecans over the mousse. Quickly dip another layer of ladyfingers and arrange on top of the mousse. Repeat the layers until the dish is filled, finishing with a layer of mousse and pecans on top. Refrigerate for up to 2 days. Remove from the refrigerator 30 to 60 minutes before serving.

TECHNIQUE TIP

Always Taste—Sometimes canned pumpkin needs a little something extra. Feel free to add a bit of sugar and spices (nutmeg, cinnamon, mace) to suit your tastes. Once your pumpkin is whipped up with the spices and mascarpone, dip a spoon in there for a taste (we're forcing you). If the mixture is a little bitter, add a touch more sugar. Taste. Repeat as necessary.

Butternut Squash Cake

Why are carrots the orange vegetable that gets all the glory? Instead of giving you another classic carrot cake recipe, we wanted to create something special (and super-moist) by grating butternut squash into our batter. Brooke's favorite winter veggie gives off the same light, natural sweetness, and the spongy cake pairs perfectly with our Ginger Cream Cheese Icing (page 289).

makes one 13- x 9-inch cake

DRY INGREDIENTS
1½ cups all-purpose flour
¼ cup wheat germ
1 cup whole-wheat flour
1 tablespoon baking soda
2 teaspoons ground cinnamon
pinch of kosher salt
pinch of ground cloves

WET INGREDIENTS
1 cup granulated sugar
4 cups grated butternut squash
1 cup chopped walnuts
3 large eggs
1 cup vegetable oil
1 teaspoon vanilla extract
1 tablespoon molasses
5 tablespoons yogurt

Preheat the oven to 350 degrees.

Butter and flour a 13- x 9-inch baking pan. Combine the dry ingredients in one bowl and the wet ingredients in another. Mix each well. Pour the wet ingredients into the dry and stir with a spoon until just combined.

Spread the mixture in the prepared baking pan. Bake until a toothpick inserted into the center comes out clean, about 30 minutes. Cool completely on a rack before removing from the pan to ice.

THE SPICE OF LIFE

Double Duty—Left uniced, this cake makes an amazing (and relatively healthy!) breakfast bread.

Ginger Cream Cheese Icing

2 cups powdered sugar
1 pound (two 8-ounce packages) cream cheese, at room temperature
8 tablespoons (1 stick) unsalted butter, at room temperature
1 teaspoon ground ginger
1 teaspoon vanilla extract

Combine all the ingredients in a bowl and beat with an electric mixer until smooth and fluffy.

To assemble, cut the cake in half, making two 6½- x 9-inch layers. Spread about one-third of the icing on one layer. Place the second, uniced layer directly on top. Use the remaining icing to cover the top and sides of the cake.

Thrifty Bartender: Chill Out: Cold White and Cool Red

You can get away with a less-expensive white wine, but the same can't be said for red. By sticking a cheap white wine in the freezer for an extra 10 to 15 minutes (say, your Aunt Vie gave you a bottle of Chardonnay as a housewarming gift and she insists you drink it together), you can tame some of those less desirable qualities—like too much oak, too much sugar, too much acidity, and too little time spent aging in oak barrels or steel casks.

And red wine, no matter how much it cost, should never be served warm, which is going to be the case if you pull the bottle from the rack over your stove. The recommended temperature for wine cellars is 55 degrees—not the ambient 72 degrees of your living room or the 80 degrees of your kitchen in action. Luckily there's an easy solution for getting "cellar temperature" red wine: lay the bottle on the bottom shelf of the refrigerator for 10 minutes and, voilà! Even a Frenchman from Bordeaux would drink your bottle of Two-Buck Chuck.

BIRTHDAY GIRL

We're about to save you $900. That's about the cost of a 3-star restaurant in Paris—at lunchtime. (I believe that's also the mortgage on a 3,000-square-foot split-level in Baton Rouge.) But what you might not know is that you're paying just as much for the service and the murals on the wall as you are for the food and wine.

We know this. We did the Gallic legwork.

For Brooke's twenty-eighth birthday, Jamie cracked open his piggie bank and whisked Brooke away to Paris. For lunch on the big day, he reserved a table at Le Grand Vefour, a gilt masterpiece of a Right Bank restaurant tucked into the arches of the Palais-Royal. The restaurant's luxury was as otherworldly as the literary ghosts—Victor Hugo, Colette, Jean-Paul Sartre, to name a few—who accompanied our meal.

The three things that Brooke remembers most about the birthday meal are the smooth, utterly decadent foie gras ravioli in truffle butter and cream sauce, the wine pairings, and the crazy feeling that comes from realizing you and Colette sat on the same banquette.

While Le Grand Vefour was truly an experience, so many restaurants overcharge for absolutely no reason. Young cooks are intimidated to cook for a big occasion so they make a reservation and leave it to a restaurant or chef to express their love and tender feelings.

Don't be intimidated and put down that phone!

We have what you've been missing: an elegant, manageable menu that has a level of French finesse. While the food is more bistro than haute cuisine, it definitely lets her know you put time and thought into the meal.

Le Grand Vefour

The Parisian institution that dates to Louis XV wins our "best in show," "best in flavor." Book a table at Chef Guy Martin's culinary palace when you want to celebrate life and the fifth basic food group—duck liver! Don't miss Chef Martin's ultimate specialty, foie gras ravioli with black truffle cream. A meal to be savored (. . . and paid off on your credit card for the next twelve months). **Le Grand Vefour**—17 rue de Beaujolais, 75001 Paris; Tel-33 01 42 96 56 27; www.grand-vefour.com.

Tapenade and Grilled Sourdough

Sodium and alcohol are our drugs of choice. And with olives, capers, and anchovies, this spread is as salty, briny, and addictive as it gets. While we haven't confirmed this with every French waiter and prep cook south of Houston and on the Left Bank, we're pretty sure that tapenade is a staple at neighborhood French bistros the world over because it's such a snap to put together and it keeps in the fridge for weeks. We recommend a dry rosé to partner this delightful olive puree. "What grows together goes together," and a nice, light Provençal rosé wine would be the perfect accompaniment to the Niçoise olives that hail from (where else?) Nice, one of Provence's premier cities.

serves 6 to 8

2 cups Niçoise olives, pitted

1 anchovy fillet, rinsed

1 clove garlic

3 tablespoons capers

2 large eggs, hard-boiled and grated

1 tablespoon chopped fresh parsley

extra virgin olive oil

1 lemon, juiced

freshly ground pepper

12 slices sourdough bread or baguette

In the bowl of a food processor, combine the olives, anchovy, and garlic and pulse until no large pieces remain (do not make a smooth paste). Transfer to a bowl and stir in the capers, eggs, and parsley. Stir in olive oil until the mixture is smooth but still thick. Season to taste with lemon juice and pepper.

Brush the bread with olive oil and toast on the grill or in the oven at 450 degrees.

THE SPICE OF LIFE

Green olive varieties are just as well suited for this recipe. We often split the duties: half Niçoise, half Picholine. Don't be afraid to mix and match your favorites to make up 2 cups total.

Demi-Bouteilles

Wine pairings are the bomb. While we're all for drinking red with fish and white with sausage (if the mood suits you), we have also had meals truly sing when the food and wine were beautifully paired. And, guess what? Pairings aren't reserved for fusty restaurants! Doing it at home is as simple as reading our "Brooke on the Bottle" boxes, doing five minutes of Internet research, and then buying half bottles, or *demi-bouteilles*.

Crispy Skate with Spinach, Brown Butter, and Lemon

You've got to believe that brown butter was just one of those amazing cooking mistakes—"Oh no! The melted butter just burned. . . . Hey, this stuff tastes really good; I sure am glad I thought of it." Or something like that. However it happened, we all stand to benefit. Browning butter by melting it and toasting the milk solids that settle to the bottom of the pan gives an incredible aroma and a rich, nutty flavor to almost any dish. It also just so happens to be perfect with light, flaky skate. A bed of simple sautéed spinach completes the dish—and makes you feel good about yourself! Butter, what butter?

serves 2

two 6- to 8-ounce portions skate wing, trimmed
kosher salt and freshly ground pepper to taste
all-purpose flour for dredging
2 tablespoons canola oil, plus more as needed
one 10-ounce bag spinach
8 tablespoons (1 stick) unsalted butter, cut into
    pieces
1 tablespoon minced shallot
juice of 1 lemon
2 tablespoons chopped fresh parsley

Season the skate with salt and pepper on both sides, dredge in a pan of flour, and set aside. Heat a large skillet over high heat and add the oil. Pat the excess flour from the fish and carefully place the skate in the hot skillet. The pan should be hot enough that the fish browns lightly in about 2 minutes. Flip and cook about 2 minutes more. Remove the cooked fish to paper towels to drain.

Discard all but 1 to 2 teaspoons oil from the pan. Add the spinach to the hot oil with ¼ teaspoon salt. Cook until just wilted. Place the spinach in a colander to drain the excess liquid and dump any spinach juice out of the pan.

Add the butter to the pan, still over high heat, and cook for 2 to 3 minutes until the butter is dark brown and smells roasted and nutty. Remove the pan from the heat and add the shallot. Let the shallot sizzle for 5 to 10 seconds and squeeze in the lemon juice. Stir in the parsley and taste and adjust the seasoning.

To serve, place a pile of spinach in the center of the plate. Lay the skate on top of the spinach and spoon the butter sauce over the skate.

WHAT?! LIKE ROLLER SKATES?

Skate is a delicious member of the ray family. Its flesh is flaky but firm with a mild flavor that cooks up quickly. Can't find it? Substitute grouper, bass, or any other mild white fish in its place.

When a Trip to the Wine Store Feels Like Completing Your Wedding Registry at a Huge Department Store

Are you looking to get into the good stuff but don't know where to start? We know, we know . . . wine can be very intimidating. Most people feel that walking into a wine store is no different from riding the escalator down to The Cellar at Macy's to start their wedding registry. When it was our turn, we had no idea where to begin, so we wandered around the waffle-maker displays and napkin-ring bins for an hour and then left empty-handed and feeling more confused than ever. "Is newlywed life all about bar codes and $1,500 espresso machines?" we wondered.

Dejected but not defeated, we relinquished our "gift gun," the zapping do-dad that registers your wedding wish list, hailed a taxi home, and started doing a little research. We talked to engaged friends; we talked to married friends; we talked to the unfortunate few who had already broken up and given away the crystal candlesticks and fondue sets. But the most important thing we did was assess our taste, our lifestyle, and our budget. We decided what WE liked, and the next week when we returned to The Cellar, we talked to the girls and guys milling around with name tags on and told THEM what we liked. And then the craziest thing happened—they helped us find the stuff we wanted! We left happy.

What does this have to do with wine? It's time to break out of your shell and find out what YOU really like; don't just grab a bottle because it's the only one you can pronounce!

The best place to do a little grape sleuthing is at a wine store, local wine bar, or restaurant that does tastings or flights. All the above venues will usually have a bottle open for sampling in the late afternoon or early evening. This is a great way to get to know wine and the people in the know about wine. A few tips:

- Write down the names of wines that you like (and don't be afraid to spell them phonetically if you're worried about pronouncing them later).
- Ask the salesman, bartender, or sommelier which wines they're really enjoying right now. Or ask what they've tasted recently that's memorable. Smart people love to show off.
- Don't be afraid to ask for just a sip before you commit to the whole glass. And if you don't like it, speak up! Tell your server why and they'll help you find something delicious.

Once you've built your roster of favorites, it's time to put them together with a meal. If it's just an intimate dinner for two or four, go with half bottles. This allows you to taste a lot of different wines with different food—and the evening won't end with unintentional nudity and lamp shades as head-gear, or with several half-drunk bottles stuck in the recycling bin.

Creamy Potato Puree

The French don't mess around with mashed potatoes, especially not that lumpy meatloaf sidekick that our moms used to serve. They make silky smooth potato puree, which, in true French fashion, seems to have roughly equal parts potato and butter. While we like to make a (barely) reduced-fat version, the magical method cannot be altered—a food mill or potato ricer is the only path to potato puree perfection. Get yourself one of these simple machines and enjoy potatoes so good, you'll almost consider giving up french fries.

serves 4

3 Idaho or russet potatoes, peeled and cut into
½-inch chunks
1 tablespoon kosher salt, plus more to taste
1 cup half-and-half
6 tablespoons (¾ stick) unsalted butter
freshly ground pepper to taste

Place the cut potatoes in a pot and cover with cold water by 2 inches. Stir in 1 tablespoon salt and bring to a boil. Reduce the heat and simmer until the potatoes can be easily broken up with a spoon. Pour into a colander and let stand for 3 minutes to drain and steam dry.

While the potatoes are cooking, bring the half-and-half and butter to a simmer over medium heat. Pass the potatoes through a ricer and add the warm butter mixture. Stir with a wooden spoon until just combined. Season to taste with salt and pepper. Make sure to work with the potatoes while they're still hot—it will make them easier to rice and keep them from getting gummy.

ESSENTIAL EQUIPMENT

A potato ricer or food mill is your only option for silky smooth and tender mashed potatoes. Beating your spuds with a masher, mixer, or whisk leaves them a little chunky (not that there's anything wrong with that), and a food processor produces a gummy, gluey mess (there *is* something wrong with that).

Like You're Rolling at a 4-Star Restaurant (on a 1-Star Budget)

Plate sparingly. That big white plate with the big white rim shouldn't overflow with risotto or chicken. Take a look at how we plate our dishes in this book. Then treat yourself to a meal at a nice French restaurant (write it off as research). Replicate that portion size at home. Remember the rule from your dating days—always leave him/her wanting more; the same applies to your taste buds.

Grand Marnier Gâteau Basquaise

Gâteau Basquaise has never reached the cult status of crème brûlée, something a little perplexing and also a little cool. Instead of serving your friends a dessert they've eaten a million times before, you can present them with "your own" little creation (that happens to be a thousand years old). Like crème brûlée, gâteau Basquaise is rich and eggy in a very good way. But instead of being just a caramelized custard, the citrus-infused gâteau—the brainchild of the very independent Basque people who live on the French/Spanish border—is like a cross between pastry cream, flan, and cake. Stick a candle in it and make sure to sing "Happy Birthday" at the top of your lungs.

makes a 9- to 10-inch cake

CRUST

1 orange, zest grated

¾ cup granulated sugar

1 teaspoon kosher salt

2 cups all-purpose flour, plus more for dusting

10 tablespoons (1¼ sticks) unsalted butter, cold, diced

1 large egg

1 large egg yolk

CREAM

1½ cups whole milk

½ vanilla bean, or 1 teaspoon vanilla extract

½ cup granulated sugar

3 large egg yolks

6 tablespoons all-purpose flour

2 tablespoons Grand Marnier, Cointreau, or Triple Sec

1 large egg, beaten

Preheat the oven to 375 degrees.

For the crust, combine the orange zest, sugar, salt, and flour in a large bowl. Cut in the butter with an electric mixer or a pastry blender. Beat the egg and egg yolk together and add. Gently knead on a floured surface until a dough forms. Wrap tightly and refrigerate for at least 1 hour.

For the cream, bring the milk and vanilla to a simmer over low heat, cover tightly, and set aside for 10 minutes. Whisk together the sugar and egg yolks and gradually whisk in the flour. Remove the vanilla bean, rinse, and save for another use. Slowly whisk the hot milk into the egg mixture until fully incorporated. This will prevent the eggs from curdling. Return the mixture to the pot and stir constantly over medium heat until it returns to a simmer; it should be well thickened at this point. Stir in the Grand Marnier. Transfer to a bowl or shallow dish and stir to release the steam. Press a piece of plastic wrap onto the surface so a skin doesn't form. Cool completely.

Remove the dough from the fridge and divide two-thirds for the base and one-third for the top. Roll each out ¼ inch thick. Carefully line the bottom of a 9-inch tart pan, pressing the pastry completely into the corners and leaving some hanging over the edges of the pan. Fill with the cooled pastry cream and cover with the second piece of dough. Moisten the edges to make sure it seals. Trim away any excess. Prick the top to release steam and brush with the beaten egg.

Bake on the center rack of the oven for 45 minutes. Cool completely before unmolding.

ESSENTIAL EQUIPMENT

If you don't have a tart pan with a removable bottom, here is your excuse to head out to your local kitchen store and pick one up! We wouldn't attempt this recipe without one.

MAKE AHEAD

If kept tightly wrapped in the refrigerator, the dough for the crust and the cream can both be prepared a day or two in advance.

Dinner Table: Location, Location, Location

It's not just about your table settings, but where you put the table! Get creative and surprise your guests with the location of tonight's feast.

1. Chiminea—Stage a campfire meal for grown-ups and gather round the chiminea for a grill-your-own dinner. Of course, S'mores (page 212) are the end-of-the-night reward.
2. "Chef's Table"—It's a cliché but it's true: at parties, everyone ends up in the kitchen. So why not create a "chef's table" in your kitchen, just like they do at fancy restaurants? Create place settings on the kitchen bar or center island or move in a utility table from the garage, cover it with Tablevogue (page 234), and let your friends marvel at your knife skills. Just be sure to prepare the majority of the dinner in advance and only cook *elements* of the meal the night of. You'll have a captive audience—but only for about an hour.
3. On the Dock—If you're lucky enough to live on the water, or near a park on the water, stage a casual seafood party on the dock! Our Bar-B-Qued Shrimp (page 104) would be the perfect main course.
4. By the Fire—There's nothing as romantic as a big fire roaring in the living room fireplace. Lay down a blanket and a few pillows for cushions and enjoy a relaxed, cozy dinner. Stumped on the perfect romantic meal to prepare? Try our Parisian-inspired Birthday Girl menu (page 291).
5. Front or Back Porch (for smaller-city folks); Card Table for Two on the Fire Escape (for big-city dwellers)—Al fresco eating is always a treat. So surprise each other—and your guests—with a table outside. Simple eats from our Everyday Dinners (page 55) would do well, or go all out and whip up our Spring Lunch (page 235).

HOLIDAY GETAWAY

The true gems of the holiday season: a soft round of warm, baked Brie smothered in brown sugar and slivered almonds; wineglasses wordlessly refilled by your tipsy uncle; a high school frenemy spotted at the hometown hot spot who's put on fifteen pounds.

But what do you do with all that family time?

We think that grandparents, aunts, uncles, screaming children (that aren't our own), and in-laws are best enjoyed with a French woman's sensibility toward her diet: a little taste of everything but not too much of anything. Or, in the words of Brooke's pappy: fish and family stink after three days.

So when we thought about three consecutive family functions in the span of one month's time—Thanksgiving, Christmas Eve, and Christmas Day (with the inevitable cookie exchange thrown in for good measure)—we had to plan a getaway, even if it's in our own kitchen.

A comfort cooking party with old friends is our answer to the ten- or twenty-year high school reunion (as well as the answer to the aforementioned family predicament). Because the people you actually liked when you were sixteen, you still keep in touch with on Facebook, right?

Once everyone lands, drops off their bags, and dodges prying family questions, offer an escape to your place.

Pomegranate Cocktails at the door signal that they've come a long way after all. Awkward starter conversations are avoided as everyone lends a hand, helping with the Brussels Sprout Salad and basil pesto while munching on Roasted Carrot Hummus and warm pita crisps. Feasting on bass—in the kitchen, or on trays by the fire—and finishing off the meal with apricot phyllo triangles means you won't miss out on yearbook superlatives or that bad downtown bar. Oh, and you've successfully escaped your loving family—at least for a night.

Pomegranate Cocktail

Fresh pomegranate juice is the key here. Yes, it's a messy job, but, trust us, it's well worth the trouble. (Just don't wear your good T-shirt while doing it.) Over a fine-mesh strainer, cut the pomegranate in half and squeeze it just as you would an orange. Crush the stray seeds that land in the strainer with the back of a spoon. You should get a little over 1 cup juice per fruit.

serves a lot or a little,
depending on the crowd

2 cups pomegranate juice

1 cup club soda

4 limes, juiced

24 ounces vodka

ice cubes

1 cup pomegranate seeds, frozen

lime wedges for garnish

In a large chilled pitcher, stir together the pomegranate juice, soda, lime juice, and vodka with a bit of ice. Keep chilled until ready to serve. Place a few frozen pomegranate seeds in each glass along with 1 large ice cube. Pour in the mixed cocktail and garnish with a lime wedge.

CALL IN THE SUBS

If substituting bottled pomegranate juice (it's not the end of the world), go for the good stuff found in the grocery store's refrigerated section. The bottle on the juice aisle sitting out at room temperature is cheaper but not nearly as flavorful.

Roasted Carrot Hummus

Hummus is kind of like guacamole—everyone has their own recipe but, boy, are they different (in flavor and quality). Jamie's riff on the classic dip throws in roasted carrots to sweeten the deal. And that light sweetness combined with the nuttiness of tahini transforms everyday into instant gourmet. Be sure to make this dip the day before, so come party time you can put it in a nice bowl surrounded by warm pita chips and get out of the kitchen. That way you can focus your attention on more important things—like fixing another Pomegranate Cocktail!

makes 3 to 4 cups

3 medium carrots, peeled and cut into 1-inch pieces
1 head garlic, cloves separated and peeled
2 tablespoons extra virgin olive oil, plus more for
     toasting the pita bread
1 tablespoon ground cumin
kosher salt to taste
two 16-ounce cans chickpeas
3 tablespoons tahini
1 lemon, juiced
freshly ground pepper to taste
hot sauce (your choice)
1 package pita bread

Preheat the oven to 400 degrees.

Toss the carrots and garlic with the olive oil, cumin, and a good pinch of salt. Wrap in a packet in aluminum foil and roast until completely tender, about 30 minutes. Remove and cool. Reduce the oven heat to 350 degrees.

Drain the chickpeas, reserving the liquid. Put the chickpeas, carrots, garlic, and oil from roasting in a food processor and puree until smooth, about 45 seconds. You may need to add a little bit of the reserved liquid as the processor runs. Start by adding only 2 tablespoons or you might end up with a soup instead of a dip.

Stir in the tahini and lemon juice. Taste and adjust the seasoning with salt, pepper, and hot sauce. The hummus will keep in the refrigerator for 10 days.

Cut the rounds of pita bread in half and then into wedges. Lay them out on a baking sheet and drizzle with olive oil and salt. Bake until golden brown. Serve with the hummus.

CALL IN THE SUBS

Tahini is a paste made of crushed sesame seeds. It is available in the ethnic aisle of most grocery stores. In a pinch? Omit the tahini and substitute sesame oil to taste (about 1 tablespoon is required). You're really stuck? Use good-quality extra virgin olive oil.

Sweet Potato and Brussels Sprout Salad with Parmesan-Pecan Pesto

This is the perfect thing to whip up when friends are coming over for dinner. Grease them up first with a cocktail and then let them do the hard work of cleaning the Brussels sprouts for you. Once the sprouts are clean, the rest of the dish is a snap. The pesto recipe makes quite a bit, but it's an ideal leftover to have hanging around the fridge. It keeps for up to 2 weeks and makes a delicious, last-minute dinner when tossed with spaghetti or fusilli.

serves 6 to 8

2 pints fresh Brussels sprouts
2 large sweet potatoes
2 tablespoons extra virgin olive oil
kosher salt and freshly ground pepper to taste
pinch of cayenne
1 cup Parmesan-Pecan Pesto (page 85)
1 tablespoon white wine vinegar
1 cup Parmesan cheese shaved into curls

Preheat the oven to 400 degrees.

Bring a large pot of salted water to a boil. Trim the stem ends, cut the Brussels sprouts in half, and discard the tough outer leaves. Prepare an ice bath. Drop the sprouts into the boiling water and cook until just tender, 3 to 4 minutes. Immediately remove to the ice bath to cool.

Peel the sweet potatoes and cut them into a large dice (about 1 inch cubes) and toss in a bowl with the olive oil, salt and pepper to taste, and the cayenne. Spread in a single layer on a baking sheet and bake until tender, about 12 minutes. Cool on paper towels.

When the sprouts are cooled, drain from the water and separate the green leaves from the tight, yellow-green cores. This is the time to get all your friends in on the fun—peeling the sprouts takes a bit of time, so the more hands in on the action, the better!

Combine the leaves and cores in a bowl with the roasted sweet potatoes. Toss with half of the Parmesan-Pecan Pesto and the vinegar. Season to taste with salt and pepper. Divide among plates and drizzle with more pesto and scatter with the Parmesan curls.

Striped Bass with Roasted Fennel, Grapefruit, and Dill

Light fish and fresh fruit will give your body a little "breather" over the holidays. Our dish is crisp and refreshing, and it takes advantage of citrus at its peak. The combination of fennel and grapefruit is spectacular!

serves 6

2 fennel bulbs

1 tablespoon fennel seeds

3 cloves garlic, crushed

olive oil or canola oil

kosher salt and freshly ground pepper

six 6- to 8-ounce portions wild striped bass or other mild white fish

2 tablespoons chopped fresh dill

2 grapefruit, cut into supremes (page 14), juice reserved

THE NEXT LEVEL

Feeling Fancy—If you own a mandoline, the handy-dandiest slicer in the kitchen, and are comfortable using it, cut the fennel bulbs in half, then shave them paper thin. Omit the fennel seeds and toss the shaved fennel with the grapefruit supremes, olive oil, and salt and pepper to taste.

Preheat the oven to 425 degrees.

Trim the green tops from the fennel and peel any brown spots from the white bulbs. Split the bulbs into quarters through the core and then split each wedge into half again, making 8 pieces from each bulb. In a large bowl, toss the fennel, fennel seeds, and garlic with 2 tablespoons olive oil, 1 tablespoon salt, and 1 teaspoon pepper. Spread in a single layer on a baking sheet and roast until tender and lightly browned, about 12 minutes.

Heat a sauté pan over high heat and add enough oil to cover the bottom of the pan. Pat the fish dry and season with salt. Lay the fish in the oil, which should be nearly smoking, skin side down (if the skin is still intact). Fit as many portions as you can in the pan, but it is very important that they not touch, or they will not cook properly. Cook until lightly browned, 3 to 4 minutes. Flip the fish, reduce the heat to medium, and cook for 3 minutes more. Remove to a warmed plate or to a 200-degree oven while the remaining fish cooks.

To plate, toss the roasted fennel bulbs with the dill, 2 tablespoons olive oil, and the reserved grapefruit juice. Arrange 3 fennel pieces in the center of each plate and scatter 5 to 7 grapefruit supremes around them. Place the browned bass on top and spoon some of the juices from the fennel bowl over the fish and on the plate.

Phyllo Triangles Filled with Rum and Dried Apricot Compote

Crispy, flaky phyllo (FEE-lo) is about as versatile as your corduroy blazer was in college. The dough is willing and able to accept any filling, sweet or savory. Here phyllo holds spiced dried fruit. But it could just as easily go with curried lamb or spinach and cheese. The process is the same no matter what you put inside, just make sure that the filling isn't too wet or you'll end up with a soggy, instead of crispy, package. Best of all, these pockets can easily be made ahead and popped into the oven 20 minutes before you want to serve them. A generous scoop of vanilla ice cream on the side never hurt anybody.

serves 6 to 8

8 ounces dried apricots, diced

2 cups dark rum

1 cinnamon stick

¼ cup crystallized ginger, chopped

½ cup pistachios, toasted and crushed

2 lemons, zest grated and juiced

1 16-ounce package phyllo dough, thawed

8 tablespoons (1 stick) unsalted butter, melted

TECHNIQUE TIP

Keeping the stack of phyllo dough covered with a clean, dry kitchen towel while you work will prevent it from becoming dry and brittle. Once the dough dries out or cracks, there's no saving it. If this happens, just toss it aside and move on to the next fresh piece.

In a small saucepot, combine the apricots, rum, cinnamon, and crystallized ginger and bring to a boil over high heat. Reduce the heat and simmer until almost dry. Remove to a bowl to cool completely. Stir in the pistachios and lemon zest and juice to taste. You won't need it all; just make sure the mixture is not too sweet. Remove the cinnamon stick and place the compote in a bowl to cool.

Preheat the oven to 425 degrees.

Remove the phyllo from the package and keep covered with a clean, dry kitchen towel. Working with one sheet of dough at a time, brush the entire piece very lightly with melted butter. Fold the dough in half lengthwise, brush with butter again, and fold in half again. The dough should now be in a very long, very narrow strip. Place a large spoonful of filling at the very bottom of the dough. Begin folding into triangles, as you would when making a paper football or folding the American flag. After 3 folds, all but one side should be enclosed. Cut off the excess dough in a triangle shape and brush with butter. Make your final fold to completely enclose the filling. Place on a baking sheet with the seam down. When all the triangles are folded, brush the tops with butter and bake until golden brown, about 10 minutes, Or freeze on the baking sheet, store in a bag or locking container in the freezer, and bake from frozen later. Serve hot.

COCKTAILS AND A COUNTDOWN

Those big New Year's Eve parties with hats and horns and choruses of "Auld Lang Syne" look really glamorous and fun in the movies, but can you imagine planning one of those babies? And where are you going to find the money to rent a ballroom and a jazz band?

We think that you should throw a casual cocktail party instead. Inviting over a manageable number of friends—say, twenty or thirty—to your new place, coupled with a well-edited, delicious menu, will signal that you've graduated from kegs and premade veggie trays to something a little more adult. Offering one gorgeous house cocktail shows some skills as well as certainty. "I am a newly hitched, decisive party host(ess). Hear me roar! If you thought I was a short-order mixologist, you've got the wrong shindig."

Let your card table host the flutes of crimson-colored bubbly, topping off the sugar cube and gin with champagne as friends arrive. Everything on the menu has been made in advance so you can safely leave behind the kitchen and pass around a tray of salmon wraps with pear and celery slaw. As everyone begins to warm up to you and your expertly prepared food, pop the premade tartiflette in the oven to give the French-style potatoes a final, bubbly golden finish. Chicken liver mousse is across the room, by the stereo, tempting the brave to take a taste and play DJ.

Right before one year passes to the next, and Ryan Seacrest makes us all feel horribly unaccomplished, flambé your dessert and show everyone they've got a long way to go to one-up you next year.

Gin, Raspberry, and Champagne Cocktail

This is one cocktail that is pretty enough for the girls and strong enough for the guys. Let the gin and raspberries sit and get to know each other for a few hours and you'll have a gorgeous pink liquor. Adding lemon juice and a sugar cube helps keep that perfect balance of tart and sweet.

serves 6

1 pint fresh raspberries
one 750-milliliter bottle gin

COCKTAILS
6 sugar cubes (substitute ½ teaspoon granulated
     sugar per glass, but the cubes are sexier)
1 lemon, zested in strips and juiced
ice cubes
brut champagne

A few hours—or a few days—before making the cocktails, place the raspberries in a glass jar and cover with the entire bottle of gin. Store in a cool place or refrigerate. If keeping for more than a week, strain the berries out after 5 days.

Place 1 sugar cube in each of 6 collins glasses, and pour 1 teaspoon lemon juice over each cube. Crush with a muddle stick or spoon until dissolved. Fill each glass with ice and pour in 1½ ounces of the raspberry gin. Fill the rest of the way with champagne. Garnish with a strip of lemon zest and stir.

A BRUT OF A CHAMPAGNE?

We don't want you to buy a misbehaving champagne. *Brut,* in French, simply means "dry." And any champagne worth its bubbles—and meant to be enjoyed with savory food, not dessert—has a low sugar content. Long story short, always look for the word *"brut"* on your champagne label. And when you crack open the bottle, think of Dom Perignon's famous quote after he took his first sip of champagne, "Come quickly, I am tasting stars!"

Tequila-Cured Salmon with Pear and Celery Slaw

Curing fish at home is such an impressive move, you'll feel like Padma and Tom will give you immunity in the next round (don't deny that you're a Top Chef *fan). It takes a little over a day to make—but it's just sitting in the fridge, not requiring an ounce of attention—and you get to add your own unique flavors to the fish. This salmon is citrusy and fresh with just the slightest hint of smokiness from the tequila. It's nothing like the stuff we're used to getting slathered in cream cheese and between crisp bagels in New York City.*

serves 12 as an h.o.d.

2 cups kosher salt

2 cups granulated sugar

3 limes, sliced, plus more for garnish

1 cup gold tequila

1 pound salmon fillet, trimmed and skin removed

Pear and Celery Slaw (recipe follows)

pale celery leaves for garnish

In a bowl, stir together the salt, sugar, limes, and tequila to combine thoroughly. Spread some of the salt mixture in the bottom of a plastic container. Lay the salmon in and cover with the remaining paste. Lay plastic wrap directly on the surface and place a weight on top (a milk jug works great). Refrigerate until the salmon is firm and the container has filled with syrupy liquid, about 24 hours. Remove the salmon from the cure, rinse well under cold water, and pat dry.

To serve, thinly slice the salmon and arrange on a chilled large platter. Build a pile of the Pear and Celery Slaw in the center and drizzle the remaining juices from the slaw around the salmon. Garnish with celery leaves and lime slices.

Pear and Celery Slaw

serves 6 to 8

2 Anjou pears, slightly underripe

4 ribs celery, very thinly sliced

juice of ½ lemon

kosher salt and freshly ground pepper

1 tablespoon chopped fresh parsley

2 tablespoons extra virgin olive oil

Cut the pears into thin strips using a mandoline, or coarsely grate them on a box grater. In a small bowl, combine the pears, celery, and lemon juice; season to taste with salt and pepper. Stir in the parsley and olive oil. This can be stored up to 12 hours before serving.

THE NEXT LEVEL

Our moms used to make ham and Swiss "roll-ups," spear them with a toothpick, and call it a casual h.o.d. Now, trying for something a little more sophisticated, we created salmon rolls by spooning a bit of this slaw onto our house-cured salmon and gently folding the coral-colored ribbons around the slaw. Sprinkle fresh pomegranate seeds on the serving platter and on top of the salmon rolls for a beautiful, seasonal touch.

Chicken Liver Mousse

Any time we visit our favorite neighborhood French bistro, Balthazar, chicken liver mousse is always the first thing we order (along with two glasses of Gigondas, a robust, aromatic wine from France's Rhone grape-growing region that's the more economical stand-in for the area's uber-expensive Châteauneuf-du-Pape). The mousse is rich, creamy, and a perfect spread for crusty sourdough bread. Tart red onions cooked in red wine until meltingly tender are the only way to make it better.

serves 12

2 tablespoons unsalted butter

1 shallot, chopped

1 branch fresh thyme

1 pound chicken livers

kosher salt and freshly ground pepper

¼ cup brandy

½ cup cream

1 sourdough baguette, or brioche, sliced, brushed
    with melted butter, and toasted

1 recipe Spicy Red Onion Marmalade (page 177)

Melt the butter in a sauté pan over medium-high heat. Add the shallot and thyme and cook until the shallot is softened, about 1 minute. In a small bowl, season the chicken livers with 2 teaspoons salt and 1 teaspoon pepper. Toss the seasoned livers into the pan with the shallot and cook until firm and the pan is dry, 5 to 6 minutes. Remove from the heat and pour in the brandy. Return to the stove and reduce until almost dry. Add the cream. Discard the thyme stem and transfer the contents to a food processor. Puree until smooth. Adjust the seasoning with salt and pepper. Refrigerate in a ceramic or plastic container with plastic wrap pressed onto the surface until ready to serve.

Serve with toasted bread and Spicy Red Onion Marmalade or spread the mousse on the bread and top with the marmalade as an hors d'oeuvre.

CHEF'S TIP

By now, we're sure you're chicken salad (page 142) addicts just like we are. So each time you roast a whole chicken for one of our delish chicken recipes, make sure to set aside and freeze the livers. Keep the livers tightly sealed in a ziplock bag until you have enough to make this recipe. Then simply thaw the livers in the refrigerator before cooking.

Confit Revealed

If you've ever seen the word "confit" on a menu and been confused, you're right to feel a little perplexed. The C-word could refer to anything from the classic duck leg braised in its own fat to sweet-and-sour red onions that are simmered until meltingly tender, perfect to serve with chicken liver mousse or fish tacos.

But confit doesn't have to be complicated. While transforming a sometimes tough or gamey duck leg into a morsel of succulent tenderness is a 2-day process where moisture is drawn out of the meat through salting and is replaced by fat, vegetable confits are quick, easy, and delicious. By slowly cooking vegetables in oil, wine, vinegar, or even their own juices, you can infuse unbelievable amounts of flavor and make them more tender than you ever imagined.

Balthazar

If you're in New York and need a French bistro fix, Balthazar is the place to go—it's the ultimate Parisian bistro that just so happens to be located in the heart of SoHo. Brooke and her best friend, Katie Clements, have a standing order when they pull up to the long zinc bar for an even longer night of sips and gossip: chicken liver mousse, steak tartare, french fries, and a nice bottle of Côtes du Rhône comprise their *très* tasty menu. **Balthazar Restaurant**—80 Spring Street @ Crosby Street, New York City 10012; Tel-212.965.1414; www.balthazarny.com.

Tartiflette

If TGI Friday's ever opens in France, you'll find these on the menu just below the croissant poppers. Think of tartiflette as baked potato skins with a French spin. Just substitute for the Cheddar a creamy alpine-style cheese like Reblochon, while shallots and white wine take the place of sour cream and chives. These make the perfect party snack and are fancy enough to be served with champagne. A nice beer like Chimay would work well too!

serves 6

6 small Yukon Gold potatoes
kosher salt
1 tablespoon unsalted butter
8 slices bacon, chopped
3 shallots, minced
1 cup dry white wine
4 ounces Reblochon cheese (substitute raclette
    or Brie if not available)

Cut the potatoes lengthwise in half, place in a medium saucepot, and cover with cold water; add salt and bring to a simmer. Cook until easily pierced with the tip of a knife. Remove to a plate or tray, arrange cut side up, and allow the potatoes to steam dry as they cool.

While the potatoes are cooking, melt the butter in a sauté pan over low heat, add the bacon, and cook until lightly browned. Stir in the shallots and sauté until tender but not colored. Deglaze the pan with white wine and cook until dry. Remove to a bowl and cool.

Preheat the oven to 450 degrees.

When the potatoes are cool enough to handle, scoop a little of the potato from the center and spoon in the bacon and shallot mixture. Top with a slice of the cheese and bake until golden brown and bubbly, about 8 minutes.

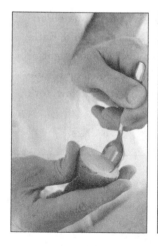

HOLY HOPS

By now, you all know that Brooke loves her vino; beer rarely enters the picture. But when she takes a sip of Chimay, the dark Belgian beer that tastes both a little fruity and spicy, she breaks into a smile and thinks, "There must be something in the water." It's that good. Come to find out, there really is something in the water. Chimay beer is made in the Scourmont Abbey from well water drawn inside the Trappist monastery's walls. This unique beer comes in four types—Rouge, Bleue, Blanche, and Dorée.

Bananas Foster Cake

By the time a holiday party gets around to dessert, we never want to work too hard. This cake gets all the heavy lifting out of the way before your first guest arrives. Then there's nothing left to do but start a fire! Flambéing is always a great party trick, just be careful not to indulge in too many champagne cocktails first. You want to "brûlée" (burn) the banana-rum mixture— not your kitchen.

serves 8 to 12

CRUST

2 packages graham crackers, ground

½ cup granulated sugar

½ teaspoon kosher salt

¾ cup (1½ sticks) unsalted butter, melted

1 pint vanilla ice cream, softened

BANANA TOPPING

2 tablespoons unsalted butter

½ cup light brown sugar

4 bananas, sliced on the bias

1 teaspoon ground cinnamon

¼ cup banana liqueur

½ cup dark rum

Preheat the oven to 325 degrees.

For the crust, combine the graham cracker crumbs, sugar, and salt in a medium bowl. Mix well and stir in the melted butter to moisten. Press the crumbs in a 10-inch springform pan, covering the bottom and coming 2 inches up the sides. Bake for 10 minutes and cool completely.

Fill the baked crust with the softened ice cream, spreading it in an even layer. Freeze to firm, at least 2 hours.

Unmold the cake and cut into slices. Hold on chilled plates while preparing the bananas.

In a large sauté pan, melt the butter over medium heat. Add the brown sugar and cook until completely melted and bubbly. Carefully add the bananas and cinnamon to the pan and toss to coat with the butter and sugar. Move the pan away from the heat and pour in the banana liqueur and rum. Return the pan to the heat and carefully tilt it toward the flame or carefully ignite with a match. When the liquor ignites, stand back and enjoy the flames. As they die down, swirl the pan to make sure that everything is well mixed. Spoon over the slices of ice cream cake and serve immediately.

INDEX